영어 표현에도 등급이 있다!

영어 표현에도 등급이 있다!

발행일   2016년 06월 14일

지은이   니콜라스 원
펴낸이   손 형 국
펴낸곳   (주)북랩
편집인   선일영   편집   김향인, 서대종, 권유선, 김예지, 김송이
디자인   이현수, 신혜림, 윤미리내, 임혜수   제작   박기성, 황동현, 구성우
마케팅   김회란, 박진관, 김아름
출판등록 2004. 12. 1(제2012-000051호)
주소   서울시 금천구 가산디지털 1로 168, 우림라이온스밸리 B동 B113, 114호
홈페이지   www.book.co.kr
전화번호 (02)2026-5777   팩스   (02)2026-5747

ISBN   979-11-5987-016-3 03740(종이책)   979-11-5987-017-0 05740(전자책)

이 도서의 국립중앙도서관 출판예정도서목록(CIP)은 서지정보유통지원시스템 홈페이지(http://seoji.nl.go.kr)와
국가자료공동목록시스템(http://www.nl.go.kr/kolisnet)에서 이용하실 수 있습니다.
(CIP제어번호: CIP2016013934)

성공한 사람들은 예외없이 기개가 남다르다고 합니다.
어려움에도 꺾이지 않았던 당신의 의기를 책에 담아보지 않으시렵니까?
책으로 펴내고 싶은 원고를 메일(book@book.co.kr)로 보내주세요.
성공출판의 파트너 북랩이 함께하겠습니다.

Thesaurus of American Adults' Daily Expressions

영어 표현에도 등급이 있다!

미국 성인들이 상황별로
대화 상대나 기분에 따라
매일 사용하는
Formal(Normal), Informal(Casual), Slang
표현들

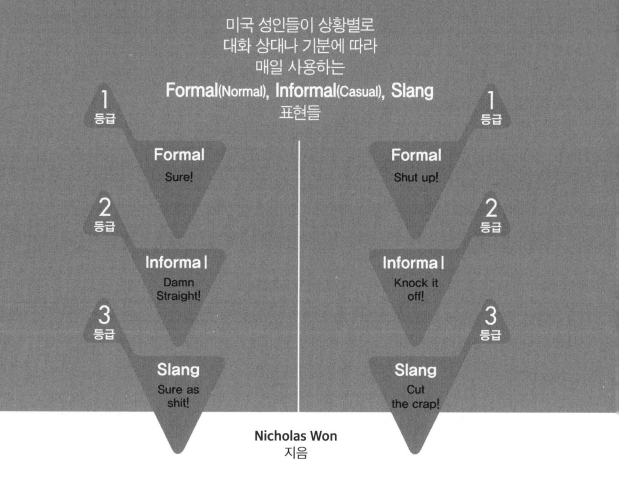

1 등급		1 등급
Formal		**Formal**
Sure!		Shut up!
2 등급		2 등급
Informal		**Informal**
Damn Straight!		Knock it off!
3 등급		3 등급
Slang		**Slang**
Sure as shit!		Cut the crap!

Nicholas Won
지음

이런 표현들을 알아야 native speaker 그들만의 대화가 들린다!

북랩 book Lab

우리가 언어를 사용해 의사소통함에 있어서 그 언어가 갖는 묘미, 대담함, 다채로움, 관용적인 표현을 더하는 것은 형식적이고 정중한 표현, 문어체 단어나 어법이 아닙니다. 언어를 하나의 살아있는 생명체로 만들어 주는 것은 일상생활 중에서 우리가 가식 없이 사용하는 표현들입니다.

다시 말하면, 우리는 친밀한 사이의 대화에서는 남이 들으면 무례하게 들릴 수도 있는 단어나 표현을 일상적으로 사용하고, 친밀한 사이가 아니라도 어떤 경우에는 의도적으로 속어나 비어를 사용하여 의미를 강조하거나 상대방에 대한 감정을 가감 없이 드러내기도 합니다. 이것이 진정한 의미의 의사소통입니다.

여느 언어와 마찬가지로 영어도 '하나의 상황이나 감정에 대응하는 정중한 표현, 친밀한 사이에서 사용하는 표현, 은유와 비유적인 표현, 그리고 비어, 속어'들이 있습니다. 그리고 native speaker라면 당연히 자신이 처한 상황과 감정에 가장 알맞은 표현을 선택하여 의사소통하게 됩니다. 또 대화하는 상대방이 사용하는 단어나 표현들로 상대방의 지식수준, 상황, 상태, 기분을 판단하는 것입니다.

하지만 영어 학습이 주로 교실 안에서 이루어지고 더구나 '수험'이 중점인 한국 영어 학습 환경에서는, 주로 정중하고 일반적인 단어나 표현들 위주로 학습할 수밖에 없습니다. 이런 학습 방법의 결과, 평가용 영어 성적은 높을 수 있지만, 실제 native speaker들과의 대화에서는 자기의 감정을 적절하게 표현할 수 없거나, 상대방이 배려하여 일반적인 표현들만을 사용해 주지 않은 이상, 그들이 하는 말 자체를 이해하는데도 많은 어려움을 겪을 수밖에 없는 것이 현실입니다.

본 교재는 위와 같이 영어를 학습하는 한국인에게 어려운 부분인 '영어로 자기감정을 적절하고 다양하게 표현'하는 데 도움을 주기 위하여, 미국 성인들이 의사소통할 때 '상황, 상태, 감정, 기분에 맞게 자주 사용하는 단어와 표현들을 아래와 같이 3등급으로 구분하여 thesaurus형식으로 구성하였습니다. Thesaurus란 의미가 같거나 유사한 단어와 숙어들을 한 곳에 정리해놓은 유의어 사전, 또는 동의어 사전이라는 의미입니다.

1등급 Formal (Normal) Words & Expressions: 우리가 학교나 교과서, 수험용 영어 교재에서 배우는 정중한(formal) 또는 일반적인 의미의(normal) 단어나 표현들입니다. 각 장에서 제시되는 제목이나 소제목의 단어나 표현들이 그 상황을 대표하는 정중한 표현이고 추가로 [Formal] 항목 아래에 그 외에 자주 사용되는 정중한 표현들을 열거하였습니다. 우선 먼저 정중한 표현들을 자유자재로 활용할 수 있도록 학습하는 것이 필요합니다. 참고로 정중한 표현들은 이미 다 잘 알고 있는 표현들이기 때문에 그 용례들은 생략하였습니다.

2등급 Informal (Casual) Words & Expressions: 격의 없고 친밀한 사이에서 사용하는 단어나 표현들입니다. Informal 또는 casual 표현들은 formal한 표현들과 slang 표현들 사이의 표현으로 일상생활에서 큰 부담 없이 사용할 수 있는 표현들입니다. 어떤 표현들은 formal한 표현들보다 더 자주 사용되는 것들도 있습니다. 물론 formal과 informal 표현들 사이를 명확하게 구분을 지을 수는 없지만, 대화 상대가 초면인 경우나 그다지 친숙하지 않은 경우, 예의를 차릴 자리에서는 formal로 구분해 놓은 표현들을 사용하는 것이 바람직합니다.

3등급 Slang Words & Expressions: 그 의미를 몰라서도 안 되지만 가능한 입 밖으로 내서도 안 되는 '속어, 비어, 욕설'들입니다. 어떤 언어에서 자주 사용되는 속어나 욕설에 대한 지식이 없으면, 그 언어를 활용한 일상적인 의사소통은 어렵다고 해도 과언이 아닐 것입니다. 어떤 경우에는 정중한 표현일 것으로 알았는데 실제로는 속어인 경우도 있어, 의도하지 않은 결례나 실수도 많이 하게 됩니다. 따라서 native speaker라면 누구나 알고 있는 속어들은 정확한 의사소통을 위해서는 반드시 이해하고 있어야 합니다. 하지만 본 교재에서 slang이라고 구분해 놓은 단어나 표현들은 native speaker들이라도 쉽사리 사용하지 않는 표현이라는 것을 꼭 명심하여, 가능한 내가 먼저 입 밖에 내지 않도록 주의해 주시기 바랍니다.

참고로 informal, slang 표현들 중에서도 특히 자주 사용되는 표현들은 **bold** 체로 표시해 놓았으며, informal, slang 단어와 표현들의 용례들은 단어와 표현이 갖는 그 의미를 이해한다면 충분히 혼자서 해석할 수 있을 것으로 판단하여 해석은 생략하였습니다.

아무쪼록 본 교재가 학교에서 배우는 정중한 표현 위주의 영어나 수험용 영어 학습에서 탈피하여, 영어라는 언어를 사용한 진정한 의미의 의사소통에 도움을 주는 교재, 생명력 있는 영어를 학습하는 데 많은 도움을 줄 수 있는 교재가 되기를 바랍니다. 고맙습니다.

Nicholas Won 올림

Contents

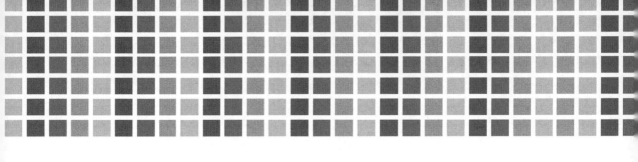

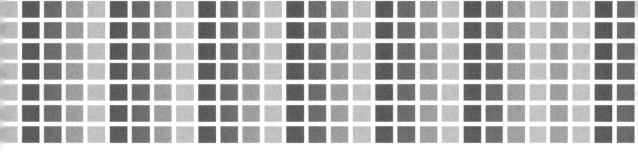

Chapter 3.　Expressing One's Feeling and States
(자신의 기분과 상태를 나타내는 감탄사 및 표현들)

Chapter 4. Qualities of People and Things
(사람과 사물의 좋고 나쁨)

Chapter 5. Types of People (사람들의 특성 표현)

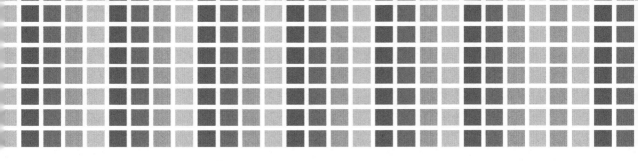

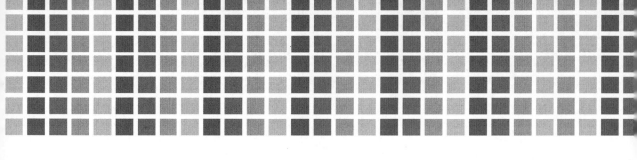

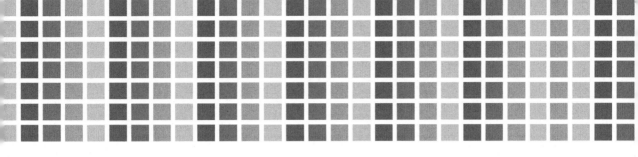

Chapter 6.   Types of Things (사물의 이름, 형태, 관련 기타 표현들)

Chapter 7.　The Use and Abuse of Power (힘, 권력의 사용, 남용)

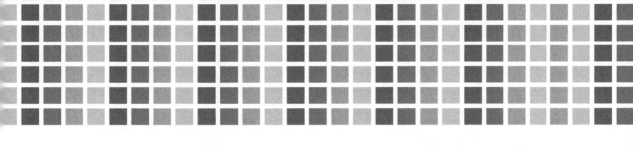

Chapter 8.　Deceit and Treachery (사기, 속임, 배반, 배신)

Chapter 9.　Confrontation and Competition (대립, 경쟁)

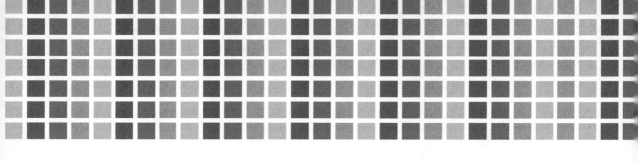

Chapter 10.   Progress & Decline (진전과 퇴보)

Chapter 11.   Thinking (생각, 사고)

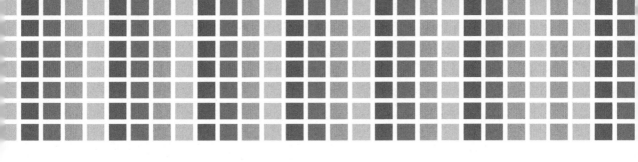

Chapter 16. Private Parts (음부, 성기 관련 표현들)

Chapter 17. Sexual Activities (성행위 관련 표현들)

Chapter 1

Communications
의사소통

첫째 장에서는 의사소통과 관련된 다양한 표현들을 정리합니다. 의사소통의 시작과 끝이라고 할 수 있는 인사말들, 의사소통의 방법을 나타내는 표현들, 문장이나 단어의 의미를 강조하기 위해 사용되는 단어나 표현들, 몸동작을 나타내는 표현들, 중요한 약어들을 3등급으로 정리하였습니다.

1 *Civilities*
인사말

1-1. Greetings (만날 때의 인사말)

Formal

Hello; How are you?; Hey there; Hi; Howdy; How is everything?; How's it going?; Hullo; What's new?; What's up?; Felicitations; Good afternoon; Good evening; Good morning; Greetings; How do you do?; How you have been?; Nice to see you; Salutations.

Informal

- **A-yo** (아주 친한 사이의) 인사말 ("Hey!"와 동의어)

  [Ex] A-yo, Jessie what's going on?

- Give me five! 우리 손바닥 부딪쳐! (축하의 하이파이브를 요청하는 말)

- Give me some skin! 우리 손바닥 부딪쳐! (축하의 하이파이브를 요청하는 말)

- **Hey, man!** 이봐, 형씨. (Hello.)

- How's it hanging? 잘 지내? (A greeting, usually between men)

- How's tricks? 안녕? (How are you?)

- Slap me five! 하이 파이브 하자! (축하의 하이파이브를 요청하는 말)

- Sup? (What's up?의 준말)

- **What gives?** 웬일이냐? (A casual greeting, similar to "What's happening?")

- What's clicking? 잘 지내?

- What's cooking? 안녕, 무슨 일이야? (What's going on?)

- **Yo!** 야!, 어이! (젊은이들의 인사말. Italian Americans들의 대화에서 많이 사용됨. Yo는 1976년도에 발표된 영화 <Rocky>의 주인공 Rocky Balboa역의 Sylvester Stallone이 영화에서 "Yo, Adrian!"라고 말하면서 유명해짐)

1-2. Partings (헤어질 때의 인사말)

Formal

Adios; Back in a few; Back in a while; Be back later; Be right back; Bye; By bye for now; Catch you later; Got to go; Gotta go now; Have a good day; Have a great one; Have a nice day; Hug and kisses; I'll be seeing you; Namaste; See you; See you around; See you(ya) later; See you soon; See you tomorrow(tonight); So long; Take care; Take care of yourself; Talk to you later; Talk to you soon; Adieu; Au revoir; Bon voyage; Farewell; God be with you; God bless you.

Informal

- Be easy 조심하시오, 조심해라. (Take care; have a good one.)

  [Ex] I'm out, be easy.

- Cheerio 안녕, 잘 있어. (Goodbye.)

  [Ex] Well, I best be off, cheerio.

- Ciao 안녕하세요, 잘 가[있어], 안녕, 그럼 또 만나. ('차우'로 발음, Goodbye in Italian, hello, Pronounced as "chow")

  [Ex] Ciao bella. (Hello / Goodbye girlfriend의 의미)
     Ciao bello. (Hello / Goodbye boyfriend의 의미)

- Hang loose 잘 지내! (Goodbye.)

  [Ex] Hang loose, dude!

- Hasta la vista, baby! 잘 가요! ("See you later."를 의미하는 Standard Spanish 구문인 hasta la vista 와 baby가 연결된 형태. Jody Watley가 1987년에 발표한 'Looking for a New Love'라는 노래에서 처음 유행되었으나, 1991년도 Arnold Schwarzenegger가 주연한 영화 <Terminator 2: Judgment Day>에서 Terminator에게 말을 가르치는 데 쓰여 더 유행하였음. Schwarzenegger는 이후 주지사가 되는 과정에서 이 말을 자주 사용하였음 / "Farewell, baby.")

- **Later** 잘 가! (젊은 사람들끼리 헤어질 때 하는 인사 / Short for "See you later.")

  [Ex] Ok, have a good time. Later.

- Later, gator! 안녕(Good-bye), 그럼 또 봐! ("See you later, alligator!"의 축약형 / See you later.)

- **May the Force be with you!** 당신 곁에 포스가 함께 하기를! (<Star Wars Episode IV: A

New Hope(1977)>에서 Death Star battle station 직전에 Han Solo역의 Harrison Ford가 Luke Skywalker 와 나누는 작별의 인사말 / Used to wish someone luck with a difficult endeavor.)

- Peace 안녕히, 잘 가. (Interjection to announce one's departure)

  [Ex] Hey, I'm leavin'. Peace, y'all. (leavin' = leaving)

- Peace out! 안녕히, 잘 가. (Goodbye.)

  [Ex] I'm leaving, guys. Peace out!

- **See you later, alligator!** (Robert Charles Guidry의 원곡인 'See You Later, Alligator'를 1955년 Bill Haley and His Comets가 rock-and-roll로 편곡하여 불러 유명하게 된 인사말. 보통 "After a while, croco-dile!"로 대답함 / A casual farewell, often responded to with the rejoinder, "After a while, crocodile!")

- **Take it easy!** 천천히 해! / 잘 가라, 또 만나자! (Goodbye.)

- Ta-ta 안녕, 잘 가. (Goodbye.)

  [Ex] Person A: See you tomorrow! / Person B: Ta-ta.

1-3. Gracious Responses (천만에요, 별말씀을, 별거 아닙니다)

Formal

You are welcome; Any time; Don't give it a second thought; Don't worry about it; It's nothing; It's okay; It's the least I could do; You're more than welcome.

Informal

- **Don't sweat it** 속 태우지 마, 별것 아니야. (상대방에게 하는 말 / Don't worry about it.)

- **Forget it** 별것 아니야. (You don't need to feel obligated.)

- **No big deal** 별일 아니다. (대수롭지 않다)

  [Ex] It's no big deal.

- **No sweat** 뭘 그런 걸 갖고 그래, 별거 아냐[문제없어]. (상대방의 감사·부탁에 대한 대꾸)

  [Ex] Person A: Thanks for everything. / Person B: Hey, no sweat.

- No worries 괜찮아요. (흔히 고맙다는 말에 대한 대꾸로 쓰임)

  [Ex] Person A: Sorry dude, didn't mean to be late. / Person B: It's cool, no worries.

1-4 Apologies (사과)

Informal

- **My bad** 내 잘못이다. (자기 잘못이나 실수를 인정할 때 씀 / An apology)

  [Ex] Sorry man, my bad.

Ways to Communicate
의사소통 방법들의 표현

2-1. Socialize (사교, 어울림)

Formal

- rub elbows 명사들과 사귀다, ~와 교제하다, ~와 친밀하게 일하다 (To socialize)

    [Ex] He rubs elbows with the rich and famous.

- small talk 한담 (특히 사교적인 자리에서 예의상 나누는 대화)

    [Ex] Well, you're in paradise with a handsome Italian. Adapt, overcome, make small talk.

Informal

- hob-knob 교제하다, 어울리다 (To mingle, usually with the upper class of society)

    [Ex] After the opera, we hobnobbed with the foreign heads-of-state.

- schmooze 향후 사업 성공을 위해 사교를 하다 (한담을 나누다, 수다 떨다)

    [Ex] His forte was PR, marketing and schmoozing. (forte: 장기, 강점)

2-2. Information and Secret (정보/비밀)

Informal

- dope (믿을 만한 소식통으로부터의) 정보, 내보內報; 예상

    [Ex] What's the dope on the new boss?

- down low(DL) 비밀로 함 (To keep quiet, Secretive, Also known as the "D.L.")

[Ex] Keep this on the Down Low.

- **intel** (군사) 정보 (Intelligence)

  [Ex] What's the most recent intel on troop movements?

- **scoop** 최신 정보(The latest information), 특종

  [Ex] What's the scoop on the upcoming hiring freeze?

2-3. Inform (정보를 제공하다, 알려 주다)

Formal

brief; inform; notify; tell; clue somebody in; fill somebody in; keep some-body posted; advise; apprise; enlighten; impart to

Informal

- **dish out** (일반적으로) ~을 분배하다, 아낌없이 제공하다, (뉴스·정보 따위를) 제공하다

  [Ex] She's always dishing out advice, even when you don't want it.

- give somebody the dope 정보를 알려 주다
- give somebody the low down 비밀이나 내부 정보를 알려 주다
- give somebody the scoop ~에게 특종을 알려 주다

2-4. Gossip (풍문을 이야기하다)

Informal

- **a little bird told me** (~의 일을) 풍문으로 들었다, 어떤 사람에게서 들었다 (정보의 출처를 분

  명히 밝히기를 피할 때 씀 / A person who I will not disclose told me.)

  [Ex] A little bird told me that it's your birthday next week.

2-5. Talk (말하다, 수다 떨다, 쓸데없이 지껄이다)

Formal

communicate; speak; talk; chat; rattle on; converse; declaim; discourse; hold forth; orate; parley

Informal

- chew the fat 수다를 떨다 (To chat)

  [Ex] There had been a lunch that day in London at which a gaggle of players had chewed the fat.

- chew the rag 수다를 떨다 (To chat)

  [Ex] We chewed the fat about the recent bribery conducted by a lawyer.

- run off at the mouth (분별없이) 말을 줄줄 늘어놓다 (To speak unwisely)

  [Ex] I hate you running off at the mouth!

- **shoot the breeze** 잡담하다, 쓸데없이 지껄이다 (To chat; to talk idly)

  [Ex] Some of my former students spotted me and came over to say hi and shoot the breeze.

- **spill one's beans** 발설하다 (To give something away; to tell secret information)

  [Ex] She threatened the president to spill the beans about her affair with him.

- **spit** (욕설·폭언 등을) 내뱉다, 내뱉듯이 말하다 (out)

  [Ex] Don't leave me in suspense. Spit it out.

Slang

- **shoot the shit** 말 같지 않은 소리를 지껄이다 (To talk meaningless things)

  [Ex] Wife: What do you guys do when you're fishing all day?
  Guy: You know… Stuff.
  Wife: No I don't know, that's why I asked.
  Guy: Just shoot the shit, nothing important.

2-6. To Talk Too Much or Indiscreetly (말을 너무 많이 하다)

Formal

talk indiscreetly; talk too much; go on (about); ramble; rattle; run-on; be diffuse; digress; drone

Informal

- **bend a person's ear** (너무 지껄여대어) 남을 넌더리 나게 하다 (To talk too much)

[Ex] Mike answered on the first ring. Rachelle had already called and bent his ear.

2-7. Listen (듣다)

Informal

- **read my lips** 내 말 잘 들어라. (To pay close attention)

[Ex] What does he say now? In America, George Bush said, "Read my lips; no more taxes", but he increased taxes and lost an election.

2-8. Stare, Watch (응시하다, 주시하다)

Informal

- eyeball (무례할 정도로) 눈을 동그랗게 뜨고 쳐다보다 (To stare)

[Ex] The guard eyeballed him pretty hard despite his pass.

- scope out ~을 자세히 살피다 (To stare, usually at a member of the opposite gender)

[Ex] He scopes out every hot chick who goes by.

2-9. Interfere (참견하다, 훈수 두다)

Informal

- kibbitz (노름을 구경하며) 참견하다, 훈수 두다

  [Ex] I don't wanna hear no more kibitz.

2-10. Tease (놀리다, 약 올리다)

Formal

mock; tease; kid; make fun of; pick on; poke fun at; rib; roast; bait; deride; ridicule; taunt

Slang

- take the piss out of 놀리다 (To tease in an aggressive way)

  [Ex] I don't want to take the piss out of the people I photograph.

2-11. Golden Rule (황금률)

Formal

- **do unto others** 남에게서 바라는 것만큼 남에게 해주어라.

  [Ex] Basic religion of whatever faith teaches the golden rule e.g., do unto others.

- magic word (공손하게 'Please'라고 덧붙이라는 것을 빗대어 하는 말)

  [Ex] Child: Can I have a snack? / Parent: What's the magic word?

2-12. Tell the Truth (솔직하다, 진실[사실]을 말하다)

be candid; be honest; be sincere; tell the truth; get something off one's chest; be aboveboard;

- be on the up-and-up 정직한, 신뢰할 수 있는 (To be honest)

  [Ex] The offer seems to be on the up and up.

- **be upfront** 솔직한 (To be honest; transparent)

  [Ex] Tell him upfront that you can't go.

- **talk turkey** 진지[심각]하게 말하다, 탁 터놓고 말하다 (To speak openly and without reserve)

  [Ex] Please talk turkey. I want to know the truth.

- **tell it like it is** 있는 그대로 말하다, 솔직히 말하다 (To speak openly and honestly)

  [Ex] They tell it like it is or at least the way they see it.

③ *Abbreviation*
약어

Informal

- **AKA** 별칭(은) (An alias; acronym of "Also Known As.")

  [Ex] That man by the bar is Frank, A.K.A. "the lady killer."

- **ASL** 나이, 성별, 사는 곳은? (Online chatting acronym of "age, sex, location?")

  [Ex] ASL?

- **B4** (Before의 on-line chatting상의 줄임 말 / Before. Online chat acronym.)

  [Ex] I knew you B4 we went to the same school together.

- **BAC** 혈중 알코올 농도 (Blood-alcohol concentration)

  [Ex] He caused a car accident while drunk driving with a BAC of 0.189 percent.

- **BF** 남자 친구 (Boyfriend)

  [Ex] Is he your new BF?

- **BFF** 영원한 절친 (Acronym for "best friend(s) forever")

  [Ex] My BFF Becky texted and said she's kissed Johnny.

- **DOB** 출생 연, 월, 일 (Acronym for "date of birth")

  [Ex] What's your DOB?

- NBD 별 일 아니다, 아무것도 아니다 (No big deal.)

- **w/** ~와 함께, 같이 (With)

  [Ex] Cover w/ plastic wrap and put a plate on top that fits into bowl.

- **w/o** ~없이 (Without)

  [Ex] Are you coming w/ or w/o your spouse?

Slang

- BS 허튼 소리, 거짓말 (Bullshit의 두음문자 / Bull shit)

  [Ex] My boss is full of BS.

- LMFAO 배꼽 빠지게 웃다 (문자 채팅에서 주로 사용 / Laughing my fucking ass off)

  [Ex] Someone told me Michelle deserved to win Pop Idol, and I was LMFAO.

- NFW 절대로 안 돼! (No fucking way.)

Increasing Intensity
-Words and Phrases 단어와 구의 강조

Formal

extreme; kind of; mighty; thumping; as much as possible; best; the best; the greatest; the maximum; the most; to the greatest degree; extremely; thoroughly; very; madly; seriously; to a great extent; completely; especially; greatly;

- and a half (보통 것보다 더) 놀라운[굉장한, 중요한]

[Ex] That was a soccer game and a half.

- as '형용사' as they come 매우[더없이] ~한

[Ex] The farmer is straight as they come.

- with a vengeance 호되게, 심하게, 맹렬히 (To an extreme degree)

[Ex] It began to rain again with a vengeance.

Informal

- **as heck** 정말로 ~인 (An intensifier; To a great extent or degree; very)

[Ex] People from my town rarely go to college. They sure as hell, sorry, miss, they sure as heck don't go to L.A. to college.

- **as hell** 정말로 ~인 (An intensifier. To a great extent or degree; very)

[Ex] Something about the girl was sexy as hell. She had such an innocent face.

- **bleeding** 몹시, 형편없는 (강조의 용법 / A somewhat less offensive replacement for "fucking")

[Ex] What the bleeding hell do you think you're doing?

- crying (나쁜 일 따위가) 심한 ('crying shame, a crying need'처럼 사용됨)

[Ex] It is a crying shame that he managed to get away with that!

- **damned** 몹시, 형편없는 (강조의 용법 / Very)

[Ex] We got out pretty damned fast!

- damnedest 몹시, 형편없는 (강조의 용법 / Most)

[Ex] Great God, it was the dirtiest, damnedest treachery I ever heard of!

- darnedest 몹시, 형편없는 (강조의 용법 / Most)

[Ex] She gave him the darndest talking to he ever got, and she told him she never would marry him as long as she lived.

- dead 몹시, 형편없는 (강조의 용법, 'dead broke, dead right'처럼 사용됨)

  [Ex] He's dead stupid.

- durndest 아주 형편없는, 극한의 (Most)

  [Ex] Sometimes I meet 'em in the durndest places. ('em: them의 준말)

- **heck** (문장이나 단어 강조 / A non-offensive replacement for the word "hell")

  [Ex] What the heck is he doing?, What the heck is that thing?

- **hell of a** 굉장한[엉망인] (말하는 내용을 강조 / Extreme; extremely; very)

  [Ex] That was a hell of a show.

- **hella** 아주, 굉장히, 진짜로 ('hell of a'의 약자 / Very, totally; lots of)

  [Ex] That party was hella sketch. What with all those skanky-ass girls.

- **helluva** 대단한 (Extreme; extremely; very; Hell of a)

  [Ex] That was one helluva dee-lish-uss cake!

- **like hell** 1. 악착같이, 맹렬히, 필사적으로 2. 결코 ~이 아닌 (Much; to a great extent)

  [Ex] A wisdom tooth was cutting through and it hurt like hell.

- **like nobody's business** 굉장히 많이[빨리/잘]

  [Ex] That ho can shake her booty like nobody's business. (ho=whore)

- **living daylights out of** 아주, 엄청난 (To a great extent)

  [Ex] It scares the living daylights out of them, so they are just stopping.

- **one hell of a** 굉장한[엉망인] (말하는 내용을 강조 / Very impressive)

  [Ex] That was one hell of a show.

- **one's damnedest** 최선(을 다하다) (With one's maximum effort)

  [Ex] I did my damnedest to stay awake.

- **stinking** 지독한, 역겨운, 엄청난 (Very. Used especially in "stinking rich")

  [Ex] Now that you're stinking rich, we'd gladly be your bitch.

- **uber** 최고의, 최대의 (Ideal; prefix meaning "super-")

  [Ex] He's an uber-carpenter.

- **way** 훨씬, 멀리, 아주 (Very)

  [Ex] This is way cool!

- as fuck 아주 x하게 (An intensifier. To a great extent or degree; very)

[Ex] That car is nice as fuck.

- as shit 정말로 ~인 (An intensifier; to a great extent or degree; very)

[Ex] It is hot as shit in here.

- as '형용사' as fuck[hell, shit] xx하게 ~인

- ass-load 대량, 많은 양 (A large amount.)

[Ex] What did Radiohead get by doing this? An ASSLOAD of publicity.

- freak 아주, 굉장히 (Very; really; extremely.)

[Ex] That is freak expensive.

- freaking 가혹한, 호된, 지독한 (명사 또는 형용사를 강조), 빌어먹을(fucking 대신에 쓰는 욕설)

[Ex] It's freaking huge.

- fricking 빌어먹을 (fucking 대신에 쓰는 욕설 / Fucking)

[Ex] This test was so frickin' horrible! (frickin' = fricking)

- frigging 빌어먹을 (Fucking의 완곡어법 / Frigging은 'masturbating' 또는 'intercourse'의 의미)

[Ex] Holy Christ, it's frigging hot as sin in here.

- fuck (Hell, Damn 등 대신에 쓰는 강의어強意語 / Very, extreme)

[Ex] What the fuck are you doing here?

- fucking x팔, 괘씸한, 지독한, 지긋지긋한, 완전한

[Ex] None of you live here. Your daughter doesn't live here. The sign says 'Resident Parking Only.' I am a resident. So move this fucking rust bucket somewhere else or by God I'll stuff your asses in the trailer and move it myself.

- fucking A 절대로, 틀림없이 (An intensifier. The "-A" is a long A.)

[Ex] You're fucking-A right you're going to pay for damages!

- fucking well '조동사' x팔 (화를 내며 하는 명령이나 진술을 강조)

[Ex] We fucking well should!

- mother fucking 비열한, 망할, 쌍놈의, 괘씸한 (Very vulgar intensifier)

[Ex] That was a mother fucking huge spider.

- one's ass off 마구, 필사적으로, 맹렬히 (To the best of one's ability)

[Ex] I've got a midterm tomorrow. I'm gonna have to study my ass off between now and then.

- the shit out of 아주 심하게

[Ex] They beat the shit out of that guy.

Increasing Intensity
Whole Sentences 문장 전체 강조

5-1. Introductory Sentence Modifiers (문장 도입부에서 강조)

Informal

- **damn** 빌어먹을, 제기랄 (실망, 짜증 등을 나타내는 욕설)

  [Ex] Damn! That guy just shot right past me!

- doggone 빌어먹을, 망할 놈의 (짜증나거나 놀랄 때 씀)

  [Ex] Doggone! I've lost my pen!

- **gosh** 어머나, 이런 (A mild expression of surprise or enthusiasm as to be put in place of "God")

  [Ex] Gosh, that was good.

- **hell** 도대체 (문장 전체의 강조 / Intensifies whole sentence)

  [Ex] Hell, I wish I'd known.

- Jeepers! 맙소사, 어머나 (놀람, 충격을 나타내는 소리 / Interjection used to express surprise)

- **Jesus** 맙소사, 어머나 (놀람, 충격을 나타내는 소리 / Interjection used to express surprise)

  [Ex] Jesus, what happened to my car!

Slang

- **Fuck** x팔, 빌어먹을, 제기랄 (실망, 짜증 등을 나타내는 욕설 / Expressing dismay or discontent)

  [Ex] Fuck, that's a lot of money.

- **shit** 이런, 제기랄 (놀람, 충격을 나타내는 소리 / Used to emphasize a point or request)

  [Ex] Shit, I missed the bus!

5-2. Other Sentence Modifiers (기타 문장 전체 강조)

Formal

goodness; my; oh; wow

Informal

- the heck Damn 등 대신에 쓰는 강의어強意語 (Hell의 의미)

  [Ex] What the heck are you doing?

Slang

- **the fuck** Damn 등 대신에 쓰는 강의어強意語

  [Ex] What the fuck is the matter with you?

6 Gesture
몸짓

6-1. Gesture (일반적인 몸짓)

Informal

- air guitar 기타 치기, 흉내 내기 (A mimed guitar)

  [Ex] They're all playing their air guitars.

- **air quotes** (허공에 양손을 들어 그려 보이는 인용 부호)

  [Ex] Charles makes air quotes with his fingers.

- facepalm 자신의 손바닥을 얼굴에 갖다 댐으로써 창피함, 놀람, 분노, 절망 등을 표현

  [Ex] In fact the Today Show and MSNBC seemed to be reveling in Cramer's very public facepalming.

6-2. Obscene Gesture (욕설의 표현인 중지를 들어 올리는 동작)

Formal

give someone the finger

Informal

- flip off (가운데 손가락을 이용하여 상대방을 조롱하고 놀리다)

  [Ex] Leslie gave Walt the finger, of course. It was rare for 20 minutes to go by without her flipping off someone. Sometimes she did it for no apparent reason.

- flip the bird (가운데 손가락을 이용하여 상대방을 조롱하고 놀리다)

  [Ex] That guy almost hit my car so I flipped him the bird.

Radio Communication

무전 통신 용어

Informal

- 10-20 현 위치는? (무전 용어 / What is your current location?)

  [Ex] What is your 10-20?

- 10-4 알았다. (무전용어 / Message received and understood. Used in radio transmissions)

  [Ex] Dr. Evil: 10-4, Goldywang, this is Rubber-Ducky. What's your 10-20, over? -- Austin Powers in Goldmember (2002 film)

- **copy that** (무전) 알았다. (To understand)

  [Ex] Captain Tidwell: I do copy that.

- over and out (무선 교신에서) 통신 끝. (Goodbye)

  [Ex] Man in helicopter: We're five by five, both packages on board. Over and out.

- **Roger!** 알았다! (통신 용어로써 상대방이 송신한 내용을 모두 알아들었음을 나타낼 때 사용)

Chapter 2

Feeling and States
기분과 상태

대화의 감정과 상태에 뉘앙스 또는 색채감을 더해주는 데는 formal 표현보다는 informal 표현 또는 slang을 사용하는 것이 제격입니다. 따라서 미국 성인들은 많은 informal 표현, 또는 속어들을 사용하여 자신의 감정과 상태 자체뿐만 아니라, 그런 감정이 시작되고 있음을 표현합니다. 이번 장에서는 인간이 갖는 여러 감정과 사물의 다양한 상태를 영어로는 어떻게 표현하는지를 살펴봅니다.

1 *Anger*

화, 성질, 짜증의 표현들

1-1. Cause Anger, Irritation and Upset (화나 짜증이 나게 하다)

Formal

affront; aggravate; anger; annoy; bother; dismay; distress; disturb; faze; irk; irritate; madden; pester; perturb; pique; rub somebody the wrong way; peeve; provoke; rankle; rile; ruffle; unnerve; unsettle; upset; vex

Informal

- **bug** 괴롭히다 (To worry or annoy someone)

  [Ex] Stop bugging me!

- get in somebody's hair 남을 괴롭히다 (To worry or annoy someone)

  [Ex] The little kids got in my hair by running and shouting.

- get in somebody's skin 남을 괴롭히다 (To worry or annoy someone)

  [Ex] It seems like they only get better at getting in people's skin.

- **give somebody a pain in the neck** 귀찮게 하다 (To cause agony)

  [Ex] He gives me a pain in the neck.

- **pick on somebody** 트집을 잡다 (To find fault with)

  [Ex] Or maybe I just wanna pick on somebody because I'm having a bad day.

- **push somebody's buttons** 남의 성질을 돋우는 행동을 하다

  [Ex] She knows how to push all his buttons.

- put somebody's nose out of joint 화나게 하다

  [Ex] There is no reason to put your nose out of joint. I meant no harm.

영어 표현에도 등급이 있다!

1-2. Moderately Angry (약간 화가 난)

Formal

angry; be angry; be cross; be irked; be mad; be galled; be irate; exasperated; mad; riled; irate;

- vexed 화가 난 (Very angry)

  [Ex] He was getting all vexed.

Informal

- amped 몹시 흥분한 (Angry, annoyed, offended)

  [Ex] He was very agitated, very amped up.

- peeved 짜증이 난 (Slightly angry)

  [Ex] Susan couldn't help feeling a little peeved.

1-3. Extremely Angry (엄청 화가 난)

Formal

furious; in a rage; outraged; raging; up in arms; ranting and raving; apoplectic; enraged; infuriated; wrathful;

- in high dudgeon 화를 내며[화가 나서], 격분해서 (In an angry or offended mood, and showing other people that you are angry)

[Ex] After being refused entry to the club, he went off in high dudgeon.

Informal

- **madder than hell** 화가 많이 난 (Extremely angry)

[Ex] Getting out of the cab, madder than hell, the trucker looked down at the two, still in the road, and yelled, "What the hell's the matter with you two? You could've been killed!"

- on the rag 화가 많이 난 (Extremely angry)

[Ex] My parents were totally on the rag at the news.

- on the warpath 화가 나서 싸우려고[응징하려] 드는

[Ex] The boss was on the warpath 'cause we're way behind. ('cause: because의 준말)

Slang

- rip shit 화가 많이 난 (Enraged or otherwise highly emotional.)

[Ex] It would only really work perfectly if you all were sincerely distraught and rip shit.

1-4. Become Angry or Lose Control (화가 나서 이성을 잃다)

Formal

become angry; become enraged; burn with a slow blue flame; erupt; flare up; fly into a rage; get angry; get mad; go crazy; go off; lose control; lose one's temper; take umbrage at; to become angry;

- go through the roof 화가 머리끝까지 치밀다 (To become very angry)

[Ex] He went through the roof when his friend totaled his new car. (total: destroy completely)

- have a conniption fit 화를 내다 (To feel extreme anger)

[Ex] Her mom is gonna have a conniption fit when she sees that white shirt, ' cause that blood is NEVER gonna come out.

- **have a fit** (심한 충격·분노 등으로) 졸도할 지경이 되다 (To become very excited or angry)

[Ex] Your mother would have a fit if she knew you'd been drinking!

- have a meltdown 굉장히 화내다 (To become extremely angry)

[Ex] I almost had a meltdown when I wrecked my jeep.

- **hit the ceiling** (몹시 화가 나서) 길길이 뛰다 (To feel extreme anger)

[Ex] She hit the ceiling when she heard about the shocking news.

- **hit the roof** (몹시 화가 나서) 길길이 뛰다 (To feel extreme anger)

[Ex] She hit the roof when he said those mean things.

- **throw a fit** 발작을 일으키다, 엄청 화내다 (To feel extreme anger)

[Ex] He threw a fit over nothing.

Informal

- **blow one's cool** 감정적이 되다, 흥분하다 (To become angry; to lose control)

  [Ex] Her mean words made him blow his cool.

- blow one's fuse[stack, stopper, top] 감정적이 되다, 흥분하다

- **blow up** ~에게 화를 내다[분통을 터뜨리다] (To lose control; to become extremely angry.)

  [Ex] He totally blew up at me after I wrecked his car.

- **crack up** 1. 발끈 화를 내다 2. 정신이 돌다, 미치다 (To become insane)

  [Ex] Everyone in my office turned to stare as I cracked up.

- flip one's lid 1. 발끈 화를 내다 2. 정신이 돌다, 미치다

  [Ex] After the divorce, she just flipped her lid. She was in hospital for months.

- fly off the handle 버럭 화를 내다 (To become enraged)

  [Ex] My dad flew off the handle when he found out I was pregnant.

- **freak** 기겁을 하다[하게 만들다] (To become angry)

  [Ex] My parents really freaked when they saw my hair.

- **freak out** 자제력을 잃다[잃게 하다], 흥분하다

[Ex] Sam: If I'm ever gonna have a chance with Andi, I gotta come clean. / Sock: Oh, she's gonna freak out, man. She's gonna think you're off your nut.

- **go ballistic** 분통을 터뜨리다, 화가 나서 길길이 날뛰다

  [Ex] When she found out he lied, she went ballistic.

- go bananas 머리가 홱 돌다 (미친 듯이 화를 내거나 터무니없는 짓을 함을 나타냄)

  [Ex] When I told him that his girlfriend left town, he went bananas.

- **go bonkers** 돌아버리다 (To go crazy)

  [Ex] He just went bonkers.

- go out of one's skull 미치도록 화가 나다 (To go crazy)

  [Ex] I went out of my skull when I heard that.

- **go postal** 몹시 화를 내다, 격분하다 (To go insane)

  [Ex] He was arrested for going postal on the policeman.

- **lose it** 화가 나다, 이성을 잃다. (To lose one's temper; lose one's control)

  [Ex] He lost it when he heard that story.

- lose one's cool 흥분하다 (To lose one's temper, lose one's control)

  [Ex] Argument is most effective when done without losing one's cool.

- lose (one's) religion 욱하고 화가 나다 (To lose one's temper)

  [Ex] I almost lost my religion.

- spaz out 경련하다, 몸이 굳어지다, 몹시 흥분하다

  [Ex] When he learned I was cheating on him, he totally spazzed out.

Slang

- **be pissed (off)** 화를 내다 (To feel angry)

  [Ex] The girl felt pissed off when the computer didn't work yet again.

- **get pissed (off)** 화가 나다 (To become angry)

[Ex] History is changed by people who get pissed off.

- **go ape shit** 화가 나다 (To lose one's temper, usually involving violent actions.)

  [Ex] Ben will go ape shit.

- **piss off** 화나게 하다.(To anger or annoy)

  [Ex] She was already pissed off at her father and mother and she didn't really feel like dealing with any more assholes.

- shit a brick 몹시 조바심 내다, 화내다, 《감탄사적》 우라질, 빌어먹을, 쳇

  [Ex] It's not that bad. Don't shit a brick!

1-5. Liable To Anger (화를 내기 쉬운)

Formal

cross; hot-tempered; ill-tempered; quick-tempered; short-tempered; bilious; cantankerous; choleric; irascible; ornery; peevish; petulant; querulous; splenetic; surly; vehement; waspish;

- **grouchy** 불평이 많은, 잘 투덜거리는 (Very bad-tempered and complaining a lot)

[Ex] You've been grouchy all day long.

- grumpy 성격이 나쁜 (Bad-tempered and miserable)

[Ex] I think being grumpy runs in the family.

- **have a short fuse** 성미가 급하다, 걸핏하면 화를 낸다 (Liable to anger)

[Ex] The guy is incredibly skillful but just has a short fuse.

- **testy** 짜증을 잘 내는 (Liable to anger)

[Ex] While you have good reasons for being testy, acting like total bitch is unacceptable.

- **touchy** 걸핏하면 화내는 (Liable to anger)

[Ex] They are touchy about what we call them.

Informal

- bitchy 욕하는, 흉보는, 쉽게 화내는

[Ex] I'm sorry. I know I was bitchy on the phone.

1-6. A Fit of Anger (발작적인 화)

Formal

fit; outbreak; outburst; tantrum; bad mood; frenzy; paroxysm;

- conniption 히스테리(의 발작), 울화통, 발끈함

[Ex] He had a conniption over the dent in the car.

Arrogance and Conceit

거만, 자만, 오만

Formal

arrogant; boastful; conceited; haughty; insolent; scornful; vain; cocky; imperious; narcissistic; presumptuous; pretentious; supercilious

Informal

- **big-headed** 자만심이 많은 (Arrogant; Full of conceit)

  [Ex] However weak your opponent may be, don't get big-headed.

- high falutin' 허세를 부리는

  [Ex] This isn't high falutin' art-about-art. It's marvelous and adventurous stuff.

- hoity-toity 거들먹거리는, 거만한 (Someone getting uppity or snobby with a person.)

  [Ex] Don't get hoity-toity with me.

- la-di-da 잘난 사람 (잘난 체하는 사람을 빈정대며 하는 말 / Arrogant and conceited)

  [Ex] Some Hollywood actors think they're so la-di-da.

- **puffed up** 자만심에 차서 우쭐한

  [Ex] He was too puffed up with his own importance, too blinded by vanity to accept their verdict on him.

- **snooty** 오만한 (With an attitude of superiority; pretentious)

  [Ex] I hate how snooty she is.

- **stuck-up** 거드름 피우는, 거만한 사람 (Pretentious)

  [Ex] She's stuck up.

Slang

- have a stick up (one's) ass 과도하게 형식적이고 딱딱하다

  [Ex] This guy really does have a stick up his ass.

영어 표현에도 등급이 있다!

3 *Attraction*

매력, 끌림

3-1. Cause Attraction (매력이 있다, 유혹하다, 매력의 원인)

Formal

appeal to; arouse; attract; charm; enchant; entrance; fascinate; lure; seduce; tempt; grab; rope in; allure; beckon; beguile; bewitch; captivate; enamor; entice; intrigue; inveigle

Informal

- hook 유혹하다, 낚다 (To ensnare someone, as if with a hook)

  [Ex] She's only here to try to hook a husband.

- suck in 끌어들이다, 유혹하다

  [Ex] I was desperate and I was sucked in by advertising.

- **turn on** (성적으로) 흥분[자극]하다[시키다] (To excite someone sexually)

  [Ex] She had been turned on as hell watching him with Jenny Cinnamon.

- mojo (사람의 성격상의) 매력 (Sex appeal)

  [Ex] I've got serious mojo.

- sweep one off one's feet ~를 정신없이 (사랑에) 빠져들게 하다

  [Ex] The first time he met her, he was completely swept off his feet.

<u>3-2</u>. Attracted (반한, 이끌린, ~에 빠진)

Formal

be charmed by; fall in love; take a liking to; succumb; attracted to; enchanted by; fond of; in love with; lovesick for; partial to; moonstruck by; bewitched by; captivated by;

- **crazy about** ~하는 데 푹 빠져 있다 (To be attracted to something)

[Ex] He's crazy about baseball. He never misses a game.

- **fall for something** ~에게 홀딱 반하다[빠지다] (To be attracted to something)

[Ex] They're the kind of people that would fall for a cult easily (anything that makes them feel like they belong to something bigger than themselves).

- **fall head over heels for** 홀딱 빠지다 (To be attracted to something)

[Ex] Sadly for them he has genuinely fallen head over heels for her.

- **hot for** ~에 열중한 (Attracted to)

[Ex] You were as hot for me as I was for you.

- **mad about** ~에 미치다, ~에 푹 빠져있다 (Attracted to)

[Ex] He's always been mad about kids.

- **take a shine to** ~에 (홀딱) 반하다 (To become attracted)

[Ex] I think you'll get the job. They seemed to take quite a shine to you.

Informal

- gaga about[for, over] (너무 좋아서) 거의 제정신이 아닌 (Crazy)

[Ex] My daughter is just gaga about entertainers.

- **hooked** (~을) 대단히 즐기는, (~에) 빠져 있는 (Addicted)

[Ex] He's hooked on prescription painkillers.

- lose one's head over ~에 매력을 느끼다, 빠지다 (To be attracted)

[Ex] People have lost their heads over it.

- **nuts about** ~에 열중해 있다, 홀딱 반하다 (A big fan of)

[Ex] I'm nuts about this new game.

- soft on ~에 빠져있다 (Attracted to)

[Ex] He must be soft on my sister.

- **stuck on** ~에 빠져[미쳐, 반해] (To be obsessed with)

[Ex] He's still stuck on his ex-girlfriend.

- sweet on ~를 아주 좋아하다[~에게 반하다] (To feel attracted to)

[Ex] Between the two of us, I know he's sweet on her.

- wild about ~에 몰두하다 (To be attracted with)

[Ex] I'm not wild about the idea.

3-3. Feel Attracted (~에 반하다, ~에 끌리다)

Formal

adore; care for; love; prize; set one's heart on; treasure; hanker after; cherish; dote on; hold dear; yearn for;

- **be all about** ~이 최고[전부]다, ~에 미쳐있다 (To be extremely enthusiastic for)

[Ex] I'm all about sports right now.

- **be smitten with[by]** 홀딱 반해서 (To become strongly attracted to)

[Ex] People over here are smitten with the game and its stars.

Informal

- **be a sucker for** ~라면 사족을 못 쓰다 (To have an infatuation with someone or something)

[Ex] I am a sucker for a seductive sound system in a beauty product.

- **be turned on by** ~에 끌려 (To be attracted)

[Ex] But not everyone is turned on by these ads.

- fancy somebody (성적으로) 끌리다

[Ex] Is there someone else you particularly fancy?

- get a bang out of ~에 흥분하다, ~에서 쾌감을 얻다 (To enjoy)

[Ex] They love the secrecy because they get a big bang out of it.

- **get a kick out of** ~에 흥분하다, ~에서 쾌감을 얻다 (To enjoy)

[Ex] I get a kick out of riding on roller coasters.

- **go for** ~을 좋아[선호]하다 (To feel attracted over)

[Ex] I don't want to go for a foreign car.

- **have a crush on** ~에게 홀딱 반하다 (To have a infatuation with someone)

  [Ex] The word around the plant was that he has a crush on her.

- **have a soft spot for** ~에 약하다[~을 좋아하다]

  [Ex] I have a soft spot in my heart for chocolate cake.

- **have a thing about** (이상할 정도로) ~을 아주 좋아하다

- **have an itch for[to]** ~이 탐나서 못 견디다 (To have a very strong desire for)

  [Ex] I have an itch to play softball tonight.

- go ape for (~에) 열중하다, 열광[심취]하다 (To feel attracted over)

  [Ex] If you like the zombie genre, you'll go ape for this book.

- **go nuts about[over]** 열중하다 (To go crazy over)

  [Ex] The kids go nuts over these little surprises.

3-4. Feel Mutually Attracted (서로에게 이끌리다)

Formal

be compatible; be on the same wavelength; take to each other; feel a rapport;

- buddy up (~와) 친구가 되다 (To form small teams)

  [Ex] One year I was buddying up with Klammer, another artist.

- **team up** (~와) 한 팀이 되다[협력하다]

  [Ex] U.S. companies are fast learning how to team up with foreign competitors to crack markets and acquire technology.

Informal

- **click** (이성과) 뜻이 맞다, 의기투합하다 (To connect, relate, hit it off with someone.)

  [Ex] When I first met her, we just clicked, and we're best friends now.

- **hit it off** (~와) 죽이 맞다 (To get along well)

  [Ex] I thought you guys hit it off really well.

- **vibe** ~에 공감하다, ~와 뜻이 통하다, ~와 죽이 맞다 (To get along well in a relationship)

  [Ex] I like him. I think we could vibe.

3-5. Attractive (매력적인)

Informal

- **knockout** 뿅 가게 만드는 사람 (Rare beauty)

[Ex] She was a knockout in navy and scarlet.

Slang

- dishy 매력적인 (Physically attractive)

[Ex] Everybody else will love those scenes starring dishy dreamboat Mark Ruffalo as Garner's true love.

Boring

지루한

Informal

- humdrum 단조로운, 따분한 (Boring)

  [Ex] The romance is humdrum, but the movie's message is sincere.

- **like watching paint dry** (페인트가 마르기를 지켜보는 것 같이 지루한 / Extremely boring)

  [Ex] This class is like watching paint dry.

- **snore** 지루한 것 (잠이 올 정도로 지루한 일)

  [Ex] That tv show was a snore.

Busy

바쁜

Informal

- **swamped** 눈코 뜰 새 없이 바쁜 (To be overloaded with work)

  [Ex] Sam: Where is Tony? / Steve: He's swamped. He's doing publicity for this Seattle Style magazine party tomorrow night.

Calmness
침착, 차분함

6-1. Become Calm (진정하다, 침착하다)

Formal

calm down; collect oneself; settle down; unwind; loosen up; quieten; relax; rest; stay calm; stay loose;

- be mellow (특히 술을 마셔서) 느긋해진 (Relaxed)

 [Ex] After two glasses of wine, I was feeling mellow.

- **chill out** (사람이) 냉정해지다, 침착해지다, (명령형으로) 침착해, 마음 편히 가져

 [Ex] Dawg, you need to chill out.

- **cool it** 냉정해지다, 말려들지 않다, 속도를 줄이다 (Loosen up and stop being uptight)

 [Ex] Don't get too hot-blooded; cool it!

- **cool out** 냉정해지다[하게 하다], 침착해지다[하게 하다] (To calm down)

 [Ex] Yo, my man, cool out, son!
- go easy on something (명령형으로 쓰여) ~를 살살 다뤄라[너무 심하게 하지 마라]

 [Ex] Police are told to go easy on the homeless.

- hang loose 차분하다, 평정을 유지하다[무사태평하다]

 [Ex] Weekends are important: time to hang loose and take stock of things.

- mellow out 여유롭게 지내다[유유자적하다] (To relax and do very little)

 [Ex] We could just put on some music and mellow out.

- play it cool 냉정[침착]하게 대처하다 (To be nonchalant)

 [Ex] He likes to play it cool, but he knows what he's doing.

- simmer down (화·흥분 후에 차츰) 진정하다[화를 가라앉히다]

 [Ex] And yet, when we simmer down, we all understand that there is a problem.

- **take it easy** (명령형으로 쓰여) 진정해라[걱정 마라] (To relax)

 [Ex] Well, take it easy today and go to bed early tonight.

- keep one's pants [shirt] on 침착하다, 냉정을 유지하다 (To not overreact)

  [Ex] Keep your pants on. It was only a minor accident.

- take a chill pill 마음을 가라앉히다, 진정하다 (To relax)

  [Ex] He needs to take a chill pill.

6-2. Calm (침착한, 차분한)

calm; collected; mild; undisturbed; laid-back; low-key; at peace; detached; dispassionate; harmonious; imperturbable; placid, serene; tranquil; unruffled;

- chilled out 차분한, 진정된 (Calm)

  [Ex] It's such a chilled out place with a great atmosphere.

- unflappable (곤경에서도) 흔들림 없는, 동요하지 않는

  [Ex] She was a true professional, very straight, authoritative and unflappable.

7 Chance

기회

- **not have a snowball's chance in hell** 전혀 가망이 없다 (To have no chance at all)

[Ex] You have a snowball's chance in hell of winning the lottery.

- toss-up 반반(의 가능성)

[Ex] So far the election is still a toss-up.

8 Cheesy, Corny

저급한

- cheeseball 싸구려의, 저급한 (Cheesy, corny)

  [Ex] Sure, looking back now, it seems cheeseball, but it was the 80s.

- **cheesy** 싸구려의, 저급한 (Corny)

  [Ex] Spiderman is so cheesy and cartoony.

- salty (때로 약간 저속하기도 하지만) 재미있는, 저속한 (Corny or childish)

  [Ex] That was the saltiest joke I've heard in a long time.

Complete
완전한

Informal

- full throttle 완전히 거침없이 어떤 일을 하는 (To do something, completely, without restraint)

[Ex] Man, that was one full throttle party.

Confused, Disorderly, Messy
혼란스러운, 엉망진창인

Informal

- ate up 엉망진창인 (Not "squared away", i.e. not organized or prepared: a mess)

[Ex] Damn, your room is ate up.

- dump 황폐한[지저분한] 거리, 초라한 장소

[Ex] Boy, what a cheap dump! You won't get me back in there again.

- kludge 조잡한 물건, 어설픈 대책

[Ex] Anti-trust laws are a kludge for the fact that somewhere else another government regulation has empowered a company with a monopoly to begin with.

- mish-mash 뒤죽박죽 (A confused mixture of different types of things)

  [Ex] It is not a religion but a mish mash of many religious texts.

- **train wreck** (열차사고가 난 것처럼) 엉망진창(인 사람)

  [Ex] Why are you dating that train wreck? He hasn't had a job in five years.

Slang

- AFU 엉망진창 (Acronym of "all fucked up" A shortened version of SNAFU.)

  [Ex] That is totally afu, dude!

- ass backwards 거꾸로, 뒤죽박죽으로 (Chaotic; in a mess)

  [Ex] He did the work ass backwards, so I had to do it again.

- clusterfuck 엉망진창

  [Ex] Hey, what is that clusterfuck on your desk?

- **crap** 잡동사니, 쓰레기 (Worthless junk and/or pointless things)

  [Ex] What the hell is this crap all about?

- FUBAR 원래의 모습을 알아보지 못할 정도로 엉망진창인 (Acronym for Fucked Up Beyond Any Recognition)

  [Ex] The place was totally FUBAR after that.

- **shit storm** 형편없는 상황 (A terrible mess)

  [Ex] We're in the middle of a shit storm now.

- skank 불쾌한 것[사람], 기분 나쁜 녀석[것] (Messy, run down, dilapidated)

  [Ex] My flat is real skank, just look at the fridge.

- SNAFU 대혼란 (Acronym for situation normal: all fucked up)

  [Ex] And there have been hiccoughs and snafus already.

11 Constant
언제나, 항상, 꾸준한

Informal

- **24/7** 하루 24시간 1주 7일 동안, 1년 내내, 언제나 (always, 24 hours a day, 7 days a week; Pronounced as "twenty-four seven")

  [Ex] That restaurant is open 24/7.

12 Cost Related
가격 관련

12-1. Cheap (값싼)

Formal

at a discount; a bargain; cut-rate; low-end; down-market; depreciated;
- **dime-a-dozen** 아주 흔해서 가치가 없는

[Ex] Rappers like Ja Rule, Chingy, and Benzino are a dime a dozen.

- dirt cheap 아주 싼, 싸구려의 (Extremely inexpensive)

[Ex] In Italy, the peaches are dirt cheap.

- **for a song** 헐값으로[싸구려로] (For very little money)

[Ex] No one else wanted it, so I bought it for a song.

Informal

- cheapo 싸구려의, 저질의 (Cheap quality or just something rubbish)

[Ex] That is some cheapo handbag.

- **steal** (값이 너무 싸서) 거저나 마찬가지 (Very cheap)

[Ex] This suit is a steal at $80.

12-2. Free (공짜, 거저)

Formal

- **for nothing** 공짜로[거저] (For free)

[Ex] He works weekends at the community center for nothing.

- **on the house** (술집이나 식당에서 술·음식이) 무료[서비스]로 제공되는

[Ex] It's on the house. Don't worry about paying for it.

12-3. Expensive (비싼, 고가의)

Formal

overpriced; big-ticket; up-market; upscale; dear; exorbitant;

- **cost an arm and leg** 아주 비싸다 (Very expensive)

[Ex] A: our clients have gone to all other stores. / B: But everything in there cost an arm and a leg.

- **high end** 고급품 (소매 / The most expensive of their kind)

[Ex] This is high-end tourism at its zenith.

- **steep** 비싼 (Expensive)

[Ex] The prices are just too steep for us.

- **stiff** 값비싼 (Very expensive)

[Ex] That's a stiff price.

13 *Courage*
용감, 용기

Formal

bold; brave; cocky; courageous; daring, fearless; heroic; overconfident; rash; spirited; unafraid; gritty; nervy; adventurous; audacious; cocksure; dauntless; doughty; gallant; indomitable; intrepid; lionhearted; mettlesome; resolute; stalwart; stouthearted; undaunted; valiant; valorous

Informal

- **balls** 용기, 근성, 배짱 (Bravado, courage; guts)

  [Ex] Randy and Andy Smith knew their dad had no balls. He had always been a pussy.

- **balls of steel** 용기, 근성, 배짱 (Metaphorical testicles that people with courage or gall have)

  [Ex] You must have balls of steel showing your face in here.

- balls out 대담한 (To be courageous)

  [Ex] People, from every industry, worked balls out until the job was done.

- ballsy 대담한, 위세 좋은, 의욕적인, 정력이 왕성한 (Brave; courageous)

  [Ex] That was one ballsy move.
- **chutzpah** 뻔뻔스러움, 철면피, 후안무치厚顏無恥 (Audacity; spirit)

  [Ex] John: I just smacked my teacher. / Mary: That took a lot of chutzpa.

- **feisty** 혈기 왕성한, 거침없는 (Tough, independent, and spirited)

  [Ex] At 66, she was as feisty as ever.

- **guts** 용기, 기력, 배짱, 근성, 인내력 (Courage)

  [Ex] You didn't have the guts to confront Cyril.

- gutsy 배짱 있는, 대담한 (Having courage or determination)

  [Ex] "Who is Mack The Knife?" she asks. "He's that man who did it so courageously, so gustily."

- **have balls** 용기가 있다 (To have courage)

  [Ex] Tucker sure has balls to demand $20 mill.

- have chutzpah 대담하다 (To be audacious)

[Ex] Einstein had the chutzpah to discard common sense and long-established theory.

- have cojones 용기가 있다 (To have courage)

[Ex] Franken is not without his faults but the man has cojones.

- **have gall** 용기가 있다 (To have courage)

[Ex] He had the gall to ask questions about it.

- **have guts** 용기가 있다 (To have courage)

[Ex] I wanted to apologize, but I didn't have the guts to admit I was wrong.

- have moxie 용기가 있다 (To have courage)

[Ex] Thank Mr. Booker for having the moxie to say so.

- **have nerve** 용기가 있다 (To have courage)

[Ex] Surely she didn't have the nerve to say that to him?

- **have spunk** 용기가 있다 (To have courage)

[Ex] We like actress Drew Barrymore, because she has spunk.

- man up (책임감 있게 행동하거나 '남성처럼 행동'할 것을 권고하는 말)

[Ex] I told him he better Man Up if he wants to fight with me.

- moxie 용기, 투지 (Courage)

[Ex] Ashley: I do still have enough fun in me to talk to a man in a Laundromat. / Britt: Well, and enough moxie to invite a relative stranger into your home.

- plucky 용기 있는 (Having or showing pluck, courage or spirit in trying circumstances.)

[Ex] The plucky schoolgirl amazed doctors by hanging on to life for nearly two months.

- spunky 용감한, 투지[열의]에 찬 (Courageous, feisty)

[Ex] Pedro is spunky, full of life.

14 Dead
사망한, 죽은

- **DOA** (Dead on arrival / (병원) 도착 시에 이미 사망, 의사 용어)

  [Ex] Not only is President Bush's Iraq plan DOA in Congress, much of his domestic agenda is, too.

- **six feet under** 매장된, 묘에 (들어간) (Dead and buried)

  [Ex] Her grandfather has been six feet under for some time now.

15 Depression
침울, 낙담

- bummed out 낙담한, 기분이 안 좋은 (Depressed)

  [Ex] I'm really bummed out.

- **case of the Mondays** 월요병 (To feel bad at the start of the week)

  [Ex] Someone's got a case of the Mondays, and I think it's me!

Displeasure and Disgust
불쾌함, 혐오

16-1. Cause Disgust (역겹게 하다, 혐오감을 주다)

Formal

be repulsive; disgust; nauseate; offend; revolt; sicken; disenchant; fill with loathing; repulse

Informal

- gross out ~를 역겹게 하다 (To sicken)

  [Ex] That food really grossed me out.

- **make one sick** 역겹게 하다 (To cause disgust)

  [Ex] It made me sick to the stomach to know what people can do to their loved ones.

- **turn off** (성적인) 흥미를 잃게 하는[싫증이 나게 하는] 것 (Something one finds unattractive)

  [Ex] Bad breath is a total turn-off.

- **turn one's stomach** 구역질 나게 하다 (To make a person vomit)

  [Ex] The very sight turns my stomach.

16-2. Gross, Disgusting, Creepy (징그러운, 역겨운)

Formal

disgusted; nauseated; queasy; repelled; revolted; sickened; be averse to; repulsed;

- creeper 기는 것[사람], 곤충, 파충류 동물

[Ex] Look out, creeper!

- **freaky** 해괴한, 기이한 (Frightening, disturbing)

[Ex] That horror movie was freaky!

- grossed out 역겨운 (Disgusting)

[Ex] Initially she was a bit grossed out as it was described to me, and vomited a number of times.

Informal

- **perv** 변태(의), 역겨운 사람 (Pervert; disgusting person)

[Ex] The alleged perv, who was charged with misdemeanor exposure, pleaded not guilty on Tuesday.

- raunchy 선정적인, 더러운, 지저분한

[Ex] Dude, that rotten trash is raunchy!

- skeevy 초라한, 더러운 (Gross, creepy; ICKY, etc.)

[Ex] He's so skeevy.

Slang

- like ass pie 역겨운 (Disgusting)

[Ex] It smelled like ass pie in there.

16-3. Displeasing, Unpleasant (기분 나쁜, 불쾌한)

Informal

- **bogus** 가짜의, 위조의, 불쾌한, 품질이 나쁜 (Displeasing; of poor quality)

[Ex] Don't talk to him, he's bogus.

- grotty 불쾌한, 저급한 (Cheap, fifth-rate, nasty, unpleasant)

[Ex] It was a really grotty little convenience store.

- icky (특히 끈적끈적하게) 기분 나쁜 (Gross, unappealing)

[Ex] Cooked carrots are icky.

- **ass** 기분 나쁜 것, 기분이 몹시 안 좋음 (Anything displeasing)

  [Ex] I feel like ass today.

- **suck** 혐오감을 주다, 아주 불쾌하게 하다, 형편없다

  [Ex] Their new CD sucks.

16-4. Be Unpleasant (불쾌하다, 기분이 나쁘다)

- **feel like ass** 기분이 더럽다 (To feel terrible)

  [Ex] Man, I feel like ass today. Must've been all the stuff I drank last night.

- **feel like crap** 기분이 더럽다 (To feel terrible)

  [Ex] He feels like crap because he can't find a job.

- **feel like shit** 기분이 더럽다 (To feel terrible)

  [Ex] He felt like a shit after he dumped her.

17 Doubtful

의심스러운, 불확실한

Informal

- iffy 불확실한 (Having doubts)

  [Ex] I'm not sure if I want to go; I'm a bit iffy about it.

- sketchy 의심스러운, 이상한 (Of questionable character; strange)

  [Ex] I'd stay away from that guy, he looks sketchy.

18 Drugged

약물에 취한

Informal

- **stoned** (마리화나, 술에)취한 (Under the influence of drugs or marijuana)

  [Ex] Well sure, now the tortoise makes sense. It's the only pet that you can catch when you're stoned.

19 *Drunken*
술 취한

Formal

- tipsy 술이 약간 취한 (Drunken)

[Ex] After drinking all that vodka, I'm feeling kinda tipsy.

Informal

- battered 심하게 취한 (Extremely intoxicated)

[Ex] I got totally battered last night.

- bombed (술, 마약에) 취한 (Extremely drunk)

[Ex] Adam got totally bombed at the party last night.

- lubricated 술에 취한 (Under the influence of alcohol)

[Ex] Dancing increased once the wedding party was sufficiently lubricated.

- plastered 술이 많이 취한 (Extremely drunk)

[Ex] Let's go get plastered!

- schnockered 술에 (많이) 취한 (Very drunk; extremely inebriated)

[Ex] 1. He was so schnockered he fell off the bar stool. / 2. I'm going to get so shnockered at the party!

- sloshed 술 취한 (Quite drunk)

[Ex] Also in attendance was KIMBERLY STEWART, who looked sloshed as she stumbled out of the club at 5 am.

- **tie one on** 고주망태가 되다 (To get drunk)

[Ex] I really tied one on last night.

- zonked (피로, 술, 마약에 취해) 완전히 맛이 간

[Ex] Did you see that guy at the party? He was zonked!

Slang

- piss ass drunk 술이 많이 취한 (Extremely inebriated)

[Ex] He was piss ass drunk last night.

Enough, Excessive

충분한, 과도한

Informal

- **fed up with** 질리다, 물리다, 식상하다

    [Ex] I'm fed up with your shit!

- **off the charts** 과도한, 측정이 안 되는 (Excessive, immeasurable, way too much)

    [Ex] His Christmas lights display was off the charts this year.

Excitement

흥분

21-1. Excited (흥분한)

Formal

charged; delighted; electrified; enthusiastic; excited; exhilarated; stimulated; thrilled; beside oneself; fired up; in a flurry; enlivened; enraptured

Informal

- full of piss and vinegar 기운이 철철 넘치는 (Full of energy)

  [Ex] There's some kind of piss and vinegar in this city.

- **gung-ho** (특히 싸움, 전쟁 등에 대해) 너무 열광하는

  [Ex] Azinger's father, Ralph, was a lieutenant-colonel in the US air-force; the son likes a bit of 'gung ho' military attitude.

- hopped up 흥분한, 흥분시키는, (자동차 등이) 마력을 높인, 마약을 사용한 (On drugs)

  [Ex] Sorry about that weird voice mail. I was hopped up on Nyquil when I left it.

- jazzed up 흥분한 (To be really excited about something)

  [Ex] Ryan got jazzed up the night before.

- **peppy** 원기 왕성한, 기운 넘치는 (Energetic)

  [Ex] At the end of every day, jot down a brief note on how peppy or tired you felt.

- pumped up 열성적인, 흥분한 (Excited; psyched)

  [Ex] He is pumped up to prove his value again.

- **rarin' to go** ~하고 싶어서 좀이 쑤시다[근질근질하다] (Excited to get started)

  [Ex] Mary is rarin' to go and can't wait for her university term to start.

- **wired** 흥분한, 활력이 넘치는 (Full of energy)

  [Ex] How can you be so wired when you got only 3 hours of sleep last night?

21-2. Exciting, Full of People (흥미로운, 흥미진진한, 사람들로 붐비는)

Informal

- **ball** 아주 즐거운 한때 (A great time)

  [Ex] Man, why did we have to leave so early? I was having a ball!

- **blast** 뭔가 특히 좋은 것 (재미있는 것 / Something very fun)

  [Ex] That party was a blast!

- bumping 바글바글하다, 와글와글하다

  [Ex] That party was bumping!

- **chilling** 흥미진진한 (Fun or exiting)

  [Ex] That movie was chilling.

- **jammed** 빽빽이 찬, 몹시 붐비는 (Full of people; packed)

  [Ex] As always, the expressway was jammed with commuters.

- **packed** (특히 사람들이) 꽉 들어찬 (Full of people)

  [Ex] The bar was packed on Saturday.

- **rocking** 굉장한, 멋있는 (Exciting)

  [Ex] Bar manager: Thank god, it's a slow night. / Peck: Really? For a Sunday, this place is pretty rockin'.

- amped 멋진, 굉장한, 몹시 흥분한 ((about)); (마약으로) 흥분한 (Exciting, fun, full of people)

  [Ex] He was very agitated, very amped up.

- crackin' 멋진, 최고의 (Exciting and/or cool and/or ecstatic)

  [Ex] The party's crackin' tonight!

- hype (마약 주사 따위를 맞은 것 같이) 흥분한, 기운이 솟은 (Excited)

  [Ex] The whole school was hype over the Homecoming game.

21-3. Agitated (안달하는, 조마조마한, 설레는)

Formal

agitated; flustered; nervous; uneasy; edgy; jumpy; discomposed; disconcerted; disquieted; unsettled; unstrung

Informal

- antsy 안달하는 (Jumpy; nervous or impatient)

  [Ex] He was antsy, waiting for the test results.

- **have butterflies in one's stomach** 마음이 조마조마하다 (To feeling extremely nervous)

  [Ex] He had butterflies in the stomach when he was on the stage for the first time.

- in a flutter 설레는 (Agitated)

  [Ex] My heart breaks out in a flutter at the thought of her.

- in a tizzy 초조한 (Distressed)

  [Ex] The reason is not the bad economy, although that was already threatening to put the Globes in a tizzy.

- **itchy** (몹시 ~하고 싶어 몸이) 근질거리다 (Having strong desire to do something)

  [Ex] He wasn't itchy at all, not about flying anyway.

- **jittery** 초조한, 조마조마한 (Nervy, jumpy, on edge)

  [Ex] This tells you the market is jittery and schizophrenic.

- **keyed up** (중요한 행사를 앞두고) 긴장한

[Ex] The Royal Festival Hall was packed, of course, and everyone was keyed up with anticipation.

- twitchy 불안해 하는 (Susceptible to twitching a lot)

[Ex] Afraid of bad publicity, the department had suddenly become very twitchy about journalists.

- worked up (몹시) 흥분한 (Agitated or angry)

[Ex] The guys especially get kind of worked up over the Superbowl.

Failure
실패

22-1. Failure (실패)

Informal

- anti-Midas touch (만지기만 하면 모든 것이 먼지로 변하는 저주 / A curse in which everything one interacts with turns out badly. From King Midas (of Greek mythology) whose touch would turn things to gold.)

  [Ex] It was like the golden one had the anti-Midas touch: everything he touched turned to dirt.

- **sophomore slump** 2년차 증후군 (A lack of success during a second attempt of something.)

  [Ex] Our first album was awesome, but we faced a bit of a sophomore slump.

22-2. Mistake (실수, 망치다, 엉망으로 만들다)

Informal

- **boner** 어처구니없는 실수, 큰 실수, 망치다 (A mistake)

  [Ex] I studied for that test for weeks, but I still managed to boner it. I got a D-!

- muck up (하고 싶던 일 등을) 망치다 (To ruin unintentionally)

  [Ex] Are you suggesting that they actually haven't mucked up the economy this time?

Slang

- ass up 실수하다, 못쓰게 만들다 (To mess up)

  [Ex] I think we assed up the acquisition.

- ass-backwards 거꾸로, 뒤죽박죽으로 (In reverse or totally incorrect)

  [Ex] That computer must have been set up ass-backwards; most of the buttons don't work.

- back asswards 잘못한, 이상한 방향으로 일이 처리된

  [Ex] Why do you have to do everything back asswards?

- **fucked up** (사물, 상황이) 엉망인, 몹시 혼란한, 심란한

  [Ex] Everything has been fucked up.

Fancy or Shiny
화려함, 반짝이는

23-1. Fancy (화려함)

- razzle dazzle (기법·효과 등의) 겉치레의 현란함, (극 등의) 화려한 연기[장면] (Fancy)

  [Ex] It's entertainment now and the younger generation expect the razzle dazzle that comes before the fights.

23-2. Shiny, Expensive (반짝이는, 비싸 보이는)

- **bling bling** 반짝이는 (보석 종류의) 장신구, 값비싼 장신구

  [Ex] She was looking hot in her bling-blings.

Far Away, Rural Area
오지, 시골

Informal

- boondocks (단수취급) 오지, 벽지, 황야, (미개척의) 삼림 지대

  [Ex] You know you live in the boondocks when you can't see your house from the road.

- **middle of nowhere** 먼 시골, 복잡하지 않은 촌 동네, 어딘지 모르는 곳

  [Ex] At dusk we pitched camp in the middle of nowhere.

- **sticks** 벽촌 (A remote area; backwoods; a city or town regarded as dull or unsophisticated.)

  [Ex] I had a boring vacation, staying out in the sticks.

Slang

- bumfuck 시골, 촌구석

  [Ex] He's from Bumfuck, Nebraska.

Fast, Quick, Quickly
빨리, 빠르게

25-1. Fast, Quick, Quickly (빨리, 빠르게)

Informal

- on the dub 황급히, 신속히 (Quickly. From "on the double")

  [Ex] I need to get those sneakers on the dub.

25-2. Expedite (서두르다, 조속히 처리하다)

Informal

- **on the front burner** 많은 관심을 받는, 우선순위의 일로 (A priority, Contrast with "on the back burner.")

  [Ex] The Jones account is now on the front burner.

②⑥ *Fear*

공포, 겁, 무서움, 두려움

26-1. Become Afraid (무서워하다, 겁을 먹다)

Formal

become afraid; become fearful; become hysterical; loose courage; shrink; break out in a sweat; go to pieces; falter; flinch; quaver

Informal

- **chicken out** 겁을 먹고 (~을) 그만두다[(~에서) 꽁무니를 빼다]

  [Ex] You're not chickening out, are you?

- **freeze up** (걱정이 되어) 얼다 (To become afraid)

  [Ex] Whenever I'm near him, I get so nervous I freeze up.

- **get cold feet** (계획했던 일에 대해) 갑자기 초조해지다[겁이 나다]

  [Ex] Why do I always get cold feet before I give a presentation?

- **lose one's nerve** 기가 죽다, 겁먹다 (To become afraid)

  [Ex] This is not a time to lose nerve or to send uncertain signals.

- punk out 겁먹다 (To become afraid)

  [Ex] Democrat Presidents with the partial exception of Harry Truman, always punk out when confronted with force.

- turn yellow 무서워서 얼굴빛이 변하다 (To become afraid)

  [Ex] But my children are very scared, their faces turn yellow.

- wimp out (하려고 하던 일을) 겁을 먹고 안 하다 (To lose courage)

  [Ex] Although the area is easily accessible by train, I wimped out and drove, nervous of unpredictable weather.

26-2. Cause Fear (무섭게 하다, 겁먹게 만들다)

Formal

alarm; frighten; give a fright to; horrify; intimidate; panic; paralyze; scare; startle; terrify; scare silly; scare witless; shake up; spook; affright; appall; daunt; petrify; terrorize; unnerve;

- creep out (공포 따위가) ~을 엄습하다 (To make someone feel uncomfortable)

  [Ex] My 14-year-old daughter is pretty creeped out about it.

- **freak out** 겁먹게 하다 (To cause fear)

  [Ex] Snakes really freak me out.

- freeze the blood 오싹 소름이 끼치게 하다, 등골이 오싹해지게 하다 (To cause fear)

  [Ex] The movie stars Kirk Douglas, an actor who could freeze the blood when he wanted to, in his most savage role.

- frighten the living daylights out of 놀라게 하다, 겁주다 (To cause extreme fear)

  [Ex] This is a game that is sure to delight fans of the macabre, while also frightening the living daylights out of them.

- give somebody the shivers 등골을 오싹하게 하다 (To cause fear)

  [Ex] That man who hangs about in the lane gives me the shivers.

- scare somebody stiff 굉장히 겁을 주다 (To scare badly)

  [Ex] The robber jumped out and scared us stiff.

- scare the living daylights out of 굉장히 겁을 주다 (To scare very much)

  [Ex] USA needed to beat the USSR who had scared the living daylights out of the West with their space capabilities.

Informal

- **scare the hell out of** 굉장히 겁을 주다 (To scare very much)

  [Ex] Sock: You don't think she's gonna come after us, do you? / Sam: God, I hope not. She scares the hell out of me. / Sock: Well, all women scare the hell out of you.

- scare the pants off somebody 굉장히 겁을 주다 (To scare very much)

  [Ex] So CIA and MI5 can stop scaring the pants off us and let us go about our daily business.

- **scare the crap out of** 굉장히 겁을 주다 (To scare badly)

  [Ex] No, but honestly, you two scared the crap out of me.

- **scare the shit out of** 굉장히 겁을 주다 (To scare badly; to scare someone tremendously)

  [Ex] Dude, you scared the shit out of me.

26-3. Feel Fear (겁을 먹다, 공포를 느끼다)

Formal

be afraid; be frightened; be scared; be terrified;

- afraid of one's shadow 제 그림자에 제가 놀라는, 몹시 겁내는, 무서워하는, 언제나 흠칫흠칫 겁을 먹는 (Scared of small or imaginary things; very easily frightened; jumpy; nervous)

  [Ex] The coward is afraid of his own shadow.

- be scared to death (of) 몹시 겁먹어 (Extremely frightened)

  [Ex] My dog is scared to death of thunder and firecrackers.

- **chicken out** 겁을 먹고 (~을) 그만두다[(~에서) 꽁무니를 빼다]

  [Ex] Freddy chickened out of the plan at the last minute.

- **cold feet** 겁, 공포, 달아나려는 자세 (To lose desire or nerve to do something)

  [Ex] Sometimes the bride or groom might not show up to their wedding because they've gotten cold feet.

- feel weak at the knees 무릎에 힘이 빠지다

  [Ex] His sudden smile made her feel weak at the knees.

- **freak out** 질겁하다 (To feel fear)

  [Ex] My mom would freak out if I say some bad words.

- **have cold feet** 무서워하다, 주눅 들다 (To suffer from fear or timidity)

  [Ex] I can't give my speech now. I have cold feet.

- **hit the panic button** (뜻밖의 일에 겁을 먹고) 허둥지둥해 버리다

  [Ex] US investors hit the panic button on signs the steepest downturn in generations is choking off profits in America Inc.

- **push[press] the panic button** 당황하여 쩔쩔매다

- **bitch out** 겁이 나 (어떤 일에서) 빠지다 (To not do something out of fear; CHICKEN OUT)

  [Ex] I knew Tony would bitch out.

- pee one's pants 놀라서 오줌을 지리다 (To feel fear)

  [Ex] I almost peed my pants when he told me that story.

- **wet one's pants** 아주 놀라다 (바지에 오줌을 쌀 정도로 놀라다 / To feel fear)

  [Ex] She was wetting her pants, so I didn't have chance to ask her why.

Slang

- **be scared shitless (of)** 몹시 겁먹어 (Extremely frightened)

  [Ex] I was scared shitless when I first moved out here, but things still worked out fine in the end.

- shit in one's shoes 아주 놀라다 (To feel fear)

- shit oneself 겁을 먹다 (To feel fear)

26-4. Liable To Fear (겁 많은, 소심한)

Formal

afraid; cowardly; fearful; spineless; timid; gutless

Informal

- **chicken-hearted** 겁 많은, 소심한 (timid, Liable to fear)

  [Ex] Yes, I'm a chicken-hearted softie. I never try anything too risky.

- lily-livered 겁이 많은 (Cowardly)

  [Ex] I wish a few of our lily livered politicians would follow his example.

- sissified 패기 없는, 유약한 (An effeminate, weak male)

  [Ex] There is no England anymore! I'm ashamed of my sissified English heritage.

- yellow 겁이 많은, 겁쟁이 같은 (Liable to fear)

  [Ex] You must be yellow letting the fight go on.

26-5. A Fit of Fear (오싹함, 전율, 소름)

Formal

anxiety; cold feet; dither; nerves; nervousness

Informal

- **creeps** 오싹한[근질근질한] 느낌, 전율, 혐오감 (A feeling of discomfort, scared or queasy)

   [Ex] Looking at that homeless guy over there gave me the creeps.

- heebie-jeebies 불안 초조한 상태 (The feeling of shivers down your spine)

   [Ex] Walking through the cemetery at night gives me the heebie-jeebies.

- **jitters** 초조함 (특히 중요하거나 어려운 일을 앞두고 느끼는 감정 / A state of nervousness)

   [Ex] I always get the jitters before exams.

- willies 소름 끼침 (Nervousness, jitters, or fright, esp in the phrase give (or get) the willies)

   [Ex] The writhing snakes gave me the willies.

Slang

- shit 놀람 (A fit of fear)

   [Ex] Jesus, you scared the shit out of me!

Happiness and Delight
행복, 기쁨

<u>27-1.</u> Happy (행복한)

Formal

    cheerful; content; delighted; glad; happy; merry; pleased; blithe; elated; joyous; jubilant;

- chipper 원기 왕성한, 명랑한 (Feeling exuberantly happy)

[Ex] I'm feelin' real chipper today! I just stole a cookie and didn't get caught!

- **feel like a million bucks** 몸의 상태가 매우 좋다 (To feel great)

[Ex] Since I got my hair cut, I feel like a million bucks.

- **feel like a million dollars** 몸의 상태가 매우 좋다 (To feel great)

[Ex] Since I got my hair cut, I feel like a million dollars.

- geek 행복한 표정을 짓다

[Ex] She geeked when he asked her out.

- **happy camper** 즐기는 사람, 기분이 좋은 손님 (A happy person)

[Ex] That man who just got rear ended in the car accident does not look like a happy camper! (get rear ended: 추돌 당하다)

- upbeat 긍정적인, 낙관적인 (Optimistic; cheery)

[Ex] The film ends on a surprisingly upbeat note.

Informal

- **high** (술, 마약에) 취한 (Intoxicated from drugs.)

[Ex] Hey man, I'm gonna get high.

- high as a kite (술, 마약)에 완전히 취한

[Ex] Sources who were with Jackson in London claim he was 'as high as a kite' when he arrived 90 minutes late.

- like pigs in clover 매우 운이 좋은 것 같아서, 대만족하여, 아주 기뻐서

[Ex] Once you get to start doing things the right way, you'll love this. If we set it up to where you are doing two or three features a year and working with people you like and respect, you'll be like a pig in clover.

Slang

- a dog with two dicks 아주 행복한, 아주 운이 좋은

[Ex] I'm happier than a dog with two dicks.

- happy as a pig in shit 아주 행복한 (Extremely happy)

[Ex] Put him in the kitchen and he's as happy as a pig in shit.

27-2. Cause Laughter (웃음을 유발하다)

Formal

amuse; cheer; tickle; tickle somebody's funny bone; divert;

- **break up** 크게 웃다[웃기다] (To cause laughter)

[Ex] I always break up when I hear her sing. She's so bad.

- convulse 포복절도하다 (To cause laughter)

[Ex] He had the audience convulsing with laughter.

- crack somebody up ~를 몹시 웃기다 (To cause laughter)

[Ex] Gill's so funny, she just cracks me up.

- have(put) somebody in stiches 큰 웃음을 유발하다 (To cause riotous laughter)

[Ex] The one who really cracks me up, though, is Debbie, aka Tamsin Greig, whose appearance in various TV comedy slots has had me in stiches.

27-3. Laugh (웃다)

Formal

laugh; chortle; chuckle; giggle; guffaw; scream; snicker; snigger; titter

Informal

- **break up** 크게 웃다[웃기다] (To cause laughter)

  [Ex] I always break up when I hear her sing. She's so bad.

- bust a gut 배꼽 빠지게 웃다 (To laugh so hard your stomach hurts.)

  [Ex] I thought I'd bust a gut laughing.

- crack up (~을) 크게 웃(기)다 (To burst into loud laughter)

  [Ex] That movie was great! I couldn't stop cracking up.

- die laughing 우스워 죽다 (To laugh so hard)

  [Ex] That comedian was so funny that the audience nearly died laughing.

- split a gut 크게 웃다 (To laugh uncontrollably)

  [Ex] I thought I'd split a gut laughing.

- split one's side 포복절도하다 (To burst into loud laughter)

  [Ex] After watching "Friends", he split his sides.

Slang

- pee oneself 오줌을 지릴 정도로 웃기다 (To laugh so hard)

  [Ex] The class peed itself laughing.

- piss one's pants 오줌을 쌀 정도로 웃기다 (To burst into loud laughter)

  [Ex] I laughed so hard I nearly peed my pants.

27-4. Enjoy (즐기다)

- dig on 즐기다 (To enjoy)

  [Ex] Right now, I'm really diggin' on that new Erykah Badu song.

- **get a kick out of** ~이 자극적이다, ~이 썩 재미있다 (To enjoy)

  [Ex] I got a kick out of persuading people to buy things.

- **live it up** (보통 돈을 펑펑 쓰면서) 신나게 살다

  [Ex] 1. They're living it up at the Hotel California.– The Eagles / 2. I decided to live it up for a while – at least until the money ran out.

- **Variety is the spice of life.** 변화가 인생을 즐겁게 한다. (Variety is what makes life enjoyable.)

27-5. Make Fun of (놀리다)

- rib (친근하게) 놀리다 (To make fun of)

  [Ex] He was ribbing in class all day.

27-6. Pleasing (기분 좋은)

- ear candy 듣기 좋은, (듣기엔 좋지만) 깊이가 없는 음악

  [Ex] Tonight's program was ear candy and a credit to all.

27-7. A party, Event, Gathering, Meeting (파티, 이벤트, 모임)

Formal

- **kegger** 맥주 파티 (A party at which draft beer is provided)

[Ex] It has almost become a tradition for college students to attend "keggers" every weekend.

- **shindig** 떠들썩한 파티 (A noisy party)

[Ex] Look, just get us into the shindig tonight.

Informal

- blowout 잔치, 파티 (A big party)

[Ex] We're going to have a huge blowout for Valentine's Day.

- **pity party** 신세 한탄 파티

[Ex] After the Bio exam, the girls had such a pity party you'd think someone's dog or grandmother had died.

- sausage party 남자들만의 파티

[Ex] Let's take off. This is just a sausage party.

27-8. Congratulations (축하, 칭찬)

Informal

- **kudos** 명성, 영예, 위신, 칭찬 (Used as a congratulation or to mean good job.)

[Ex] Kudos to you on your winning the spelling bee.

- back-slap (친밀한 표시로) 등을 툭 치다[치기]

[Ex] They exchanged hugs and backslaps, waved in unison, and stood close to one another.

Hard core

강경한, 노골적인

- smash-mouth 격렬한, 공격적인, 난폭한 (Hard-core)

  [Ex] Kentucky is a smash-mouth, half court defensive team that can really guard people.

Honest

정직한

- **on the level** 정직한, 합법적인 (Honest, Possibly from the opposite of "crooked.")

  [Ex] I'm sure he's no crook. He's on the level.

Humiliation

굴욕

30-1. Cause Humiliation (굴욕을 주다)

humble; humiliate; make ashamed; shame; cut down to size; snub; abase; chagrin; chasten; debase; degrade; demean; denigrate; discomfit; mortify; put out of countenance

- **bring(take) someone down a peg** ~의 자만심[콧대]을 꺾다, ~에게 자기 수준을 깨닫게 하다 (To lower someone's high self-opinion)

  [Ex] He needed to be brought down a peg or two.

- put in the dog house 찬밥 신세가 되게 하다 (To lower someone's high self-opinion)

  [Ex] We are put in the dog house if we are not as clean as another country.

30-2. Become Humiliated (굴욕을 당하다)

embarrassed; humiliated; abashed; ashamed; chagrined; mortified

- come down (on) a peg 높은 콧대가 꺾이다, 체면을 잃다 (To become humiliated)

[Ex] A man came down a peg, as his wife made a silly mistake.

- **eat crow** 굴욕을 참다

[Ex] I say I'm a great cook. Then you eat my food and it is no good. I sit there and eat crow.

- **eat humble pie** 잘못[실수]을 인정하고 굴욕을 참다

[Ex] It was the government's turn to eat humble pie.

- **pocket one's pride** (목적 달성을 위해) 자존심을 억누르다 (To become humiliated)

[Ex] I pocketed my pride when I got this job.

- **tuck in one's tail** 꼬리를 감추다, 굴욕을 당하다 (To become humiliated)

Slang

- eat crap 굴욕을 참다 (To become humiliated)

- eat(take) shit 굴욕을 참다 (To become humiliated)

[Ex] Man, are you going to take shit from him like that?

---

31 *Ignorance*
무지, 모름

Informal

- 404 컴맹의, 전자 기기에 깜깜한, 모름, 정보가 없음 (No information)

[Ex] Don't asking him about it, he's 404.

Slang

- Fucked if I know! 정말 아는 바 없다! (I don't know!)

32 *In Trouble*
곤경에 처한

Formal

- in a bind 곤경에 처한 (To be in a bad situation; in trouble)

[Ex] *Killing this hobo put me in a bind.*

- **in a hole** 곤경에 처한 (To be in trouble)

[Ex] *Don't put me in a hole.*

- in over[above] one's head 어쩔 수 없이 (In a situation one can't cope with)

[Ex] *I can see she is a small-town kid in over her head. She wasn't raised on the mean streets of a middle-class San Diego suburb like I was. She needs a few friends and you guys are the best friends to have.*

Informal

- in (deep) doo-doo 곤경에 빠져 (To be serious trouble)

[Ex] *Hain is clearly deep in doo doo and there is probably, as we suggested yesterday, no other way for him than out of the Cabinet.*

Slang

- **in deep shit** 어려운 지경이 되어 (To be serious trouble)

[Ex] *You are in deep shit when you come into work tomorrow.*

Instinct

직감, 육감

Informal

- **gut feeling** 직감, 육감六感 (An instinct or intuition)

[Ex] *I have a gut feeling that he is not the murderer.*

영어 표현에도 등급이 있다!

34 *Large*
커다란, 거대한

Formal

bulky; gigantic; colossal; monumental; stupendous

Informal

- **daddy of all** 거대한 (Large)

  [Ex] My first stop was to see the daddy of all geysers.

- hefty 크고 무거운 (Heavy, bulky)

  [Ex] The maintenance cost must be pretty hefty for such a big house.

- hulking (흔히 불안감을 줄 정도로) 거대한

  [Ex] When I woke up there was a hulking figure staring down at me.

- **humongous** 거대한 (Huge, enormous)

  [Ex] They got these humongous waves in Waimea.

- **mother of all** 최대의, 가장 큰

  [Ex] I got stuck in the mother of all traffic jams.

- **whopping** 엄청 큰 (Very large)

  [Ex] The Russian leader won a whopping 89.9 percent yes vote.

Menstruation, Menstrual Period

생리, 월경

Formal

- **delicate** 생리중인 (On monthly period)

  [Ex] I'm feeling delicate.

- **that time of the month** 생리 기간 (A menstrual period)

  [Ex] It's that time of the month again.

Informal

- Aunt Flo 월경 (Menstrual period, Sometimes abbreviated as AF, Also Aunt Flo and cousin Red.)

  [Ex] I had unexpected company last night... Aunt Flo and cousin Red came to visit.

- on the blob 생리중인 (Having one's menstrual period.)

  [Ex] My girlfriend is on the blob, so we couldn't have sex.

- on the rag 생리중인 (To menstruate, Origin: possibly from old-style pads)

  [Ex] Man, stay away from Casey. I think she's on the rag.

- red tide 생리기간 (Menstrual period)

  [Ex] She's still having her red tide so she is going to buy more pads.

36 Mental Illness

우울, 미침

36-1. Depressed (우울한, 침울한, 낙담한)

Formal

cheerless; dejected; glum; grim; moody; sad; unhappy; gloomy; crest-fallen; depressed; despondent; disconsolate; dispirited; downcast; downhearted; heavy-hearted; melancholy; morose; woebegone(비통에 잠긴)

Informal

- case of the Mondays 월요병

 [Ex] Sounds like you've got a serious case of the Mondays.

- down in the dumps 우울한 (Depressed)

 [Ex] I've been down in the dumps for the past few days.

- down in the mouth 우울한 (Depressed)

 [Ex] Mark was certainly down in the mouth when he lost his dog.

- in a funk 침울한 (Depressed)

 [Ex] He is sitting in his room in a funk.

- **PMS** 월경 전 증후군 (Pre-menstrual syndrome, to be grumpy or moody)

 [Ex] She's really PMS-ing today.

- singing the blues 울상을 짓고 있는, 침울한 (Depressed)

 [Ex] He is singing the blues because his girlfriend has left him.

36-2. A Fit of Depression (우울, 의기소침)

Formal

dejection; black mood; doldrums; ennui; lassitude; low spirits; melancholia; stupor; torpor;

- **blues** 우울 (Sadness; a mood of depression)

[Ex] You'll have to excuse Bill. He's getting the blues thinking about Jane.

- funk 의기소침, 실의, 낙담 (Sadness; a mood of depression)

[Ex] Don't get in a funk about your job. Things'll get better.

36-3. Have a Mental Breakdown (미치다, 정신이 나가다)

Formal

experience a mental collapse; have a breakdown; suffer a breakdown; go crazy; go insane; go mad; go out of one's mind; lose control; become demented; become psychotic; suffer from nervous prostration;

- **blow one's mind** 미치게 하다 (To become insane; to amaze)

[Ex] That concert blew my mind.

- **come apart at the seams** 분노가 폭발하다, 감정을 억제하지 못하다

[Ex] I couldn't take any more. I just came apart at the seams.

- come unglued 미치다 (To have a mental breakdown)

[Ex] If she hears what you're saying, she's going to come unglued.

- come unstuck 미치다 (To have a mental breakdown)

[Ex] But he comes unstuck when the kid's bargaining skills prove better than his.

- **go to pieces** 몸과 마음이 허물어지다 (To go crazy)

[Ex] She's a strong woman, but she nearly went to pieces when Arnie died.

Informal

- **crack up** (중압감을 못 이기고 정신적으로나 육체적으로) 무너지다, 쓰러지다

  [Ex] She was under so much pressure at work that she cracked up.

- **drive nuts** 미치게 하다 (To make crazy)

  [Ex] That guy's voice is driving me nuts. Makes me want to kill myself!

- flip one's lid 자제력을 잃다, 발끈하다 (To lose one's temper)

  [Ex] Your dad is going to flip his lid when he sees what you did to his car.

- flip one's wig 자제력을 잃다, 발끈하다 (To lose one's temper)

  [Ex] Poor old David Dee has flipped his wig.

- **freak out** 미치다 (To become insane)

  [Ex] People were crying and freaking out.

- go batty 미치다, 돌다 (To go crazy)

  [Ex] They went batty, absolutely mad because they said they didn't want to show women's boxing.

- go crackers 미치다, 돌다 (To go crazy)

  [Ex] Then Sexby went crackers and almost raped her.

- **go nuts** 미치다 (To go crazy)

  [Ex] About once a week we get this way. I mean we just go nuts on each other.

- go off one's bean[head, nut] 미치다 (To go crazy)

- **go off one's rocker** 미치다 (To go crazy)

  [Ex] The neighbors must think I've gone off my rocker.

- go out of one's skull 미치다 (To go crazy)

  [Ex] She went out of her skull after her divorce.

- **lose one's marbles** 미치다 (To go insane)

  [Ex] He lost his marbles when he heard the shocking news.

- schiz out 미치다 (To go insane)

  [Ex] I schizzed out during the test. Got an F.

36-4. Crazy, Retarded (미친, 정신이 모자란)

Formal

certifiable(정신이상인); insane; mentally ill; not in one's right mind; crazy; crazy as a loon; mad; mental; not right in the head; sick in the head; demented; deranged; non compos mentis(정신상태가 정상이 아닌);

- touched in the head 머리가 약간 이상한 (Crazy)

[Ex] He's a little touched in the head.

- unhinged 불안정한, 흐트러진, 혼란한 (Angered or crazy)

[Ex] Hillaryland has been sounding more and more unhinged recently.

Informal

- bananas 바보 같은[같이], 멍청한, 멍청아! (Stupid)

[Ex] That Chris Tucker movie was bananas.

- bats (in the belfry) 정신 이상의, 미친 (Crazy)

[Ex] Maybe she has bats in her belfry.

- batty 머리가 돈, 미친, 어리석은 (Crazy, usually in reference to a person)

[Ex] That music is driving me batty.

- **bonkers** 술 취한, 정신이 돈, 미친(mad), 제정신이 아닌

[Ex] He just went bonkers.

- crackers 미친 (Crazy, Nuts, Extremely foolish)

[Ex] Our English teacher is crackers.

- cuckoo 미친 (Crazy)

[Ex] One was going cuckoo and the other making a warbling sort of noise.

- few beers short of a six-pack; few cents short of a dollar; few fries short of a happy meal; few peas short of a casserole: few sandwiches short of a picnic 정신이 나간 (Stupid; Retarded)

- have a screw loose 머리가 돌다, 미치다 (To go crazy)

[Ex] He dresses his cats up in little coats for the winter. Sometimes I think he must have a screw loose.

- kooky 괴짜의, 머리가 좀 돈 (Slightly strange or eccentric)

[Ex] She's been mocked for her kooky ways.

- lights are on, but nobody's home 약간 정신이 나간 (Stupid; Retarded)
- **loco** 미친 (Someone who is crazy. From the Spanish "loco" meaning "crazy")

  [Ex] What's up, loco?
- loony 미친 (Crazy)

  [Ex] He does have some pretty loony ideas.
- **nuts** 미친, 제정신이 아닌 (Crazy)

  [Ex] My friends think I'm nuts for saying yes.
- **nutty** 미친 (To be funny acting or stupid; retarded; crazy, daring)

  [Ex] That dude is nuttier than squirrel turds.
- **nutty as a fruitcake** 미친 (Crazy)

  [Ex] He's as nutty as a fruitcake. Do you know what he did yesterday? He had lunch outside in the pouring rain.
- **off (one's) rocker** 미친, 통제가 안 되는 (Crazy, out of control)

  [Ex] He's really off his rocker!
- psycho 미친, 미친 사람 (Psychotic)

  [Ex] My ex-girlfriend is psycho.
- schizo 정신분열증 환자 (A person with schizophrenia)

  [Ex] It's usually dim-wits who are fanatical, don't you agree? Dim-wits, schizos and sociopaths.
- screwy 나사가 풀린 듯한, 이상한 (Strange)

  [Ex] My car has been acting screwy lately.
- **sicko** 이상 심리 소유자, 정신병자 같은 사람 (A disturbing or gross person)

  [Ex] I don't need to feel like some sicko just because I read someone's clothes.
- **wacko** 미친, 제정신이 아닌, 분별없는 (Crazy)

  [Ex] He's wacko.
- whack 미친 (Crazy)

  [Ex] She is whack.
- whacked out 미친, 제정신이 아닌 (Crazy; alternative spelling of "wacked out")

  [Ex] Look, it ain't my fault they seem to need to believe their artists are a little whacked out and confused.

- batshit crazy 아주 미친 (Extremely crazy)

  [Ex] Either way, it's nice to see that not all of the batshit crazy religious folks out there are American.

- crazy as a catshit 머리가 돈, 미친, 어리석은 (Crazy)

37 *Muscular*
근육질의, 우람한

Informal

- beefy 우람한

  [Ex] Look at him! He is so beefy!

- **buff** 근골이 늠름한 (Muscular)

  [Ex] He is buff.

- built 좋은 체격의 (Large, well built, highly muscular, great presence, huge)

  [Ex] He is so built.

38 Naked, Unclothed, Disrobed
나체의, 알몸의, 옷을 벗고

Informal

- **birthday suit** 맨살, 알몸 (Nudity)

  [Ex] The guests at the pool party were dressed in their birthday suits.

- **buck naked** 완전히 벗은 (Completely nude)

  [Ex] The man was running down the street buck naked!

- **in the buff** 옷을 하나도 안 걸친, 알몸의 (To be nude)

  [Ex] Strippers are in the buff.

- **skinny-dip** 알몸으로 헤엄치다[헤엄치기] (To swim naked)

  [Ex] At least once a month I would catch girls skinny dipping in the pool.

- **stark-naked** 홀딱 벗은, 실오라기 하나 안 걸친 (Completely naked)

  [Ex] They often wandered around the house stark naked.

None, Nothing At All

없음, 무

Formal

not any; not a bit; not a thing

Informal

- damn-all 쥐뿔(도 ~아니다[모르다]) (Nothing at all)

  [Ex] I know damn all about computers.

Slang

- diddley-shit 전혀 없음, 전혀 아님 (A small or worthless amount; nothing at all)

  [Ex] I don't give a doodly-shit.

- fuck-all 전혀 없음 (nothing, nothing at all)

  [Ex] These instructions make fuck all sense to me.

Not To Care
상관하지 않음, 관계없음

- **Been there, done that.** 거기엔 이미 가 봤고, 다 안다.

  [Ex] Been there done that, now wearing the T-shirt.

- Does it look like I give a damn? 내가 신경이라도 쓰는 것처럼 보이냐? (나는 하나도 상관 안

  해. 나는 전혀 상관없어. / I don't give a damn.)

- **I could care less!** 전혀 관심 없어. (I don't give a damn.)

- **No skin off my ass[butt].** 그것은 내 알 바 아니다. (I don't give a damn.)

- **No skin off my nose.** 그것은 내 알 바 아니다. (I don't give a damn.)

- Does it look like I give a fuck[shit]? 내가 신경이라도 쓰는 것처럼 보이냐? (나는 하나도 상

  관 안 해. 나는 전혀 상관 없어. / I don't give a damn.)

- **give a flying fuck** 신경 쓰다, 상관하다 (To care; Used always to imply that one doesn't care.)

  [Ex] I don't give a flying fuck.

- give a rat's ass 신경 쓰다, 상관하다

  [Ex] I don't give a rat's ass what you think!

- **give a shit** 신경 쓰다, 상관하다 (To care)

  [Ex] I don't give a shit about any of this.

- It sucks to be you. 그것 참 안되었네. (I don't care; that's too bad.)

Okay, Fine

좋아, 괜찮아

Formal

- kosher 1. 유대교 율법에 따라 만든 2. 정직한, 합법적인 (Very good, excellent; cool; fine; okay)

  [Ex] *Is everything kosher?*

- **peachy** 좋은, 아주 멋진 (Good)

  [Ex] *Everything's peachy.*

- **swell** 아주 좋은[즐거운, 멋진]

  [Ex] *A: how are you(or how's it going)? / B: Swell, just swell.*

Informal

- ain't nothing but a chicken wing 문제없다, 대수롭지 않다

  [Ex] *To me it ain't nothing but a chicken wing.*

- **chill** (계획 따위가) 완벽한, 좋은, 굉장한 (Great, awesome; cool)

  [Ex] *My boyfriend's new Mustang is way chill.*

- straight 좋다 (Fine; okay)

영어 표현에도 등급이 있다!

Patient
참는, 참을성 있는

Formal

- sit tight 움직이지 않고 가만히 있다 (To stay in one place and wait patiently)

  [Ex] Annie: Sit tight. I'll be back. I said sit tight! / Carlo Reni: That's not something I'm good at – sit tight.

- **stay put** 꼼짝 말고 그대로 있어

  [Ex] Stay put for a few more moments.

Pregnant
임신한

Informal

- **knocked up** 임신한 (Pregnant)

  [Ex] She's knocked up.

Relation
관계

Informal

- **shotgun wedding** (신부의 임신 등으로 인해) 급히 치러야 하는 결혼식, 속도위반 결혼

  [Ex] Wasn't that a shotgun wedding?

- **vibe** 분위기, 낌새, 느낌 (A distinctive emotional atmosphere)

  [Ex] 1. I'm picking up some pretty negative vibes. / 2. The coffee shop has a nice vibe.

45 *Relaxation*
느긋함, 여유

45-1. Relaxed (느긋한, 긴장이 풀린)

Formal

easing up; loosening up; relaxed; slowing down; unwinding; de-stressed; putting one's feet up; unbending; reposing

Informal

- **chill** 진정하다 (To calm down)

  [Ex] You need to chill before you're completely pissed.

- **cool** (열정·분노 따위를) 식히다, (사람을) 달래다, 진정시키다

  [Ex] After the argument, Bill asked Andrew, "We cool?", and Andrew replied, "Ya, we cool."

- hang loose 차분하다, 평정을 유지하다, 무사태평하다

  [Ex] Weekends are important: time to hang loose and take stock of things.

- **kick back** 긴장을 풀다, 쉬다 (To recline, as in a reclining chair)

  [Ex] Kick back and put your feet up.

- **laid back** 느긋한, 태평스러운 (Relaxed, calm, not anxious)

  [Ex] My brother is so laid back.

- **R and R** 휴식 (Rest and relaxation)

  [Ex] I could use some serious R and R.

- **take it easy** 일을 쉬엄쉬엄하다 (To relax)

  [Ex] I'm just taking it easy… watching some TV.

- **unwind** 긴장을 풀다 (To relax)

  [Ex] I'm tired of work. I'm going home to unwind.

45-2. Sleep (잠자다)

Formal

doze; drift off; fall asleep; go to sleep; nap; rest; take a nap; take a rest; take a siesta; catnap; drowse; slumber;

- **turn in** 잠자리에 들다 (To go to bed)

[Ex] I think I'm going to turn in. See you in the morning.

Informal

- catch some z's 잠자다, 눈 좀 붙이다 (To sleep)

[Ex] I want to hit the sack and catch some z's.

- conk out 잠이 들다 (To fall asleep)

[Ex] She's conked out.

- cop some z's 잠깐[선잠] 자다 (To sleep)

[Ex] She copped some Z's at the bar.

- **crash** 자다, 무료로 묵다 (To sleep)

[Ex] You can always crash at one of our places.

- get some shuteye 한숨 자다 (To sleep)

[Ex] Pawpaw said as he tried to get some shuteye while my brother and I contin-ued to fish.

- **hit the hay** 잠자리에 들다, 자다 (To go to bed)

[Ex] I'm for hitting the hay too, this cold has me very tired.

- **hit the sack** 잠자리에 들다, 자다 (To go to bed)

[Ex] I'm tired, I'm going to hit the sack.

- sack out 자러 가다, 잠자리에 들다 (To sleep)

[Ex] Rachel sacked out with her mother's lullaby.

- **spoon** (남자가 여자를 뒤에서 껴안고) 잠자다 (To sleep with another person at your back, faced the same direction, usually a male behind a female.)

[Ex] Kenneth and Will spoon together every night.

46 Rich
부자인

Informal

- **filthy rich** 대단히 부유한 (Extremely rich)

[Ex] Look at Posh and Becks who are filthy rich.

47 Rumor
소문

Informal

- **viral** 입소문에 의한 (Popular due to being forwarded between people who know each other)

[Ex] Concerns about the Internet's harmful effects on our brains and lives have gone, well, viral.

Sentimental

감상적인

Informal

- hokey 유난히 감상적인 (Corny)

  [Ex] Most set ups are hokey and contrived. This one was good. I mean, it wasn't new but the acting was a lot better than what I expected.

- schmaltz 몹시 감상적인 곡, 감상주의 (Too sentimental)

  [Ex] A schmaltzy wedding.

- schmaltzy[schmalzy, shmaltzy, shmalzy] 몹시 감상적인 (Too sentimental)

  [Ex] A bathroom stop took almost 30 minutes because they had to peruse every item in the schmaltzy gift shop.

49 *Small*
작은, 조그만

Formal

pint-sized; pocket-sized; runty; shrimpy; diminutive

Informal

- bitty (아주) 조그만 (어린이 말 / Little, small, insignificant)

  [Ex] It's a bitty little thing, isn't it?

- dinky 작은 (Small)

  [Ex] There's no way your dinky car will make it up the mountain.

- **measly** 쥐꼬리만 한 (Unimpressive; small in number)

  [Ex] My measly paycheck can barely cover my rent and living expenses.

- mickey mouse 중요하지 않은, 작은 (Unimportant; small)

  [Ex] Who's in charge of this mickey mouse operation, anyway?

- teeny 작은 (Small)

  [Ex] The teeny molecule might have other medical uses.

- **teeny-weeny** 작은 (Small)

  [Ex] Someone give us one single little teeny weeny bit of evidence, please.

Stupid
멍청한, 지능이 낮은

Formal

unintelligent; retarded; stupid

Informal

- all foam, no beer 멍청한, 지능이 낮은 (Stupid; retarded)
- few beers short of a six-pack; few cents short of a dollar; few fries short of a happy meal; few peas short of a casserole; few pecans short of a fruitcake; few sandwiches short of a picnic; few slices short of a loaf; few spokes short of a wheel 약간 정신이 뒤떨어지다 (Stupid; Retarded)
- **half there** (정신 상태가) 덜 떨어진 (Stupid; retarded)
- lift doesn't go to the top floor 약간 정신이 덜떨어지다 (Stupid; retarded)
- **lights are on, but nobody's home** (정신 상태가) 덜떨어진 (Stupid; retarded)
  [Ex] Don't try discussing anything intelligent with Alice. The lights are on but nobody's home, I'm afraid.
- **not all there** (특히 정신병 때문에) 별로 똑똑하지 못한
- not playing the full deck; not the brightest bulb in the chandelier; not the brightest light in the harbor; not the sharpest knife in the drawer (정신 상태가) 덜 떨어진 (Stupid; retarded)
- one brick short of a load 약간 정신이 모자란 (Stupid; retarded)
- terminally stupid 아주 멍청한 (Stupid; retarded)
- wheel is turning but hamsters' dead 약간 멍청한 (Stupid; retarded)

Stylish, Styling
멋진, 근사한

Informal

- banging 멋진, 근사한 (To be stylish)

  [Ex] Her outfit is bangin'!

- **cool** 멋진, 근사한, 훌륭한, (사교적으로) 세련된, 똑똑한 (Excellent, wonderful)

  [Ex] That new bike is cool.

- fitted 잘 맞는 옷을 입은 (Dressed well)

  [Ex] That boy is fitted!

- **hip** 유행에 밝은, 최신 유행인 (To be stylish)

  [Ex] Hey, man, that guy is really hip!

- sassy 멋지게 옷을 입는 (Styling)

  [Ex] Those clothes are sassy!

- snazzy 맵시 있는, 세련된 (To be stylish)

  [Ex] If you give the correct answer, you will get a snazzy car as a prize!

- **swag** 스타일이 좋음 (Style, From swagger)

  [Ex] That boy got some swag.

- swagger 'Cool'한 스타일이나 태도 (Style, attitude, or general demeanor that is "cool")

  [Ex] Demarcus' swagger is strong – he always has on something nice.

- swanky 매력적인, 스타일 있는 (Attractive or stylish, Also swanky)

  [Ex] Those are some swanky shoes!

Successful
성공적인

Informal

- **ball** 성공하다 (To be successful. Typically used to refer to men, and often implies an abundance of money, women, nice clothes, expensive cars, etc. Also big balling)

  [Ex] You know that's a baller; he keeps three or four females at all times.

- home run 성공 (A success)

  [Ex] I think we're going to hit a home run with this new album.

- score a touchdown 성공하다, 득점하다 (To success)

  [Ex] He had scored a touchdown the first time that he was given the ball!

- **smash** (노래, 영화, 연극의) 엄청난 히트[대성공]

  [Ex] That movie was a huge smash!

- touchdown 성공, 득점 (A success)

  [Ex] When you lose a game by a single touchdown, it always hurts more.

Tired / Out of It

피곤한, 녹초가 된

Formal

drained; drooping; droopy; drowsy; exhausted; fatigued; tired; worn; worn out; burned out; dead on one's feet; dog-tired; out of it; run-down; sleepy; enervated; flagging; haggard; prostrated; spent

Informal

- **beat** 지쳐 빠진 (Tired; spent)

  [Ex] After two games of football, man, I am beat.

- bushed 몹시 지친 (Tired)

  [Ex] The next day I was completely bushed.

- done for 1. 몹시 지쳐, 다 써버려, 탕진된 상태로 결딴나서 2. 죽어서, 다 죽어가서

  [Ex] Those chicks are done for. They had too much to drink.

- **pooped** 녹초가 된, 기진맥진한 (Tired; exhausted)

  [Ex] I'm too pooped to pop.

- **strung out** (육체적·정서적으로) 소모[고갈]된 (exhausted; Tired)

  [Ex] Carrie Fisher looks like she's strung out on drugs.

- wasted 너무 피곤한 (Too tired to proceed)

  [Ex] I'm wasted, man.

- wiped out 녹초가 된, 기진맥진한 (Tired; exhausted)

  [Ex] I'm pretty wiped out. I think I'll go to bed.

- zonked 지쳐 빠진, 녹초가 된 (Exhausted)

  [Ex] We were so zonked after The Late Show.

To Go to the Bathroom, Use the Restroom 용변, 화장실

Informal

- bio break (채팅이나 회의 도중) 화장실에 가기 위한 짧은 휴식

  [Ex] Do you guys need a bio break? Let's break for ten, and then I'll continue the presentation.

- potty break 화장실에 가기 위한 짧은 휴식 (A bathroom break)

  [Ex] Things reach crisis point when a monk announces over the public address system that 'Santa needs a potty break'.

Treated Badly
학대받는

Informal

- like a doormat 불쌍한, 천대[학대]를 받는 (Poorly, regarding how someone treats another)

  [Ex] Why do you let her treat you like a doormat?

56 *Wild, Ridiculous, Extreme* 거친, 무모한, 극단적인

Formal

- **no holds barred** 어떤 제약도 없이 모든 수단을 동원하여 (Without restrictions)

  [Ex] It is a war with no holds barred and we must prepare to resist.

Informal

- balls out 무모하게 (With reckless abandon and extreme courage)

  [Ex] You just have to go balls out to win this game.

- balls to the wall 끝까지, 극단적으로, 최후까지 (Extreme, all out)

  [Ex] This is the last game of the season, boys! So, it's balls to the wall!

- buck wild 거친, 통제가 안 되는, 무례한 (Uncontrollable, uncivilized; wild; crazy)

  [Ex] I'm tired of going to parties where everybody is buck wild.

- fired up 열광한, 흥분한 (Wild)

  [Ex] When the issue arose, they suddenly became fired up.

- **hard core** 핵심의, 절대적인, 무제한의, 단호한, 철저한, 본격적인, (사회의) 최하층의, 만성 실업의, (포르노 영화, 소설 등) 극도로 노골적인

  [Ex] I can't believe he went to a strip club at 12:30 in the afternoon. That's pretty hard core.

- **off the hook** 아주 좋은, 굉장한 (Very good, excellent)

  [Ex] Whoa, that shirt is off the hook.

57 Wonderful, Excellent, Splendid
Fabulous 훌륭한, 멋진, 끝내주는

Informal

- bananas 열광한, 흥분한 (Excellent; unbelievable; ridiculous)

  [Ex] Penny: Dave, this sandwich is bananas. / Dave: Thanks, Pen.

- bangin' 끝내주는 (The bomb; extremely good)

  [Ex] That new cd is bangin'!

- whiz-bang 소형의 초고속 포탄, 주목을 받는 신기술, 훌륭한

  [Ex] This software update has a lot of new whiz-bang features!

- yummy 아주 맛있는 (Delicious, desirable)

  [Ex] Q: Let's take the rest of the week off and go to Cancun for a stint… sounds yummy. / A: Absolutely, yum yum!

Chapter 3

Expressing One's Feeling and States
자신의 감정이나 상태를 나타내는 감탄사 및 표현들

내부의 감정이나 상태는 비언어적인 동작이나 표정들로 표현되기도 하지만, 감탄사나 감탄문의 형식으로 바로 입 밖으로 나오게 되는데, 이런 경우 정중한 표현들만큼이나 informal expression이나 속어들도 많이 사용되고 있습니다. Informal 표현들이나 slang이 갖는 가장 흥미로운 부분은 감정이나 상태를 직접적으로 표현해주는 데 있기 때문입니다. 이번 장에서는 감정이나 상태를 표현할 때 거의 감탄사처럼 습관적으로 사용하는 표현들을 정리하였습니다.

1

Agreement and Approval

긍정, 허락

Formal

Affirmative; Agreed; By all means; Certainly; Definitely; Indeed; Naturally; Of course; Yes; All right; Amen; No kidding; Okay; Okey-dokey; Sure; Sure thing; Uh-huh; Assuredly; Beyond a doubt; Granted; Indubitably; Just so; Undoubtedly; Unquestionably; Willingly; Without fail; Cross my heart; Definitely; I know for sure; No ifs, ands or buts; No two ways about it; Sure as I live and breathe; Beyond doubt; Indubitably; Irrefutably; Undeniably;

- **Amen to that!** 그 말이 맞다! (동의를 나타냄 / I am agreeing.)

 [Ex] Amen to that, I want him to stay healthy, too.

- **Check!** 좋다, 알았다! (Ok, or yes; acknowledgment of an item from a checklist)

 [Ex] Let's go to the club next weekend. Check.

- **Cool!** 좋아, 좋다! (제안에 찬성·동의를 나타냄 / Good or great)

 [Ex] Cool!

- **Don't mind if I do!** 그거 좋죠!

- **down** (계획에) 동의하는

 [Ex] I'm down for[with] that.

- **For sure!** (의심할 여지없이) 확실히[틀림없이] (Certainly)

 [Ex] A: Want to get some food? / B: For sure.

- **I'll drink to that.** (상대에 동의하여) 그렇다, 동감이요, 찬성이다. (I agree with you.)

 [Ex] A: My conclusion is that we need to respect each other for our accomplishments more. / B. I'll drink to that.

- **No buts about it!** 두말 말고 해 주게! (Without a doubt!)

- **Right on!** 옳소[잘한다]! (강한 찬성·격려를 나타냄)

 [Ex] A: You're going dancing tonight? / B: Right on.

- **Scout's honor.** 정말이다. ((보이) 스카우트의 영예를 걸고 말하는 것)

 [Ex] Lee: Scout's honor? / Don: On my mother's grave.

- **Sounds like a plan!** 좋은 생각이야! (That sounds great!)
- **You bet your life!** 틀림없다! (Certainly, Definitely)
- **You bet!** 물론이지[바로 그거야]! (Certainly, Definitely)
- **You betcha!** 물론이지[바로 그거야]! (Certainly, Definitely)
- **You can say that again!** 정말 그렇다, (당신 말에) 전적으로 동의한다.
- **You said a mouthful!** 맞았어, 바로 그거야! (That's right!)
- **You'd better believe it!** 믿어도 돼, 틀림없다니까. (It's sure!)
- **You're telling me!** 내 말이 바로 그 말이에요[전적으로 동의해요]!

Informal

- **Damn straight!** 그래 맞다.

  [Ex] A: Wow, this band is awesome! / B: Damn straight!

- Dead sure! 틀림없다. (Certainly, Definitely)
- Hot diggety! 이것 좋은데! 좋지!

  [Ex] Speaker: Do you want to go to the party? / Response: Hot Diggety!

- No diggity! 정말로! 정말이지! (Roughly equivalent to "serious." Used similarly to phrases such as, "Seriously?", "Are you serious?" etc. Can also be used as a statement rather than a question, meaning "Seriously!" Popularized by R&B/rap group Blackstreet in their song "No Diggity" on the 1996 album Another Level.)

  [Ex] Sally: Einstein was smart! / Bennie: No diggity? / Sally: No diggity!

- **Rock and roll!** 멋지다, 좋다! (Statement of support, agreement, encouragement)
- **Rock 'n' roll!** 멋지다, 좋다!

  [Ex] 1. A: Ready to go? / B: Rock 'n' roll.
  2. A: We're going to a theme park tomorrow. / B: Rock 'n' roll!

- Hot dog! 좋아! 대단해! (Delighted agreement; exclamation of excitement)
- **Is the Pope Catholic?** 뻔한 이야기를 묻지 마시오, 당연하지 않은가? (A rhetorical question in response to a question where the answer is an emphatic yes; This is the answer you give when somebody asks a stupid question when they already know the answer is yes. Or it's the emphatic way of answering yes to a question.)

  [Ex] A: Would you like to go to the beach? B: Is the Pope Catholic?

- No duh! 쳇![그걸 누가 몰라!] (Scornful agreement with something the speaker thinks should go without saying)

  [Ex] Speaker: Don't run that red light. / Response: No duh!

- **Oh, what the heck!** 에라 모르겠다! (하지 말아야 할 것을 하려고 할 때, 내뱉는 말)

  [Ex] It means I'll be late for work but what the heck!

- **Oh, what the hell!** 알 게 뭐야, 아무려면 어때!

  [Ex] I shouldn't tell this story, but what the hell.

Slang

- **Abso-fucking-lutely!** (Absolutely를 강조한 것 / Absolutely; The insertion of "fucking" places emphasis on the use of "absolutely". "absolutely, without a doubt")

  [Ex] I have abso-fucking-lutely too much homework.

- **Fuckin' A** ('Fucking Affirmative'에서 온 말로 강한 긍정을 나타냄 / An exclamation of satisfaction or happiness; Expression used to denote correctness; "Fucking affirmative". Originated in US army.)

  [Ex] Person A: Hey dude, I got the beer. We're all set. Person B: Fuckin' A, man!

- Fucking ay, aye! ('Fucking Affirmative'에서 온 말로 강한 긍정을 나타냄)

- **No shit!** 뻔하지! 당연하지! (강한 Yes의 의미)

  [Ex] 1. Speaker: Don't run that red light. / Response: No shit.
  2. Speaker: I bet it hurt when you got shot in the chest. / Response: No shit.

- **Sure as devil[hell, shit]!** 틀림없다! (Certainly, Definitely)

- **You bet your (sweet) ass!** 당연하지! (Certainly, Definitely)

② Disagreement and Disapproval 부정, 반대

Formal

I don't think so; Never; No; Not at all; Of course not; Not really; That's a negative; By no means; Most certainly not; Under no circumstances;

- **Forget it!** 생각도 하지 마! (No의 뜻을 강하게 나타냄 / Strong statement of "no")

- **Get over it!** 그건 잊어버려.

- **In your dreams!** 꿈 깨[꿈같은 얘기로군]! (가망 없는 꿈을 꾸고 있다는 뜻)

[Ex] Daniels: One day I'll be mayor of this city! / Smith: In your dreams! Who would vote for you?

- Nah! 아니(오) (No; To disagree, disapprove, or doubt)

- **Negative!** 아니(오) (no, Another way of saying no.)

[Ex] Jena: I know you like that bull Jerome! / Mia: Negativity. He looks like a monkey.

- **Never in a million years!** 절대로 ~하지 않다 (By no means)

- Nix! 퇴짜 놓다, 거부하다, 안 된다 (To reject or cancel)

- **No way!** 절대로[결코] 아니다[안 되다] (Interjection of doubt; an emphatic "no")

[Ex] A: Do you want to go to the party? / B: No way. My ex is going to be there.

- Not in my backyard! 내 뒷마당에서는 안 된다! (NIMBY)

- **Not in my job description!** 내가 하는 일이 아니다! 그 일은 하지 않겠다! (According to the terms of my contract, I don't have to do this, and I'm not going to.)

[Ex] Cleaning the office is not in my job description.

- **Not on (one's) life** 절대로[결코] 아니다[안 되다]

[Ex] Teenager: Mom, can I stay out after curfew? / Mother: Not on your life.

- **Over my dead body!** 내 눈에 흙이 들어가기 전에는 (안 된다.)

[Ex] Tobias: Um, I'm going to Vegas with Kitty. / Narrator: But Lindsay wasn't about to lose her man without a fight. / Lindsay: Over my dead body!

- Get your head out of your ass! 자기중심적인 태도는 그만! (Stop being so self-involved.)

- No fucking way! 절대로 아니다. (By no means)

- What in the fuck is this shit? 이건 도대체 뭐야? (What is this?)

3 *Amusement*

웃김, 재미있음

Formal

- FOFL 배꼽 빠지게 웃다 (Falling on floor, laughing)
- get (one's) groove on 즐겁게 춤추다 (To have fun dancing. Also get (one's) swerve on.)

[Ex] Yeah, I was at that party; I really got my groove on.

- **have a ball** 신나게 즐기다 (To have a great time)

[Ex] Don't you guys worry, I have a gift with dogs, okay? Wilfred's gonna have a ball.

- **have a field day** (특히 남들이 좋게 보지 않는 것을) 신나게 즐기다 (To have a great time)

[Ex] The health-scare "experts" are having a field day with their Doomsday predictions.

- Rolling on the floor laughing (온라인 채팅을 할 때 이전의 포스팅이나 채팅 상대방의 농담에 대한 열렬한 반응을 나타내는 말로 포복절도하는 모습을 나타냄)

Informal

- Laughing my ass off! 배꼽을 잡고 웃고 있는 중!
- LMFAO 배꼽 빠지게 웃다 (Laughing my fucking ass off)

[Ex] Someone told me Michelle deserved to win Pop Idol, and I was LMFAO.

- ROTFLMAO (온라인 채팅을 할 때, 이전의 포스팅이나 채팅 상대방의 농담에 대한 열렬한 반응을 나타내는 말로 포복절도하는 모습을 나타냄 / Rolling on the floor, laughing my ass off)

Anger, Displeasure, Dismay, Disappointment 화남, 기분 나쁨, 실망

Formal

Oh my!; Oh no!; Oh my lord!; Goodness!

Informal

- Cripes[Cripe]! (놀라움을 나타내어) 이크, 그것참, 우라질, 제기랄!

  [Ex] Cripes, I forgot my keys again!

- **Damn!** 빌어먹을, 우라질! (무엇이 짜증스러움을 나타내는 욕설)

  [Ex] Damn! I hate him.

- Damn and blast! 빌어먹을, 우라질! (무엇이 짜증스러움을 나타내는 욕설)

- **Damn it!** 빌어먹을! (An exclamation of displeasure)

  [Ex] Lana: Damn it, we're never gonna find Benoit! / Archer: ··· and we might if you two would stop being bitches for five seconds!

- Damn it to hell! 빌어먹을!

  [Ex] Damn it to hell! My old lady got drunk and fucked Wayne!

- doggone 빌어먹을, 망할 놈의 (짜증스럽거나 놀랄 때 씀)

  [Ex] My dad worked at a doggone poultry farm his whole life.

- **Go to hell!** 우라질, 제기랄! (A contemptuous dismissal)

- **Goddamn!** 우라질, 제기랄! (Exclamation of displeasure)

- Golly! 야, 와! (놀람을 나타냄 / Interjection of surprise)

- Hang it! 제기랄! (Exclamation of displeasure)

- **Heck!** 젠장, 제기랄! (An interjection expressing mild to moderate displeasure)

  [Ex] Heck, guys. It's just hell.

- **Hell!** 제기랄, 빌어먹을! (General exclamation, usually (but not always) conveying displeasure)

  [Ex] A: What movie should we go see? / B: Hell, I don't know.

- Hell's bells! 우라질, 제기랄! (Exclamation of surprise or delight)

- **Jesus!** 제기랄, 우라질, 세상에, 이럴 수가! (놀람·실망·불신·공포·강조 등의 소리)

  [Ex] Jesus, that was a good meal!

- **OMG** 어머나, 세상에 (Acronym for "Oh my God", a general-purpose exclamation)

  [Ex] OMG - this is the best pizza I've ever had!

- **Son of a gun!** 제기랄!

- **This sucks!** 정말로 후졌다, 이것 정말 싫어, 지긋지긋해!

Slang

- **Bullshit!** 헛소리 마, 집어치워, 거짓말 마라! (불쾌감을 나타냄)

- Eat shit and die! 똥이나 씹어라! (A contemptuous dismissal)

  [Ex] That mother-fucker just cut me off! Hey you! Eat shit and die!

- **f' word** (욕설 "fuck"을 대신해서 쓰는 말)

  [Ex] Barney Frank (D-Mass), an openly gay congressman, was called the f' word.

- Frig! (욕설 "fuck"을 대신해서 쓰는 말 / Euphemism for fuck.)

- **Fuck!** X팔, 제기랄, 젠장, 우라질!

- **Fuck it all!** 우라질, 제기랄!

- **Fuck it!** 제기랄, 젠장, 닥쳐, 꺼져, 알 게 뭐야!

- **Fuck me!** 이런 제기랄! (An exclamation of extreme displeasure; "oh shit")

- **Holy shit!** 우라질, 제기랄! (Exclamation of displeasure)

- **Piss on you!** 엿 먹어라! (Exclamation expressing displeasure)

- Poop on you! 똥이나 쳐먹어라! (Piss on you!)

- **Shit!** 제기랄, 빌어먹을(Bullshit)! (Vulgar exclamation of displeasure)

- **Son of a bitch!** 제기랄!

  [Ex] Oh, son of a bitch! Mom lied again.

- **Stuff it!** ~따위는 엿이나 먹어라, 멋대로 해라 (강한 거절이나 반감 / Angry retort)

- **Suck it!** 그만 뒤라, 집어치워!

  [Ex] If you don't like my project, you can suck it.

Certainty

확신, 확실

Formal

- **You bet your life!** 틀림없다! (Certainly, Definitely)
- **You bet!** 물론이지[바로 그거야]! (Certainly, Definitely)
- **You betcha!** 물론이지[바로 그거야]! (Certainly, Definitely)
- **You can say that again!** 정말 그렇다[(당신 말에) 전적으로 동의한다]!
- **You'd better believe it!** 믿어도 돼, 틀림없다니까! (It's sure!)

Informal

- **Sure as hell!** 틀림없다! (Certainly, Definitely)
- Sure as the devil! 틀림없다! (Certainly, Definitely)

Slang

- **bet (one's) ass** (~을) 확신하다, 절대 ~이다 (Statement that something is true)

  [Ex] And you can bet your ass that belongs to him, too.

- Shitsure! 그렇고 말고, 물론이야, 옳소! (Certainly, Definitely)
- Sure as shit! 틀림없다! (Certainly, Definitely)
- **You bet your (sweet) ass!** 당연하지! (Certainly, Definitely)

Desire for Silence

입을 다물어라, 입 닥쳐

Formal

Please be quiet; Enough said; Hush; Shhh; Silence;

- **Mum's the word!** (명령형으로 써서) 아무에게도 말하지 마 (너만 알고 있어)!

[Ex] It's a secret, OK? Mum's the word!

Informal

- Button your lip! 입 닥쳐! (Shut Up!)
- clam up 입을 다물다, 답변을 거부하다

  [Ex] I clammed up during the presentation.

- Cram it! 입 닥쳐! (Shut Up!)
- **Don't make a peep!** 찍소리도 내지 마라! (Shut Up! Don't make a sound!)
- Nuff said 그만하면 알았다[됐다] (Enough said)
- Pipe down! (특히 명령문으로 쓰여) 조용히 해[입 다물어]!

Slang

- **Shut the fuck up!** 아가리 닥쳐! (Shut up with "the fuck" infix intensifier.)
- Shut your trap! 아가리 닥쳐! (Shut up your mouth!)

Desire for Someone To Stop Doing Something 그만해!

Formal

Can we stop now?; Let's move on; Cut it out!; Leave me alone!; Quit it!; Quit that!; Shut up!; Stop!; Stop it!; That's enough!; Cease and desist(정지 명령); Let us move on;

- **Don't go there.** 특정 주제에 관해 이야기(토론)하지 마라, 그 이야기는 하지 마.

Informal

- **Get lost!** 꺼져, (거절을 나타내어) 턱도 없다! (Go away!)
- **Get off my back!** 귀찮게 하지 마[나 좀 내버려둬]! (Stop annoying me!)
- **Get out of my face!** 내 앞에서 꺼져! (Leave me alone!)
- Get out of my hair! 괴롭히지 좀 마! (Leave me alone!)
- Give it a rest! (짜증스러우니) 그쯤 해 둬[그만해]!

  [Ex] Give it a rest! Ye talk too much.

- **Knock it off!** 그만해, 집어치워! (Stop whatever you're doing.)

  [Ex] Devil: (Imitating Sam's girlfriend) A quickie, right, Sam? / Sam: Knock it off!

- Lay off! (명령형으로 쓰여) (~을) 그만둬[그만해]!

  [Ex] Lay off joking!

Slang

- **Cut the crap!** 헛소리 마! (To tell someone to stop talking)

  [Ex] A: Where's my money, Marv? B:Yo, hey, I've been meaning to call you, something came up, and I, uh. / A: Cut the crap, douchebag, where's my money?

- **Cut the shit!** 그만 둬! (To tell someone to quit playing; to knock it off)

  [Ex] You: What were you doing last night? / John Doe: You⋯. / You: Cut the shit; what were you doing?

8 *Understanding*
이해

8-1. Desire for Understanding (이해하는지 확인)

Formal

Do you know what I mean?; Do you see what I'm saying? Is that clear?; Is that understood?

Informal

- Are we on the same sheet of music? 우리 서로 이해하는 바가 같은가요?

- **Are we on the same wavelength[page]?** 우리 서로 이해하는 바가 같은가요?

- Are you tuned in? 주파수를 맞추셨습니까?[알아들으십니까?]

- **Capisce?** 알아들었어? (To understand. Used as a question. Pronounced colloquially as "ka-PEESH"

  , and frequently misspelled capish, capeesh, kapish, etc.)

  [Ex] Joey expects his money by Monday. Capish?

- **Dig me?** 무슨 말인지 이해하니? (Do you understand me?)

- **Do you catch[get] my drift?** 무슨 말인지 이해하니? (Do you understand me?)

- **Do you read me?** 무슨 말인지 이해하니? (Do you understand me?)

- **Get it?** 무슨 말인지 이해하니? (Do you understand me?)

- Get the message? 무슨 말인지 이해하니? (Do you understand me?)

- **Get the picture?** 무슨 말인지 이해하니? (Do you understand me?)

- **Got it?** 알았어? (Do you understand me?)

- **Got me?** 알았어? (Do you understand me?)

- Read me? 내 말 알아들어? (Do you understand me?)

- Savvy? 무슨 말인지 이해하니? (Do you understand me?)

8-2. Failed Understanding (이해를 못할 때)

Formal

Could you repeat that?; I don't understand; Could you run that by me?(다시 한 번 말씀해 주시겠어요?); I didn't catch that; Let's have that again; What did you say?; You('ve) lost me; Excuse me?; I can't quite make this out; I am sorry?; Pardon me?

Informal

- **Come again?** 뭐라고(요)? (상대방의 말을 잘 못 알아들었을 때, 다시 한 번 말을 해 달라는 뜻으로 씀 / Could you repeat that?)

  [Ex] FRIEND: Guess What! On the weekend I··· and··· mumble mumble··· pink spotty pineapple···. / YOU: What the hell? Come again?

- Say what? 뭐라고? (Could you repeat that?)

8-3. Understanding Achieved (이해할 때)

Formal

I know what you mean; I see; I understand; Now it's clear; That makes sense. Understood.; I get it; Yes, Sir/Ma'am

Informal

- Capish 이해하다 (보통 의문문으로 사용, 이탈리아어 방언에서 유래)
- **Got it** 알았다 (To understand)
- **Gotcha!** 잡았다, 알았어! ("Got you"; to be holding onto a person physically)
- Savvy! 알았다! (To understand)
- Ten-four! (특히 무선 통신에서) 알았다, 오케이, 오버!

9 *Disgust*

혐오, 징그러움

Formal

That's disgusting; That's repulsive; How foul!

Informal

- **Gross!** 징그럽다, 징그러워! (Disgusting)

  [Ex] A : He ate it with mustard. / B: Oh, gross!

- Ucky! 우엑! (Disgusting)

- **Yuck!** 윽 (역겨울 때 내는 소리 / Disgusting)

Dismissal and Rejection

묵살, 일축, 꺼져!

Formal

I need to be alone now; Please go; You're fired; Be off!; Get going!; Go away!; Make tracks!(가라!); Off with you!; Take off!; Class dismissed(수업 끝!); Could we have a moment?; You may go

Informal

- Beat it! 나가, 썩 꺼져! (To send away without ceremony)

  [Ex] If you don't like somebody just tell them beat it.

- **Get the hell out!** 꺼져, 여기서 꺼져! (A contemptuous dismissal)

- **MYOB** 참견 마세요, 네 일이나 신경 써 (Mind your own business)

Slang

- Chuck you, Farley! 엿 먹어라! (A contemptuous dismissal, Fuck you!)

  [Ex] Chuck you, Farley, I'm not having anything to do with it.

- Eat shit! 똥이나 씹어라! (A contemptuous dismissal)

- **Fuck off!** 꺼져버려! (An intense way of telling someone to get lost or go to hell)

  [Ex] Kyle: (You) sound like a clown. Not even nymphos would go for that. / Roman: Fuck off! Nymphos would go for that.

- **Fuck you!** 엿먹어라! 꺼져버려! (A contemptuous dismissal.)

- **Get the fuck out!** 썩 꺼지지 못해! (A contemptuous dismissal.)

- **Kiss my ass!** 엿먹으라고 해! 엿먹어!

- **Piss off!** 꺼져! (A contemptuous dismissal; to leave or (more accurately) leave a person alone)

  [Ex] Why don't you just piss off and leave me alone?

- **Piss on you!** 엿 먹어라, 꺼져버려! (A contemptuous dismissal)

- **Screw you!** 엿 먹어라, 꺼져버려! (A contemptuous dismissal; An expression of anger.)

  [Ex] Person A: You suck at fishing. / Person B: Screw you!

영어 표현에도 등급이 있다!

- **Shove it!** 집어치워[말도 안 되는 소리 하지 마]! (Angry retort)

- **Shove it up your ass!** 집어치워[말도 안 되는 소리 하지 마]! (A contemptuous dismissal)

- **Stick it up your ass!** 엿이나 먹어라! (A contemptuous dismissal)

- **Take a flying fuck!** 뒈져버려! (A contemptuous dismissal)

- **Up your ass!** 엿 먹어라! (A dismissive retort)

- **Up yours!** 빌어먹을, 뒈져라! (A dismissive retort)

- You know where you can stick it? 알아서 꺼져라! (A contemptuous dismissal)

Excitement
흥분

I'm so excited; This is wonderful; How exciting; Wow; Yippee; Yahoo! 야
호 (신이 나서 외치는 소리 / An exclamation of excitement)

Frustration and Exasperation 불만, 짜증

I'm exasperated; I'm frustrated; I need a break; It doesn't matter; It makes no difference; It's neither here nor there. (그게 중요한 것이 아니다.); It's not important; This is annoying; Enough already!; I'm fed up; I'm sick of this; So what do you want from me?; That's enough! That's it!; Thank you, no;
- For crying out loud! 세상에, 맙소사! (화가 나거나 놀랐음을 나타냄 / Exclamation of frustration; "Oh, No!")

영어 표현에도 등급이 있다!

- **Get a life.** (명령형으로 쓰여) 정신 차려라, 따분하게 굴지 마.
- **Give me a break.** 그만 좀 해, 좀 봐주세요.

  [Ex] Give me a break, I was just trying to help!

- **I've had it!** 더는 못 참아! (I am losing my ability to cope! Cry of frustration.)
- That tears it! 그걸로 이젠 끝이다, 더 이상은 대응을 못한다.

Informal

- For Christ's sake! 제발, 하느님 맙소사! (Oh, No!)

  [Ex] For Christ's sake! How could you already have another parking ticket?

- For God's sake! 세상에, 맙소사! (화가 나거나 놀랐음을 나타냄)

  [Ex] For God's sake, why won't this work?

- For Pete's sake! 제발, 부디, 도대체 (Oh, No!; An exclamation of displeasure)

  [Ex] Oh, for Pete's sake! Could you please turn down your stereo? I'm trying to study.

Slang

- **Take your thumb out of your ass[butt].** 가만히 앉아 있지만 말고 뭔가 행동을 시작

  하라. (Stop sitting around or messing around and get ready for serious action.)

Ignorance
알지 못함, 무지

Formal

I don't know; I have no idea; How should I know?; I don't know the first thing about it; What do I know?; Who knows?; I'm at a loss; I'm not familiar with this topic;

- **I don't have the foggiest.** 전혀 짚이는 데가 없다. (I don't have any idea.)
- I don't know the beans about it. 아무것도 모른다. (I don't know anything about it.)
- No clue 모른다, 단서가 없다 (I don't know; no awareness; no idea)

Informal

- **Beat the hell out of me!** 도무지 무슨 말인지 모르겠다! (I don't know.)
- **Beats me!** 몰라, 두 손 들었어! (I don't know.)

  [Ex] A: Wow, how did you get that bruise? / B: Beats me!
- Dunno 몰라 (I don't know.)
- **Search me!** 난들 아나[난 모른다]! (I have no idea.)

Slang
- **Fucked if I know!** 정말 아는 바 없다. (I don't know.)
- No fucking idea. 정말로 모른다. (I don't know.)

Indifference
관계없음, 상관하지 않음

Formal

- I don't care.
- **So what!** 그래서 (어쩌라고)? (I don't' care.)
- **Whatever!** 아무래도 좋아! (I don't' care.)

Informal

- **Big deal!** 그게 무슨 대수라고! (감탄사적, 야유[조소]를 나타냄)

  [Ex] So you gained a few pounds. Big deal!

- I don't give the bull. 나는 상관 안 한다. (I don't care.)
- **I don't give a damn.** 전혀 관심 없어, 전혀 상관 안 한다. (I really don't care.)
- Who gives a damn? 전혀 관심 없어, 전혀 상관 안 한다. (I don't' care.)

Slang

- **I don't give a crap[flip, fuck, rat's ass, shit].** 전혀 관심 없어, 전혀 상관 안 한다.

  (I don't give a damn.)

- Who gives a (flying) fuck[fart, frig, shit]? 나는 상관없어. (I don't' care.)

Retorts and Taunts

말대꾸, 조롱

Formal

- Huh? 어? 뭐?

Informal

- Arrgh! (짜증을 나타내는 의성어 / Sound to indicate irritation)
- Bite me! 꺼져, 저리 가!
- **Bummer!** (실망, 불쾌한 경험, 불유쾌한 일, Expression of sadness or dismay)

  [Ex] You gotta go? Oh bummer!

- Dang! 제기랄! (Damn의 완곡한 표현 / Equivalent of damn)

  [Ex] Oh dang, I'm flat out broke.

- Darn! 제기랄! (Damn의 완곡한 표현)

  [Ex] We've missed the bus? Darn!

- **Duh!** 1. 당연하지 2. 흥, 누가 그걸 몰라

  [Ex] A: Don't run that red light. / B: Duh!

- Go make me a sandwich! 잔말 말고 샌드위치나 만들어와! (General insulting retort to a female)

  [Ex] Female: <compelling argument> / Male: Whatever. Go make me a sandwich.

- **Go to hell!** 거꾸러져라, 뒈져라! (Dismissive retort)
- **Goddamn it!** 빌어먹을, 제기랄! (분노·당혹·놀람 따위를 나타냄)
- **Jeez!** 에이, 이크! (화, 놀람 등을 나타내는 소리 / A general exclamation, From "Jesus")

  [Ex] Jeez, that was a terrible meal!

- pound sand 꺼져 버려 (A dismissive retort; "screw off")

  [Ex] He probably told them to go pound sand.

- screw 사라지게 하다, 꺼져버리게 하다

  [Ex] A: He just called and said he's not coming. / B: Well, screw him!

- **Screw off!** 꺼져 (A dismissive retort; "buzz off"; go away)

- Take a hike! 가다, 사라지다, (명령형으로) 썩 꺼져, 저리 가! (Angry retort, Literally: "Leave!")
- **Thanks for nothing.** 아무것도 안 해 줘서 고마워! (Retort used to indicate displeasure with someone's lack of help.)

- Bite my ass! 꺼져, 저리 가! (A contemptuous dismissal)
- Blow it out your ass! 꺼져, 저리 가! (A contemptuous dismissal)
- Blow me! 제기랄! (저리 꺼져! 등의 의미)

  [Ex] Hey buddy, if you don't like my attitude, you can blow me.
- Eat a dick! 젠장 할, 헛소리 마! (A generic yet abrasive comeback to a verbal attack)

  [Ex] My girlfriend was complaining that we don't spend enough time together and I disagreed by saying "EAT A DICK!"
- Eat my shorts! 빌어먹을, 뒈져라, 이 바보야! (Insult used by cartoon character, Bart Simpson, from The Simpsons.)

  [Ex] Principle Skinner can eat my shorts.
- Eat off! 꺼져라! (Go away! Euphemism for "fuck off!")
- Eat shit! 똥이나 씹어라!

  [Ex] You THINK I'm the selfish one in this relationship, Jack? Well, eat shit and die!
- **Fuck!** X팔, 제기랄, 젠장, 우라질 (Derogatory dismissal; a general insult or insulting retort)

  [Ex] Fuck, that hurts.
- Get stuffed! 꺼져, 집어치워! (An angry retort)

  [Ex] I didn't like his cringe, so I said to him, "Get stuffed!"
- Go fly a kite! 꺼져, 귀찮게 굴지 말고 저리 가! (An angry retort)

  [Ex] A: I don't like you. / B: Go fly a kite.
- Go fucking figure! 참 이해가 안 돼! (Who would have thought!)
- Go screw! 꺼져(버려)! (To leave)

  [Ex] I've gotten calls for her from 'Daddy's Little Fuckhole', which I told to go screw as soon as I heard the guy's name 'Real Racks', 'Blonde Ambition' and probably a dozen more.
- Piss off! 꺼져버려! (Exclamation used to tell somebody rudely to go away)
- **Shit!** 제기랄! (An angry retort)

  [Ex] You're telling me that you hooked up with her and her mom? Shit.
- Shucks! 이런, 어머, 아뿔싸 (당혹감, 실망감을 나타내는 소리 / Bashful exclamation)

- Stuff it! 엿 먹어라! (Angry retort)

- Suck on that! 엿 먹어라! (An angry retort; Also, suck that)

- Suck one's dick! 엿 먹어라! (An angry retort; Also, suck that)

- Suck that! 엿 먹어라! (An angry retort; Also suck on that)

- **Tough shit!** 그것 참 안됐네 (하지만 나는 상관없어)! (Too bad (for you), but I don't care.)

  [Ex] Oh, your new job is hard? Tough shit.

- Tough titty! 그것 참 안됐네 (하지만 나는 상관없어)! (Too bad (for you), but I don't care.)

  [Ex] You don't like it? Tough titty.

Skepticism and Disbelief

의문과 불신

Formal

I don't believe it; That can't be true; That doesn't seem right; That's not true; I smell a rat; I'll believe it when I see it;

- **As if!** 절대로[결코] 아니다! (Exclamation which connotes a derisive assertion that whatever is being talked about is impossible or very unlikely. Replacements for, e.g. "As if that were remotely possible!" or "Doesn't he/she wish!" or simply "Yeah, right!")

[Ex] That guy asked me out on a date. As if!

- **I don't buy it!** 난 받아들이지 않아, 나는 믿지 않아! (I don't believe it[you].)

- **Negative.** 아니(오). (Another way of saying no)

[Ex] Jamal: Yo, you wanna go to the gallery. / Jay: Negative.

- **Not on one's life.** 절대 안 돼! (Strong statement of "no")

- Tell it[that] to the marines. 네가 하는 말은 못 믿는다. (I don't believe it[you].)

- Tell me another (one)! 너의 말은 못 믿는다. (I don't believe it[you].)

Informal

- **Hell no.** 빌어먹을, 안 돼. (An emphatic "no")

- Hell to the no. (Hell no의 강조 / An emphatic "hell no")

- **Like hell!** 말도 안 된다!

[Ex] Like hell! You're missing your sister's wedding.

Slang

- **Are you fucking kidding me?** 지금 날 놀리고 있는 거냐?

- **Balls!** 헛소리 마! (I don't believe it[you]; Exclamation of disappointment)

- BS (Bullshit의 두음문자 / Bull shit)

[Ex] My boss is full of BS.

- Bullshit! (불쾌감을 나타내어) 헛소리 마, 집어치워, 거짓말 마라!

[Ex] *"Oh, bullshit, Andy replied. You bullied us until we showed you what would happen the next time. She's right. You treat us like your slaves because old man Travers treats you like his. Well, I'll be damned if I'm going to be Eric Travers' piss boy. No way in hell."*

- My ass! 설마, 바보 같은 소리, 아니야! (강한 부정)

[Ex] *Single, he told you? Single? My ass, he had six wives. One of those Mormons, ya know?*

- You're FOS! 너의 말은 다 거짓말이다! (You are full of shit. I don't believe you.)

- You're full of shit! 너의 말은 다 거짓말이다! (I don't believe it[you].)

Surprise, Shock, Discovery 놀람, 충격, 새로운 발견

Formal

Excuse me; My apologies; Oh dear; Oh my; Sorry; Oh no; Forgive me; Heavens; I beg your pardon; Oh my goodness!

- **Oh my God!** 오, 이런! (An exclamation of surprise, shock)
- **Oops!** 이크, 이런! (사고를 당할 뻔했거나 무엇을 깨뜨렸거나 할 때 내는 소리)
- **Whoops!** 아이쿠, 어머나!
- Yeep! 이크! (An exclamation of surprise)
- Yikes! 1. 이키! (갑자기 놀라거나 겁을 먹었을 때 내는 소리) 2. 아야, 이크, 어럽쇼! (아픔·놀람 등을 나타내는 소리 / An exclamation of surprise)

Informal

- **Gee (whiz)** 1. (놀람, 감탄을 나타내어) 야! 2. (짜증스러움을 나타내어) 에이!

  [Ex] Ah gee, Steve, you are so ignorant!

- Golly! 1. (놀람, 감탄을 나타내어) 야! 2. (짜증스러움을 나타내어) 에이! (Interjection of surprise)
- **Gosh!** 이크, 어이쿠! (General exclamation, Origin: euphemism for "God")
- Jeepers! 맙소사, 어머나! (놀람, 충격을 나타내는 소리 / An expression of mild surprise or shock from 60's-70's. Popularized by cartoon character Velma of the 70's children's show Scooby-Doo. Rarely used today, except in an ironic fashion. A very wholesome word.)

  [Ex] Jeepers, that's a large box of ants!

- **What (in) the hell is going on?** 여기서 도대체 무슨 일이 일어나고 있는 거야?
- What the devil? 뭐[뭐라고]? (놀람, 분노를 나타낼 때 / Vulgar expression of "What?")
- **What the hell?** 도대체 무엇[왜]? (Vulgar expression of "What?")

18 *Misc*
기타

- Alley oop! 영차, 이영차! (물건을 들어 올리거나 일어설 때 내는 소리)

  [Ex] I'll lift you onto the stage, ready? Alley oop!

- **Check it out!** 여기 좀 봐, 한번 봐! (Pay attention)

  [Ex] Check it out. So at the club last night, there was this dude….

- **Rise and shine!** 정신 차리고 일어나라[일어나서 움직여라]! (보통 잠자리에 있는 사람에게 하

  는 명령문 / Interjection used to wake someone up.)

  [Ex] Rise and shine! Time to start the day with all the latest tech news, rounded up in one place.

- **Wake up and smell the coffee!** 정신 차리고 상황을 직시하라!

  [Ex] Wake up and smell the coffee, man! Your ex-wife is not coming back.

Chapter 4

Qualities of People and Things
사람과 사물의 좋고 나쁨

이번 장에서는 사람과 사물의 좋고 나쁨, 품질 등에 대한 표현들을 정리합니다. 사람이나 사물의 좋고 나쁨을 표현하는 데 속어를 사용한다는 것은 가장 매력적일 수도 있지만, 동시에 가장 나쁜 방법이기도 합니다. 따라서 속어적인 표현을 사용하는 것은 최대한 피해야 합니다. 그렇지만 성인 native speaker들이 자주 사용하는 단어와 표현은 알아놓아야 합니다.

Excellent People and Things 멋진 사람과 물건

1-1. Wonderful, Excellent, Splendid, Fabulous People and Things
(멋진, 탁월한, 굉장한 사람, 사물)

Formal

adorable; attractive; charming; enchanting; fascinating; interesting; inviting; magnetic; seductive; tempting; stunning; alluring; captivating; enthralling; enticing; luring; tantalizing

Informal

- all that (and a bag of chips) 끝내주다, 굉장히 매력적이다 (Of the highest quality)

  [Ex] He thinks he's all that.

- **bad ass** 끝내주는 (Very good, excellent; cool; awesome)

  [Ex] He's a bad-ass guitar player.

- **bitching** 기막히게 좋은, 끝내주는 (Excellent, wonderful)

  [Ex] That's a bitchin' bike! (bitchin' = bitching)

- **bomb** 대성공 (The best; outstanding)

  [Ex] That movie is really bomb!

- boss 아주 좋은 (Excellent, wonderful)

  [Ex] He has such a boss car.

- **cool** 멋진, 근사한, 훌륭한, (사교적으로) 세련된, 스마트한

  [Ex] That's a cool car.

- copacetic 훌륭한, 틀림없는, 아주 만족스러운 (Excellent, first-rate)

  [Ex] Henry: If any of this is making you uncomfortable. / Ron: Not at all, no, no. I'm totally copacetic.

- crackerjack 뛰어난 사람, 일류 인사, 뛰어난 것

  [Ex] John was a crackerjack of a mechanic: he could make a Mustang hum going in reverse.

- **cushy** (일, 자리 따위가) 편한(easy), 즐거운 (Extremely comfortable)

  [Ex] Her figure made her look really cushy, so we decided to call her that.

- dynamite 발군의, 뛰어난, 최고의, 놀라운 (Especially fine, excellent)

  [Ex] That new restaurant is dynamite!

- hunky-dory 더할 나위 없이 좋은 (Fine, wonderful)

  [Ex] I'm happy and everything's hunky dory.

- **kickass** 아주 좋은, 굉장한 (Very good, excellent; cool; awesome)

  [Ex] The Canadian Olympic Hockey team is kickass!

- **nifty** 스마트한(smart), 멋진, 멋들어진, 재치 있는, 멋[재치]있는 것[말]

  [Ex] I got a nifty new sledgehammer, care to see?

- **out of sight** 발군拔群의, 넘어서 있는, 훌륭한, 출중한 (Excellent, outstanding, amazing)

  [Ex] The view of the sunset from here is out of sight.

- out of this world (이 세상의 것이 아닌 것처럼) 너무도 훌륭한[아름다운]

  [Ex] I know a spaghetti place around here that is simply out of this world.

- **peachy**(-keen) 좋은, 아주 멋진 (Wonderful, excellent)

  [Ex] Everything in her life is just peachy.

- **plush** 아주 안락한, 고급의 (Expensive; luxurious)

  [Ex] It's also a pleasant and even quite plush place to be.

- ripper 훌륭한, 일류의 (An excellent one of its type)

  [Ex] There's a party at the docks tonight – it's gonna be a ripper.

- **rocking** 굉장한, 멋있는, 재미있는 (Excellent, fun, exciting, lively etc.)

  [Ex] Bar manager: Thank god, it's a slow night. / Peck: Really? 'Cause for a Sunday, this place is pretty rockin'.

- **something else** (비슷한 유형의 다른 것들보다) 훨씬 더 대단한 것[사람, 일]

  [Ex] Those girls are something else.

- splendiferous 대단히 훌륭한

  [Ex] That's splendiferous, man!

- swank(y) 매력적인, 스타일 있는 (Elegant, sophisticated, classy)

  [Ex] The money for this swanky pad comes from their illegal, extra-curricular activities.

- ta da 최고, 멋진 것 (The best; the bomb)

  [Ex] That chick's ass is ta da!

- **top-notch** 최고의, 아주 뛰어난 (Excellent, highest-rated)

  [Ex] That girl is top notch.

- **way good** 아주 좋은 (Extremely good)

1-2. Fashionable People and Things (패셔너블한 사람[물건])

Formal

fashionable; well-dressed; chic; dashing; natty; sharp; classy; dapper

Informal

- fancy schmancy 최고급의 (A derisive recognition of a high class)

  [Ex] Well, have fun at your fancy schmancy meeting! I wish I could come, but I'm not freakin' good enough!

- **hip** (최신 유행의 사상·스타일 따위에) 통달한, 정통한, 진보된, 세련된, 때를 벗은, 멋있는, 흥미 있는, 마음이 내키는

  [Ex] I know you are all hip over Becca Blaze and you overpaid to get her. But her scene was lackluster.

- **posh** 1. 멋진, 우아한, 호화로운 2. (경멸적) 상류의

  [Ex] That outfit is so posh!

- snazzy 아주 맵시 있는, 세련된 (Fashionable, of fashion, good)

  [Ex] My goodness, that bikini really looks snazzy on you!

- **spiffy** 멋진, 세련된 (Smart, stylish; very good, excellent; cool)

  [Ex] That's spiffy!

1-3. Successfully Completed Things (성공적으로 완료된 일)

Formal

completed; concluded; finished; settled; assured

Informal

- **in the bag** (성공·당선 따위가) 확실하여, 보증되어 (Guaranteed, made certain)

  [Ex] I knew that random hot chick would make sex w/ me. I had it in the bag.

- in the can (계약 따위가) 체결되어 (Finished, completed)

  [Ex] The movie that I have been waiting for long is in the can right now.

- nailed down ~으로 확정된, 최종적으로 해결한 (Dealt with successfully)

  [Ex] I expect everything to be nailed down by this weekend.

- **sew up** 성사시키다, 매듭짓다 (To accomplish)

  [Ex] They think they have the election sewn up.

Terrible, Unpleasant, Problematic, Irritating People and Things

기분 나쁜, 문제 있는, 짜증 나는 사람이나 물건

2-1. Broken Things (고장 난 물건)

Formal

broken; cracked; crushed; damaged; demolished; fractured; in pieces; mutilated; shattered; shredded; split; mangled; smashed; defective; disintegrated; fragmented; riven(분열된, 갈라진)

Informal

- borked 망가진, 부러진, 고장 난, 깨진 (Broken, not functioning)

  [Ex] I think your computer is borked.

- busted 고장 난 (Broken, not correctly functioning, doesn't work)

  [Ex] This radio is busted.

- conked out 못 쓰게 된, 아주 망가진 (Broken, not functioning)

  [Ex] Germany is in recession – the motor of European economic life just conked out.

- cooked 녹초가 된, 망가진 (Broken)

  [Ex] Well, you drove without any oil. Why do you think your car is cooked?

- **fried** 고장 난, 망가진 (Non-functioning, in reference to electronic devices)

  [Ex] That phone is fried.

- horked 고장 난, 망가진 (Broken)

  [Ex] I had to take my computer to the shop – it was horked.

- **hosed** 망가진 (Broken)

  [Ex] The computer is hosed.

- kaput 고장 난, 망가진 (Broken, not functioning)

  [Ex] The ponzi scheme is dead, defunct, no more, kicked the bucket, kaput.

- **messed** 지저분한, 엉망인 (Something as broken down)

  [Ex] You should see Nate's old car, it's messed.

- **show stopper** 하드웨어나 소프트웨어를 사용할 수 없게 만드는 오류

  [Ex] I do not think that climate and environment of itself is a show stopper to our being able to deploy.

- **toast** 완전히 망가지다 (Permanently broken)

  [Ex] I think the motherboard in my computer is toast.

- twacked 망가진, 고장 난 (Messed up, wrong, not working correctly)

  [Ex] That computer program is twacked, I'll have to reinstall it.

Slang

- **fucked up** (사물·상황이) 엉망인, 몹시 혼란한, 심란한, 큰 충격을 받은

  [Ex] Did you hear Ramsey dumped his girlfriend because she was getting too fat? That's pretty fucked up.

2-2. Disgusting People and Things (혐오스러운 사람, 물건)

Formal

disgusting; horrid; repulsive; revolting; detestable; distasteful; ghastly; gruesome; loathsome; noisome; odious(혐오스러운); offensive; repellent; repugnant; vile

2-3. Disorganized or Messy People and Things
(엉망진창인 사람, 물건)

Formal

confused; disorganized; untidy; addled; befuddled; messy; chaotic; disordered; in a mess; jumbled; muddled; snarled; topsy-turvy; anarchic; disarranged; disorderly; in disarray

Informal

- balled-up 못쓰게 된, 대혼란의 (Confused; in a mess)

  [Ex] He got balled up in his speech.

- flummoxed 당황한, 혼란스러운 (Confused or perplexed)

  [Ex] The Conservatives appear flummoxed on what to do next.

- helter-skelter 허둥지둥하는, 어질러진 (Carelessly scattered, disordered)

  [Ex] When the fire broke out, people in the theater ran helter-skelter toward the exit.

- **messed up** 지저분한, 망가진, 더러운 (Damaged or ruined)

  [Ex] He looked really out of it with his face bright red and his hair all messed up.

- **sloppy** 엉성한, 대충하는 (Messy, imprecise)

  [Ex] Yeah, he was pretty sloppy last night.

Slang

- FUBAR 엉망인, 손댈 여지가 없는 (Fucked up beyond all recognition)

  [Ex] That project is totally fubar.

- **fucked up** (사물·상황이) 엉망인, 몹시 혼란한, 심란한 (Messed up, botched)

  [Ex] Everything has been fucked up.

2-4. Ill-conceived Things (계획이 잘못된)

Formal

feeble-minded; ill-conceived; impractical; not well thought out; poorly planned; senseless; short-sighted; brainless; flaky; hare-brained; insane; kooky(괴짜의, 머리가 돈); lunatic; eccentric; underdeveloped

Informal

- birdbrained 바보의, 멍청한 (Stupid; Ridiculous or preposterous)

  [Ex] Making fun of your birdbrained theories is a far cry from hostility, but it is a lot of fun.

- crackpot 머리가 돈, 제정신이 아닌 (Crazy or eccentric)

  [Ex] That girl comes up with so many crackpot ideas.

- **half-baked** 섣부른 (Incompletely thought out)

  [Ex] He's full of half-baked ideas.

- jerky 바보스러운, 멍청한 (Foolish, idiotic)

  [Ex] Once jerky bankers go back to being jerky bankers, everything will be fine again.

2-5. Incompetent, Inadequate People and Things
(무능력, 부적절한 사람, 물건)

Formal

below par; incompetent; low-grade; mediocre; second-class; bottom-rung; second-rate; second-string; amateurish; inadequate; second-fiddle; substandard

Informal

- D-list 아주 등급이 낮은 유명인 (A very minor celebrity)

  [Ex] That actress is a D-list.

- half-assed 저능한, 어리석은, 엉터리의, 제멋대로의, 불충분한, 현실성 없는

   [Ex] You did a half-assed job on this building.

2-6. Inferior Performance and Quality (저급한 실적, 품질)

Formal

　poor quality; poor showing; nothing to brag about; nothing to write home about; inferior; paltry; wretched;

- cheesy 값싼, 싸구려의 (Lacking in taste; lame; corny, Of poor quality; shoddy)

   [Ex] His clothes are so cheesy, but hey, I dig clothes from the seventies.

- **lousy** 몹시 더러운, 불결한, 천한, 비열한, 불유쾌한, 비참한 (Awful; contemptible)

   [Ex] They are lousy tippers and hell to wait on.

- **two-bit** 별 볼일 없는, 하찮은 (An inferior item or trivial sum)

   [Ex] He goes around acting like a two-bit hood.

Informal

- **piss-poor** 형편없는 (Of unbelievably poor quality)

   [Ex] I think that was just a piss poor choice of words.

- raggedy-ass(ed) 낡은, 오래된, 애처로운 (Over-used, worn-out, pathetic)

   [Ex] Your heritage is nothing but a bunch of raggedy-assed spirituals and grass huts.

Slang

- **bullshit** 형편없는, 지랄 맞은 (Inferior; worthless)

   [Ex] Looks like bullshit to me. anyway.

- **crappy** 더러운, 불결한, 불쾌[지독]한 (Bad or displeasing; inferior; worthless)

   [Ex] Bailey: A mysterious lady with a shotgun. / Stark: Yeah, who knows? Maybe she's just a crappy neighbor.

- dogass(ed) 쓸모없는 것, 불쾌한 것 (Worthless; inferior)

- **shitty** 1. 엉망진창인, 형편없는 2. 개 같은, 더러운

   [Ex] That movie was shitty.

2-7. Risky People or Things (수상한 사람, 물건)

Formal

delicate; hazardous; risky; uncertain; chancy; dicey; iffy; fraught with danger; perilous; precarious; speculative; treacherous;

- **hinky** 수상쩍은, 의심스러운 (Unusual, weird)

[Ex] She has done like 900 girl-girl scenes in the last 11 years. I'm sure one or two of them were hinky.

2-8. Uncared-for People and Things (방치된 사람, 물건)

Formal

frayed; mean; miserable; neglected; pitiful; poor; worn-out; dingy; dog-eared; gone to seed; gone to dogs; moth-eaten; ragged; rickety; run-down; seedy; bedraggled; decrepit; desolate; dilapidated; poverty-stricken; squalid; uncared for;

- **shabby** 다 낡은, 허름한 (Things or places looking old and in bad condition)

[Ex] He was so shabby-looking that at first I thought him a hobo.

2-9. Undistinguished People or Things (평범한 사람, 물건)

Formal

boring; dull; bland; characterless; indifferent; plain; routine; usual; run-of-the-mill; so-so; pedestrian; prosaic; undistinguished; unexceptional; uninspired; unremarkable;

- **plain vanilla** 단순한, 전형적인 (Without adornment or extra trimmings, uninteresting)

[Ex] *My family through marriage includes blacks, Hispanics, and plain vanilla sorts like me.*

2-10. Unpleasant People or Things (기분 나쁜 사람이나 물건)

Formal

extremely unpleasant; hideous; horrendous; troublesome; unlikable; dreadful; disagreeable; harrowing; horrific

Informal

- poopy 기분 나쁜, 짜증 나는 (Unpleasant, irritating)

[Ex] *She always went for the poopy jokes, which is fine by me.*

2-11. Worthless People and Things (쓸모없는 사람, 물건)

Formal

pointless; useless; worthless; good-for-nothing; no-good; trivial; unessential; unimportant; unusable; valueless; fertile; ineffective; meaningless

Slang

- dogass 쓸모없는 것, 불쾌한 것

2-12. People Facing Difficulties (곤경에 처한 사람)

Formal

facing a mountain of work; facing an uphill battle; in difficulties; in trouble; back to the wall; up against it; having a Herculean task to perform; in a predicament; in dire straits;

- in a hole 곤경에 처한 (To be in trouble)

[Ex] Don't put me in a hole.

Informal

- hope in hell 기회가 전혀 없는, 희망이 전혀 없는 (Having no chance at all)

[Ex] Everybody knows they haven't got a hope in hell of forming a government anyway.

- in (deep) doo-doo 곤경에 빠져 (To be serious trouble)

[Ex] They tell you who really is up to their necks in deep doo doo.

- **screwed up** 혼란한, 당혹한, 난장판이 된 (To be serious trouble, broken, ruined, defective)

[Ex] I wonder why everything he does is so screwed up.

Slang

- **fucked up** (사물·상황이) 몹시 혼란한, 심란한 (Messed up, botched)

[Ex] Everything has been fucked up.

- have one's ass in the sling 곤경에 처하다 (To be in trouble)

[Ex] If I tell you the secret, then I have my ass in a sling.

- **in deep shit** 어려운 지경이 되어 (In serious trouble)

[Ex] You are in deep shit when you come into work tomorrow.

- **shit out of luck** 아주 재수 없는 (Without hope, in an irreparable bad situation)

[Ex] You have no money for cab fare? Well then I guess you're shit out of luck!

- SOL 더 이상 방법이 없는, 아주 재수 없는 (Acronym of "shit out of luck")

[Ex] I guess that means you're SOL.

- up shit creek 궁지에 몰려 (Possibly a shortened version of "up shit creek without a paddle")

[Ex] I don't have much choice. I am up shit creek without a paddle.

Chapter 5

Types of People
사람의 특성 표현

이번 장에서는 사람의 특성, 특징에 따른 단계별 표현들을 정리하였습니다. 사람의 특성에 대한 표현이기 때문에 부정적인 의미를 가진 표현들보다는 긍정적인 의미의 표현들을 많이 사용할 수 있도록 노력할 필요가 있습니다. 물론 부정적인 의미의 표현들도 알아놓아야 합니다.

Ambitious, Energetic
야심 찬, 정력적인

Formal

bundle of energy; doer; hard worker; mover; mover and shaker; achiever

Informal

- ball of fire 행동파, 정력가 (A person possessed of great energy and drive)

  [Ex] He did that job so fast! He is really a ball of fire!

- dynamo 정력이 넘치는 사람 (An energetic and aggressive person)

  [Ex] He teaches gymnastics and is a dynamo at work.

- **eager beaver** 아주 열심인 사람, 일벌레 (An earnest and hard-working person)

  [Ex] He's such an eager beaver.

- energizer bunny 끈기 있게 집념을 가지고 결코 포기하지 않는 사람 (Energizer 광고에 나오는

  토끼 / Extremely determined, persistent; Someone who will never quit trying.)

  [Ex] She tries again, because Emily is like that, an Energizer Bunny-type friend,
  but instead of keep going and going, she keeps trying and trying.

- **go-getter** (특히 사업에서) 성공하려고 단단히 작정한 사람

  [Ex] A go-getter like you will succeed no matter what you do.

- **live wire** 활동가, 정력가

  [Ex] Watch what you say, because he's a live wire, he gets so mad over the tiniest
  things, especially if you tease him about his extensive shoe collection. But if you
  talk about something he likes, he'll become really excited and happy!

- spark plug (동료 등을) 분발시키는 사람

  [Ex] Henry Ford turned out to be the spark plug of the automobile industry.

② *Annoying*

귀찮게 하는, 골치 아픈

Formal

aggravation; annoyance; inconvenience; irritation; pest; burden; irritant; plague; vexation

Informal

- bugaboo 귀찮게 하는 것, 사람

  [Ex] Jeremy L. is such a bugaboo!

- **pain in the neck** 골칫거리, 문제 인물 (An annoying person or problem)

  [Ex] That guy is a pain in the neck with his constant demands.

- **pain in the rear** 골칫거리 (An annoying person)

  [Ex] Some people may say that he is literally a pain in the rear.

- **snot(nose)** 오만하고 버릇없는 자식 (An arrogant and annoying person)

  [Ex] The new supervisor is such a snotnose that nobody likes her at all.

Slang

- fart 귀찮은 자식, 어쩐지 싫은 녀석 (An annoying person)

  [Ex] He's a crazy old fart.

- **pain in (one's) ass** 골칫거리 (An annoying person; a nuisance. Also "pain in the ass")

  [Ex] He's a massive, massive pain in my ass.

- PITA 골칫덩어리 (Pain in the ass)

3 *Aspiring*
패기 있는, 초보의, 풋내기

Formal

amateur; apprentice; beginner; newcomer; new kid on the block; abecedarian(ABC를 배우는, 초보의); fledgling; neophyte; novice; trainee

Informal

- greenhorn (속기 쉬운) 풋내기 (A novice)

  [Ex] You have done pretty well for a greenhorn.

- **newbie** 뉴비, (특히 컴퓨터 사용의) 초보자

  [Ex] Katie, I can't believe you've never done this before. You're such a newbie.

- **rookie** 초심자, 초보자 (A newcomer to a group or team)

  [Ex] It was two rookies who provided the real telling moments, however.

- **wannabe** 유명인을 동경하는 사람 (유명인을 동경하여 행동, 복장 등을 그들처럼 하는 사람)

  [Ex] I'm just a wannabe Emacs user, so could you explain why that's a bad idea?

Attractive – Female

매력적인 - 여성

Formal

beauty; dreamboat; stunner; bella; vision

Informal

- 10 아주 매력적인 여성이나 남성 (10점 만점에 10점 / A very attractive person; a person who on a scale of 0 to 10, is the best. From the movie "10", featuring Dudley Moore and Bo Derek.)

  [Ex] Look at her. she's a 10!

- astronaut lady 우주 최고의 미모를 갖춘 여자

  [Ex] You're an astronaut lady, that's how beautiful you are.

- **babe** 계집아이, 성적 매력이 있는 여성

  [Ex] Hey babe, could you grab me a beer?

- **bimbo** 섹시하지만 멍청하고 헤픈 여자, 백치 미인

  [Ex] She looks like a bimbo.

- bird 매력적인 소녀, 여자, 여자 친구 (A female, usually attractive. Origin: British)

  [Ex] That bird is fine!

- buttercup 순진한 소녀 (A sensitive female)

  [Ex] Don't cry, my little buttercup.

- easy on the eyes 보기 좋은 (Extremely attractive)

  [Ex] She may be easy on the eyes but she is totally conceited.

- **fox** 여우 같은 사람, 매력적인 사람 (An attractive person)

  [Ex] She is quite the fox.

- **glam** 글래머러스한 (Shortened form of "glamorous")

  [Ex] She is glam!

- **hot stuff** 섹시한 사람 (An attractive person)

  [Ex] The kid is hot stuff!

- karena 순수하고 귀여운 여자애 (A pretty girl)

  [Ex] She is such a karena!

- **knock-out** 아주 매력적인 사람 (An attractive person)

  [Ex] She is such a knock-out.

- smoking 아주 매력적인 (Extremely attractive)

  [Ex] That woman is smoking-hot.

- tasty 섹시한, 육감적인 (Something really good, attractive or just cool)

  [Ex] Check out that tasty chick!

- trim (늘씬한) 여자 (Slender woman)

  [Ex] I saw some nice trim today.

- twinkie 매력적인 젊은 여성 (An attractive girl)

  [Ex] That's a hot little twinke.

- vamp 요부妖婦 (An attractive female who is constantly flirting with men)

  [Ex] She is so vamp!

<hr>

Slang

- banging 아주 매력적인 (To be very attractive)

  [Ex] She was banging at that party!

- box 매력적인 여성 (An attractive female)

- butterface 얼굴만 빼고 전반적으로 매력적인 여성 (대개 몸매는 훌륭하나, 얼굴은 못생긴 여성의 경우에 사용 / Chick with a hell of a nice body but the face is ugly.)

  [Ex] She looked real good… but her face (butterface).

- butterhead 얼굴만 빼고 전반적으로 매력적인 여성

  [Ex] Everything looks good, butterhead (but her head).

- chiquita banana 매력적인 여성 (An attractive female)

  [Ex] Look at that chiquita banana over there.

- dime piece 아주 매력적인 여성 (An attractive female; "10". From a dime being worth 10 cents)

  [Ex] Halle Berry is a straight dime piece.

- dish 예쁜 소녀, 성적 매력이 있는 여성

  [Ex] That's one hot little dish!

- mackable 매력적인 (Hot; attractive)

  [Ex] That girl is so mackable.

- **piece of ass** (섹스 대상으로서의) 여자 (An attractive person)

  [Ex] Boy! She's a real piece of ass.

- sexy mama 아주 섹시한 여자 (An extremely attractive woman with striking sex appeal)

    [Ex] Man, what a sexy mama!

- totty 섹시한 여자 (특히 남성들이 쓰는 말로 보통 여성들에겐 모욕적으로 여겨짐)

    [Ex] Your new girlfriend is quite the totty.

- yummy mummy 매력적인 여성

    [Ex] She is yummy mummy.

Attractive - Female (Old)

매력적인 - 나이 든 여성

Slang

- **cougar** 젊은 남자와의 연애나 성관계를 원하는 중년 여성

  [Ex] Lydia: Hey, now you're single, I'm single, it's like, "Look out, world! Two cougars on the prowl."

- MIF 보통 나이에 비해 젊어 보이거나 매력적인 아줌마 (Acronym for "mom I'd fuck." – that is, an attractive older woman. Possibly from "MILF.")

  [Ex] That woman is a MIF. She looks fine.

- **MILF** 보통 나이에 비해 젊어 보이거나 매력적인 아줌마 (Acronym for "mom I'd like to fuck." or "mother I'd like to fuck." Popularized by the movie "American Pie". See also yummy mummy.)

  [Ex] She was only 35 but that was ancient in the business. Sure, there were MILF scenes available. She got one or two offers a month from sites that featured young men (or young women) having sex with a woman twice their age.

Attractive – Male

매력적인 남성

Informal

- babe magnet 사람을 유혹하는 것, 매력적인 남자 (Attractive male)

  [Ex] That guys a babe magnet.

- beefcake (남성의) 육체미[누드] 사진, 잘생기고 늠름한 남성 (A muscly man)

  [Ex] Massive-breasted heiress, 38, seeks witty Nobel-awarded intellectual beefcake gardener chef-poet with stonking pecs.

- GQ 맵시 있는 남성, 멋진 남성, 세련된 남자 (A man that is dressed well, attractive and well off. From the magazine GQ, originally called Gentlemen's Quarterly.)

  [Ex] Man, that guy was GQ.

- **hunk** (체격 좋고) 섹시한 남자 (Attractive, well-built man)

  [Ex] Wow, who's that hunk you just said hello to?

- jiggy 멋진, 근사한 (Attractive, sexy)

  [Ex] Did you see the new guy? He's so jiggy!

- **stallion** 잘 생기고, 체격이 좋은 남성 (An extremely handsome, well-built man - usually a stripper - whose body is in great shape.)

  [Ex] Damn, he's got the body of a stallion!

- **stud** 성적으로 매력 있는 남자 (An attractive male; a sexually talented male)

  [Ex] Look at that stud - that's all man.

Slang

- DILF 매력적인 유부남 (Acronym for "dad I'd like to fuck."; a heterosexual female's version of a MILF)

  [Ex] That father is quite a DILF, if I do say so….

- FILF 성적 매력이 있는 중년 남성 (MILF의 남성형 / Attractive older man; Abbreviation for "father I'd like to fuck."; male version of MILF)

  [Ex] Have you ever been to her house? Her dad's a total FILF!

Attractive Person

(Either Gender) 매력적인 - 남녀 공통

Informal

- dime 아주 매력적인 사람 (A very attractive person; "a perfect ten". Frequently, attractiveness is rated on "a scale of 1 to 10". In the United States, a dime is worth 10 cents. Hence, a "dime" is one whose attractiveness rates 10 on the scale. Also dime piece.)

  [Ex] He's a perfect dime.

- **dreamboat** 멋진 사람[것], 이상적인 연인 (An attractive person, usually male)

  [Ex] I hope he asks me to prom. He's such a dreamboat.

- eye candy 눈으로 보기 좋은 것, 매력적인 사람 (An attractive person)

  [Ex] That guy was complete eye candy.

- hottie 성적 매력이 있는 사람 (An attractive person)

  [Ex] I am definitely down with that chick, she's a hottie.

- item 매력 있는 사람 (A person whose positive attributes make them a coveted rarity)

  [Ex] That girl is quite an item. Good find, man.

- snack 매력적인 사람 (Attractive female or male)

  [Ex] The boy I like is a total snack!

- **stunner** 굉장한 미인, 굉장히 매력적인 것 (an attractive person)

  [Ex] One of the girls was an absolute stunner.

Unattractive

매력 없는

Informal

- beater 매력 없는, 탐탁지 않은 사람 (Unattractive or undesirable; Applied to a person)

  [Ex] I got together with her at a party once, but she was kind of beater.

- pigeon 못생기고 돈 없는 여자 (An unattractive, trashy, usually poor female; HOOCHIE)

  [Ex] I don't want no pigeons!

Bisexual, Bisexual Person

양성애의, 양성애자

Informal

- **bi** 동성애자 (Bisexual)

  [Ex] I wondered if she was bi.

- heteroflexible 동성애 관계에도 개방적인 태도를 보이는 이성애자

  [Ex] Most girls I know are heteroflexible.

- swing both ways 양성애이다 (To be bisexual)

  [Ex] Britney, obviously swings both ways, so she's bi.

Boyfriend, Girlfriend, Boo, Significant Other 이성 친구, 배우자

- **baby** (예쁜) 젊은 여자, 계집애, 연인, 자기 (Affectionate term for one's significant other)

  [Ex] 1. Hey baby, could you grab me a beer? / 2. When my girlfriend started calling my best friend "baby", I knew it's over.

- ball and chain 아내 (속박의 의미 / Significant other)

  [Ex] Where's your ball and chain?

- **better half** 배우자 (특히 아내를 나타내며 드물게는 남편을 나타냄 / One's significant other)

  [Ex] Where's your better half?

- **BF** 남자 친구 (Boyfriend)

  [Ex] Is he your new BF?

- **BFF** 영원한 절친 (Acronym for "best friend(s) forever")

  [Ex] My BFF Becky texted and said she's kissed Johnny.

- boo 여자 친구나 남자 친구 (Boyfriend or girlfriend)

  [Ex] Me and my boo are going out to watch a movie.

- **cupcake** 연인을 부르는 말 (Form of reference for a loved one)

  [Ex] Hey, cupcake!

- **ex** 전남편, 전처, 전 애인 (A person with whom one is no longer in a relationship. From ex boyfriend, ex-girlfriend, ex-husband, ex-wife, etc.)

  [Ex] Ryan: My ex, Paula, she's getting married. / Wilfred: How'd she dump you? / Ryan: Actually, I dumped her. / Wilfred: Yeah, right.

- main squeeze (정해진) 여자 친구, 남자 친구, 배우자 (One's boyfriend, girlfriend or spouse)

  [Ex] I spent Friday night with my main squeeze after seeing that chick I sometimes mess around with in the afternoon.

- **trophy wife** 트로피 와이프 (나이 많은 남자의 젊고 매력적인 아내, 성공한 중 장년 남성들이 수차례의 결혼 끝에 얻은 젊고 아름다운 전업주부)

  [Ex] New research reveals that Alpha Males don't want trophy wives any more.

Complaining
불평하는

Formal

complainer; crybaby; grumbler; moaner; whiner; fault finder

Informal

- bellyacher 불평을 늘어놓는 사람, 불평가

  [Ex] Grace can be cute but she always is bellyaching.

- griper 불평가 (Complaining person; grumbler)

  [Ex] Hey, gripers, you've been invited to a party.

- kvetch 투덜거리다, 푸념하다 (A person who complains constantly)

  [Ex] What he does is hang out at a table in a coffee shop and kvetch with old pals.

Contemptible
야비한, 비열한

Formal

brute; dirt; low life; rabble; riffraff; the dregs of humanity; the lowest of the low

Informal

- bottom-feeder 밑바닥 인생 (다른 사람의 불행이나 다른 사람들이 버린 물건을 이용하여 돈을 버는

  사람 / A despicable person; a useless or low-class person)

  [Ex] You are either incompetent – or a dedicated bottom feeder of the bankers.

- scab 항상 빌리기만 하고 갚지는 않은 사람

  [Ex] He is always scabbing cigarettes.

- **scum** 인간쓰레기, 쓰레기 같은 인간 (A bad person or group)

  [Ex] Stay away from that scum.

- **scumbag[scuzzbag]** 쓰레기 같은 인간, 더러운 놈

  [Ex] Tevon's the dealer they work for. He runs the projects – real scumbag.

- **trash** 쓸모없는 인간, 인간쓰레기, 건달 (A low-class person)

  [Ex] Why are you dating that guy? He's trash.

Slang

- **cunt** 1. (성교 대상으로서의) 여자, 계집 2. (경멸적) 계집 (Derogatory term for a woman)

  [Ex] My ex-girlfriend is a fucking cunt.

- **dick** 자식, 사내, 녀석, 얼간이

  [Ex] That guy is such a dick for calling me that!

- **fucker** 새끼, 자식, 바보 같은 놈, 싫은 사람, 녀석, 놈

  [Ex] He's just a fucker.

- fuckhead 바보 자식, 얼간이 (특히 남성 / Somebody who is stupid, careless or inconsiderate)

  [Ex] That stupid fuckhead pulled in front of me.

- **jerk** 바보, 멍청이 (Fool, idiot)

- **shit-bag** 바보 자식, 멍청이 (Dumb ass; jack ass)

  [Ex] You fucking shit-bag.

- **shithead** 똥 쌀 놈, 싫은 자식 (A despicable person)

  [Ex] You're a real shithead!

- turd 똥, 똥 같은 놈 (A piece of fecal matter)

  [Ex] I'm probably shaking too hard in fear at their menacing glares. To give you an accurate description but I'll try. Five-five, 110 pounds, look like a couple of turds.

- **twat** 등신, 멍청이 (A displeasing person; idiot)

  [Ex] "Oh you sneaky little twat", she hissed.

Courageous, Brave
용기 있는, 용감한

Formal

- **backbone** 기골, 강한 의지[정신]력 (Having a "backbone" endows one with courage, will)

[Ex] You've got to grow a backbone if you don't want to become the one who gets trampled over in the end.

- cowboy up 용기를 내다 (Quit bitching and be a man when it gets tough; start playing hard.)

[Ex] Before the big game against our rivals, someone said "Cowboy up" to the pessimistic boys.

- **edgy** 신랄한, 가시 돋친, 겁 없는

[Ex] "Alamo Bay" was an edgy movie on immigration.

- grit 투지, 기개 (Spirit, courage)

[Ex] It takes grit to stand up to a bully.

- **have balls** 용기가 있다 (To have courage)

[Ex] But let's be honest here: the old man has balls.

영어 표현에도 등급이 있다!

14 *Cowardly*

비겁한, 겁 많은

Formal

deserter; quitter; skulker(몰래 숨는 사람); alarmist(기우가 심한 사람); malingerer(꾀병을 부리는 사람)

Informal

- candy-ass 소심[비겁]한 사람, 계집애 같은 사내(sissy)

  [Ex] He is such a candy-ass when it comes to these things.

- **chicken** 겁쟁이, 비겁한 사람, 겁먹다 (A coward)

  [Ex] Michael: Why does everybody think that I'm scared of girls? / George, Sr.: Because you're a chicken.

- **gutless** 배짱이 없는 (A weak character and lack courage or determination)

  [Ex] Cameron is a pretty gutless little man.

- lily liver 겁, 겁쟁이 (Coward)

  [Ex] I can't watch horror movies because of the lily liver.

- **sissy** 계집애 같은 사내(아이) (An effeminate; weak male)

  [Ex] To my dad, people who taught at colleges and people who wore ties were "sissies" – all of them.

Slang

- chicken dick 겁쟁이 (Scared or cowardly)

  [Ex] Don't be a chicken dick.

- **chicken-shit** 소심한 사람, 겁쟁이 (Feeble, cowardly)

  [Ex] That chicken-shit can't kill a fly.

- **pussy** 겁쟁이, 꼬맹이 (A coward or physically weak person; wimp)

  [Ex] I never said you were a pussy.

Crazy
미친

Formal

- **nervous wreck** 신경쇠약인 사람, 신경과민인 사람

  [Ex] Bob: I'm allergic. Remember our first date? / Linda: Yeah, I remember our first date. You were a nervous wreck.

Informal

- **kooky** 괴짜의, 멍청한, 미친 (Strange, out of the ordinary; weird)

  [Ex] That's a kooky haircut.

- **nut** 미친 사람 (A crazy person)

  [Ex] He's a real nut.

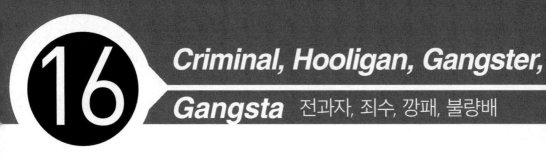

Criminal, Hooligan, Gangster, Gangsta 전과자, 죄수, 깡패, 불량배

Formal

hoodlum; rowdy; tough; bully; punk; ruffian

- **thug** 폭력배 (A gang member or "ruffian")

[Ex] I got mugged by a thug.

Informal

- **con** 죄수(convict), 전과자(ex-convict) ('A convict'의 뜻)

[Ex] He was labeled a con.

- **hood** 불량배, 망나니, 깡패, 갱, 범죄자

[Ex] That guy is a hood.

- **perp** 범인 (Perpetrator, i.e. person who committed a crime)

[Ex] The perp is in custody.

- rat 쥐새끼 같은[비열한] 놈 (A scab, criminal)

[Ex] What a rat, leaving us stranded here!

- **scum** 인간쓰레기, 쓰레기 같은 인간 (A bad person or group; bastard)

[Ex] They really are the scum of the earth.

- **scumbag** 쓰레기 같은 인간, 더러운 놈

[Ex] So the politicians may be lying scumbags but the people are idiots.

Crude
무례한, 거친, 촌놈

Informal

- butthead 바보 같은[꼴 보기 싫은] 녀석

  [Ex] That guy's a member of the Young Republicans…. what a butthead.

- Neanderthal (무례하고 거칠어) 원시인같이 구는 (Behaving in a very uncivilized way)

  [Ex] I am university-educated, and while no rocket scientist, I am no Neanderthal either.

- **roughneck** 거친 남자 (Crude male)

  [Ex] And then I met these people, these patriotic roughnecks, and I was undone by them.

Slang

- shitkicker 촌놈 (Cowboys or cowgirls and by extension rednecks in general)

  [Ex] What do you mean you've got no money, you fucking shitkicker?

Demanding
혹사시키는, 요구가 많은

Informal

- **ball-buster** 매우 힘든 일, 남을 혹사시키는 사람

  [Ex] My slave-driving boss expects me to work over the weekend. What a ball-buster!

19 **Determined**
다루기 어려운, 고지식한

Formal

dictator; realist; tyrant; tough cookie(자신만만한 사람); pragmatist

Informal

- **handful** 다루기 힘든 사람 (A person hard to handle or deal with)

  [Ex] Her children can be a real handful.

- hard nut 다루기 어려운 사람

  [Ex] He's a hard nut to crack.

- **hard-ass** 융통성 없는 (사람), 냉혹한 (사람) (Very hard; a stubborn person)

  [Ex] The shop teacher is a real hard-ass.

- hardhead 융통성 없는 사람, 고지식한 사람 (A stubborn person)

  [Ex] He's a real hardhead.

- tough nut 다루기 힘든 사람 (A very difficult person to deal with)

  [Ex] The self-employed are a tougher nut to crack.

Displeasing

싫은, 기분 나쁘게 하는

Informal

- dirtbag 싫은 놈, 더러운 놈 (A dirty, grimy, sleazy or disreputable person)

  [Ex] She is a dirtbag. She works as a hooker in Reno.

- **perv** 변태 (Pervert)

  [Ex] He's such a perv.

- potty mouth 상스런 말씨(를 쓰는 사람) (The mouth of a person who frequently swears)

  [Ex] I'm going to wash that potty mouth of yours with soap!

- **slob** (지저분한) 게으름뱅이 (A dirty or messy person)

  [Ex] What do you expect of Moyles? He's a disgraceful slob.

- toad 보기 싫은 놈[것], 주는 것 없이 미운 사람[것] (A very unpleasant man)

  [Ex] I've never met that toad you used to date.

Slang

- **asshole** 멍청이, 똥 쌀 놈, 지긋지긋한 것[곳]

  [Ex] Look, I've got four assholes from your hometown here to collect your belongings. What do you want me to tell them?

21 Drug Dealer
마약 밀매자

Informal

- **hustle** (흔히 불법적으로) 팔다 (To deal drugs)

  [Ex] I hustled till dawn.

- **pusher** (마약) 밀매자 (One who sells illegal drugs)

  [Ex] I picked up two grams yesterday, from my pusher.

Drug User

마약 사용자

Informal

- doper 마약 상용자

  [Ex] I hate cheats! That's all the dopers are.

- **druggie** 마약 상용자 (A habitual drug user)

  [Ex] She lost her desk job because her spouse Darrell is a druggie lowlife.

- **junkie** 마약 중독자, 마약쟁이 (A drug addict)

  [Ex] His younger brother is a smack junkie.

- pot-head 마리화나 상용자 (A person who smokes a lot of marijuana)

  [Ex] What are they smoking? Questions on marijuana flood White House website. Apparently, America is a country full of potheads.

- **stoner** 마리화나 상용자 (A person who frequently smokes marijuana)

  [Ex] Look at his bloodshot eyes. You can tell he's a stoner.

Slang

- acid freak LSD 상용자 (LSD user)

  [Ex] It's more common that hackers are like hippies or acid freaks or mad scientists or car mechanics.

- acid head LSD 상용자 (LSD user)

  [Ex] Paul was an acid head and enjoyed LSD.

- crack head 크랙[코카인] 상용[중독]자 (A person who does too much crack)

  [Ex] Mr. Johnson sold his car for 20 dollars, he must be a crack head.

 **Enthusiastic**

열성적인, 열광하는

Formal

fan; fanatic; aficionado; connoisseur(감정가); devotee; votary(숭배자, 애호가)

Informal

- **buff** ~광, 애호가 (Enthusiastic)

  [Ex] The carefully filmed battle scenes are sure to please Civil War buffs.

- fandom (스포츠·영화 등의) 팬층, 팬들 (A group of fans for a specific show[book, movie, etc.])

  [Ex] The Harry Potter fandom is huge!

- fiend ~광 (An addict)

  [Ex] You shouldn't smoke so much – you're becoming a fiend.

- **freak** ~광 (A person very enthusiastic about a thing or activity)

  [Ex] Tom is a real speed freak.

- **groupie** 가수를 따라다니는 소녀 팬

  [Ex] Other bandmates prefer to concentrate on bedding groupies rather than concentrating on the music.

- junkie 열성 팬 (A tremendous enjoyer)

  [Ex] I'm a college football junkie.

- party animal 파티 광 (A person who parties hard and often)

  [Ex] My new roommate is a total party animal. I get no studying done in our room.

Excellent People

최고의 사람들

Informal

- **a-list** 최고 부류[대열](에 속하는 인사들) (A metaphorical list of the post popular people)

[Ex] *The practice of hiring celebrities is so common that there's even an industry price list for A listers.*

영어 표현에도 등급이 있다!

Expert

전문가, 귀재

Formal

authority; expert; master; professional; specialist; virtuoso(거장)

Informal

- **artist** (~의) 명인, 달인, ~통通

  [Ex] He's a real artist.

- dab hand (무엇을 아주 잘하는) 명수, 달인

  [Ex] That Paul's a dab hand with PCs – he always manages to solve my problems.

- **hired gun** 살인 청부업자 (A person hired for their expertise)

  [Ex] They are hired guns and no amount of jingoism will change that.

- **hot-shot** (특정 직종이나 스포츠에서) 아주 잘 나가는 사람 (Impressive, expert)

  [Ex] He's some hot-shot lawyer.

- maven 전문가 (Expert)

  [Ex] Foreign affairs mavens however should note a couple of developments over the weekend.

- **whiz-kid** 신동, 젊은 수재

  [Ex] Wozniak was an engineering whiz kid continually inventing gadgets.

- **wizard** 귀재 (A person with deep, expert knowledge of that subject matter)

  [Ex] We're looking to hire a Unix wizard.

- wonk 전문가 (An expert)

  [Ex] You don't need policy wonks, you need people of experience who are there for you and have innate intelligence.

Expert But Socially Awkward 괴짜

Formal

techie; trekkie(미국 드라마 <Star Trek> 마니아);

- **bookworm** 공부벌레

[Ex] Although Mohammed was a charismatic and influential leader, he was not much of a bookworm.

Informal

- **dork** 유행에 뒤진 사람, 촌뜨기, 바보, 얼간이

[Ex] What else has you thinking about marrying that dork?

- dweeb 샌님, 꽁생원 (A person who is bookish; antisocial)

[Ex] You're just upset that you're not dealing with some spineless dweeb anxious to get out of his Mommy's basement.

- **geek** 괴짜, 어느 한 가지 분야에만 몰두하는 괴짜

[Ex] Are you telling me, in this town full of super-geeks, you can't find one person who can do a simple math problem?

- gomer 괴짜, 어느 한 가지 분야에만 몰두하는 괴짜 (Geek, nerd, or weirdo)

- **nerd** 1. 멍청하고 따분한 사람 2. 컴퓨터만 아는 괴짜 (A clever but socially awkward person)

[Ex] Don't waste time with those guys - they're all nerds.

- otaku 오타쿠

[Ex] Brian will never have a girlfriend, he's too much of an otaku.

- tech weenie 컴퓨터와 관련된 것에만 빠져 있는 바보

27 Fashion

패션

- **fashionista** 패션 리더 (항상 최신 유행대로 옷을 입는 사람 / A person obsessed with fashion)

  [Ex] The Mercer has its super-hip lobby crammed full of New York's premier fashionistas.

- recessionista 리세셔니스타 (적은 예산으로 자신을 꾸미는 사람)

  [Ex] It's no wonder some recessionista brides are turning to websites like The-DressList.com for second-hand wedding gowns.

Father

아빠, 아버지

Informal

- baby daddy (여성의 입장에서) 아기 아빠 (The father of a woman's child)

  [Ex] That man isn't my boyfriend, he's my baby daddy.

- **pop** 아빠 (Father)

  [Ex] Mom and Pop Stores are dying out.

- stage father 어린 연기자의 아버지 (The father of a child actor)

  [Ex] So the new gossip is that Marcus is becoming a real stage father, after his daughter has been in only 1 play. She didn't even have a speaking role!

- stepdude 계부 (Stepdad)

  [Ex] I've got to go to my stepdude's family's Thanksgiving this year.

- Sunday dad 일요일에만 아이들을 보게 되는 아빠

Slang

- sugar daddy 돈 많은 중년 남자 (보통 성관계 대가로 자기보다 훨씬 젊은 여자에게 많은 선물과 돈을 안겨 주는 남자)

  [Ex] These days, even sugar daddies are feeling the pinch of the economic downturn, and they are tightening their expenditures.

Female

여자

Informal

- **broad** 女子(woman), 품행이 나쁜 여자, 매춘부 (An insulting use of "female")

  [Ex] Come on, you're old enough to figure this out. I'm nailing this broad.

- **gold digger** 돈을 목적으로 남자와 교제하는 여자

  [Ex] Man, you need to break up with her. She's a gold digger.

Female - Young Lady

어린 여자

Informal

- **jail bait** 성관계 허가 연령 이하의 아동 (jail bait와 성관계를 하면 본인 동의 여부와 상관없이 강간 죄가 성립됨 / One who is too young to have sex with. As in if you do you will go to jail.)

  [Ex] Speaker: That chick is hot! / Response: Yeah, but she's jail bait.

- **teeny bopper** 팝 음악, 패션 등에 관심이 아주 많은 어린 십 대, (10~13세 사이의) 소녀

  [Ex] Sure, we fans may not be teeny boppers anymore, but we are mature and successful women who adore this group.

Flattering
아첨, 아부하는

Formal

charmer; sweet talker; teacher's pet; adulator(아첨꾼); sycophant

Informal

- apple polisher 아첨꾼 (A sycophant; toady)

  [Ex] That apple-polisher gave me quite a laugh, but I can't stand him.

- **bootlicker** 아첨꾼, 알랑거리는 사람 (A servile flatterer; a toady or sycophant)

  [Ex] BDK is always kissing Capt. Connoly's ass, what a bootlicker!

- **brown nose** (남에게) 알랑거리다, 아첨 떨다 (To fawn over a superior)

  [Ex] John is a total brownnoser because he is always sucking up to the teacher.

- toady 1. 아첨꾼, 알랑쇠 2. 아첨하다, 알랑거리다

  [Ex] The House cannot operate if it is simply full of self-congratulatory toadies.

- **yes-man** 예스맨 (윗사람에게 잘 보이려고 무조건 예라고 하는 사람)

  [Ex] I'd fire both Margaret and Nick for being totally useless unoriginal "Yes men".

Slang

- **ass-kisser** 아첨꾼 (An obsequious person)

  [Ex] That ass-kisser, Peter, is always telling the boss how great he is.

- **ass-sucker** 아첨꾼, 알랑쇠

  [Ex] He was a real ass-sucker.

- **kiss ass** 아첨하다, 아첨하는 사람

  [Ex] You are such a kiss-ass, freak.

- **suck ass** 1. 아첨하다, 알랑거리다 2. 아첨꾼 (Someone that sucks up to another)

  [Ex] This girl at work is a suck-ass to the boss.

- **suck up** 1. 알랑대다, 아부하다 2. 아첨꾼

  [Ex] He was sucking up to the professors to get good grades.

32 Friend, Friends

친구

Formal

- ace 친구, 어려울 때 의지가 되는 것

  [Ex] Derek used to be my number one ace until he tried to take my girl.

Informal

- Batman and Robin 항상 같이 다니는 친구 사이 (Batman and Robin refers to the partnership

  between Batman and Robin, two superhero characters; inseparable friends)

  [Ex] Those two are so Batman and Robin.

- **bro** 친구 (남자를 다정하게 부를 때 / Friend; commonly used in greetings)

  [Ex] What's up, bro?

- bud ('buddy'의 준말 / Friend; short for buddy)

  [Ex] Hey, bud, what's up?

- **chum** 친구, 벗, 옛 친구 (A good friend, pal, buddy or chummy)

  [Ex] They are old chums.

- **fella** 남자, 남자 친구 ("Fellow", i.e. a man. a particular group of male friends)

  [Ex] Where are the fellas tonight?

- homie[homey] 고향 친구, 함께 뭉쳐 다니는 친구 (A close friend)

  [Ex] Obama needs his street cred with his homies on the one hand and needs the soothing rhetoric with the white folks on the other.

Slang

- asshole buddy 친구, 짝패, 호모들

  [Ex] Lonnie and Joe Bob? You hardly ever see one without the other. They've been asshole buddies for years.

Generous

후한, 자애로운

Formal

contributor; donor; sponsor; benefactor; benefactress; humanitarian; patron; philanthropist

Informal

- **do-gooder** 박애주의자

[Ex] The "do-gooders" must come to their sense before the situation is irretrievable.

- soft touch 쉬운[만만한] 사람, 돈을 내기 쉬운 사람

[Ex] There is not a soft touch in terms of law enforcement.

③4 *Gullible*
잘 속는

Formal

casualty; injured party; innocent prey; sacrifice; target; victim; sitting duck; martyr; pawn; quarry;

- chump 바보, 멍청이, 얼간이 (A stupid or gullible person)

  [Ex] He was a chump to believe those lies.

- **doormat** 학대받아도 가만히 있는 사람 (A person who is easily abused by others)

  [Ex] The director treated the actor like a doormat.

- **easy mark** 잘 속는 사람, 봉 (Gullible person)

  [Ex] Maybe I just look like an easy mark.

- easy touch (특히 돈을 우려내기) 쉬운[만만한] 사람 (Gullible person)

  [Ex] Unfortunately, my father is no easy touch.

- **fall guy** (남의 잘못을 뒤집어쓴) 희생양 (A person who is blamed for something bad)

  [Ex] He is such a fall guy.

- **mark** (비웃음 따위의) 표적[대상](이 되는 사람), 봉 (An easy target or victim)

  [Ex] You're such a mark.

- **pushover** 호락호락한 사람, 호구 (A person easy to persuade to do what you want)

  [Ex] Despite her fragile, feminine appearance, she was no pushover.

Informal

- patsy (남의 잘못을 뒤집어쓴) 희생양 (Someone who takes the blame; fall guy)

  [Ex] This country is increasingly regarded as a bunch of patsies.

- schnook 별 볼일 없는 인간, 멍청이 (A stupid or gullible person)

  [Ex] Do these schnooks read legal papers? There's a notice of default and a notice of trustees' sale on Neverland.

- **sucker** 잘 속는 사람, 바보 (Imbecile; a person that got screwed)

  [Ex] He's such a sucker that I could sell him the Eiffel Tower.

Hard To Handle
대하기 어려운

Informal

- piece of work 대하기 어려운 사람

  [Ex] He's a real piece of work.

Helpful
도움이 되는, 조수, 보조

Formal

backer; supporter; angel; mentor; patron;
- **back-up** 후원, 지지, 백업, 예비 (A person or item relied on for support)

  [Ex] Thanks for the concern, but we have a back-up plan.

Informal

- flunky (요리사 등의) 조수 (A person that does anything to be accepted or appreciated)

  [Ex] He got his flunky to pick up his package!
- gofer (회사의) 사환

  [Ex] He was reading from a note passed to him by a gofer.
- **grunt** 병사, 보병

  [Ex] They were the grunts of the society.
- **sidekick** 조수 (A person who accompanies one helps him/her)

  [Ex] Austin's new beautiful sidekick is played by the singer and actress Beyonce Knowles.

영어 표현에도 등급이 있다!

Important
중요한, 거물

Informal

- big boy 실력자, 거물 (Person with power or influence)

  [Ex] The employers who know about it are local authorities and the big boys.

- big bug 실력자, 거물 (Person with power or influence)

  [Ex] They come to us with letters from Directors or some big bug or other.

- big cheese 실력자, 거물

  [Ex] My dad can get us on the moon within the hour. He's a big cheese at NASA.

- big chief 실력자, 거물 (Person with power or influence)

  [Ex] Meanwhile back at the ranch the big chief Brown rules like an emperor waiting for orders from Washington DC.

- big enchilada; big fish; big gun; big guy 실력자, 거물

- **big shot** 중요 인물, 거물 (An important person)

  [Ex] He's a big shot in Chilean politics.

- **big wheel** (회사, 기관의) 중요 인물 (An important person)

  [Ex] His father's a big wheel in the textile industry.

- **big wig** 중요 인물 (An important person)

  [Ex] Animation bigwig Jeffrey Katzenberg is talking about a revolution.

Officer
장교, 간부, 우두머리

Formal

administrator; chief; director; employer; executive; foreperson; leader; manager; overseer; owner; person in charge; superintendent; supervisor

Informal

- **brass** 고급 장교들, 고위층

  [Ex] Setanta's emergence should worry the BBC top brass.

- **exec** (기업의) 경영자 (Executive)

  [Ex] Our execs work non-stop, and are in the public eye.

- fat cat 배부른 자본가, 많은 정치 자금을 내는 부자 (A rich person)

  [Ex] They'll just be used to line the pockets of the fat cat directors & shareholders.

- grand poobah 중요한 인물, 고위직 (A person who is important or high-ranking)

  [Ex] The grand poobahs think we'll lose our shirt. We're not. I've been running this program for 18 months now and it outperforms every facet of our operations except for the most lucrative high-end loan division.

- **head honcho** 우두머리, 두목 (An important person; the person in charge)

  [Ex] The glossy mag is about to get Catherine Ostler as its new head honcho.

- heavy hitter 중요한 인물, 고위직 (A person who is important or high-ranking)

  [Ex] The Chief Secretary to the Treasury is one of the Government's heavy hitters.

- heavyweight 중요한 인물, 영향력이 많은 인물

  [Ex] You've got a lot of heavyweight contenders here: Finding Neverland starring Johnny Depp as the author of Peter Pan.

- **honcho** 책임자 (A leader)

  [Ex] So I called to tell them what's what. All I get is the head honcho telling me.

- kingfish 우두머리 (A leader of a group)

- **kingpin** 우두머리 (A leader of a group or drug lord)

  [Ex] The Kingpin wouldn't let us down in New York City at night time.

- Mister Big (숨은) 보스, 거물 (An important person)

- **panjandrum** 대장, 두목, 높으신 분, 어르신네

[Ex] It should leave civil servants in no doubt that power has shifted from the panjandrums to the people.

- **pooh-bah** 높은 사람, 고관, 거만한 사람, 지도자, 대가, 중요한 인물

[Ex] She's the candidate that makes the party pooh-bahs feel comfortable.

- **powerhouse** 유력 집단 (A country or organization that has a lot of power or influence)

[Ex] Angeles and New York remain the powerhouse centers of the music business.

- **powers that be** (조직·국가 등의) 실세들

[Ex] The decision is in the hands of the powers that be.

- PTB 실세, 책임자, 담당자 (Powers that be)

- **skipper** 선장, 주장 (Captain)

[Ex] The Spurs skipper is battling a knee injury which prevents him playing successive games.

- TPTB (조직·국가 등의) 실세들 (The powers that be)

- top banana (뮤지컬 등의) 주역 배우, (단체의) 제1인자, 중심인물

[Ex] Thompson is top banana at the BBC.

- **top brass** 고급 간부들 (People in the highest positions)

[Ex] If the business flourishes, the top brass pick up big, big bonuses.

- **top dog** 톱의, 최고의, 가장 중요한 (The leader)

[Ex] America has always been the "top dog" that most countries would not consider challenging.

Impotent and Foolish
바보, 멍청이

Formal

buffoon; clown; goon

Informal

- bozo 녀석, 멍청이, 거친 사람, 골치 아픈 사람 (Fool)

  [Ex] You are such a bozo.

- dufus 바보, 멍청이 (Fool)

  [Ex] Gibbs is a dufus and cannot handle real reporters.

- **goof** 바보, 멍청이 (A funny or silly person)

  [Ex] Brown's a goof – that much is clear.

- goofball 멍청이 (A fool)

  [Ex] My father, who is 53, always thought that Conan was a goofball and that Jay was better.

- goofus 어리석은 사람, 바보 (A fool)

  [Ex] I was such a goofus for keeping my cell phone on during the movie.

- **horse's ass** 바보, 멍청이 (An idiot; jackass)

  [Ex] I refuse to be friends with a horse's ass like that.

- muddlehead 멍청이, 바보 (A fool; idiot)

  [Ex] The income, of course, would seem small to some women, muddleheads, but she could manage.

- noodle 바보 (A geek; weirdo)

  [Ex] Don't be such a noodle!

- schmo 멍청이, 얼간이 (An unintelligent person)

  [Ex] Who are the losers? The ordinary schmoes of the world.

Indecisive and / or Weak

우유부단한, 줏대 없는

Formal

pushover; momma's boy; namby-pamby; equivocator(얼버무리는 사람)

Informal

- creampuff (줏대나 기개가 없는) 물렁이

  [Ex] You are a creampuff.

- jellyfish 나약하고 결단성이 없는 사람 (Indecisive and[or] weak)

  [Ex] They are a pathetic bunch of jellyfish.

- lamer 시대에 뒤처진 사람, 아무것도 모르는 사람

  [Ex] He is such a lamer.

- weak sister 도움이 필요한 사람, 거추장스러운 사람

  [Ex] Please come to America and give our weak sisters in the GOP lessons on how to stand up to tyranny. (GOP: Grand Old Party; 미국 공화당)

- weeny 나약한 사람 (A wimp)

  [Ex] Weeny? Useless? Insignificant? Yeah, probably all three of those.

- **wimp** 겁쟁이, 약골 (Lacking physical prowess or stamina)

  [Ex] I am not a wimp, but decided that a confrontation was not in order.

- wuss 쪼다, 병신 (Wimp, sissy, coward; Also wussy)

  [Ex] Michael: Oh, that's a pretty tough race. / Steve Holt: Only for a wimp, a wuss….

Inept
서투른, 부주의한

Formal

bull in a china shop; clumsy; fumbler; a person with two left feet; an unco-ordinated person

Informal

- butterfingers (단수취급) 물건을 (손에서) 잘 떨어뜨리는 사람, 부주의한 사람, 서투른 야구 선수, 서투른 사람 (A clumsy person, especially one who tends to drop things)

  [Ex] It was you who dropped it, butterfingers.
- **klutz** 어설픈 사람, 얼뜨기 (An uncoordinated person)

  [Ex] I dropped my tray and broke five plates. I am such a klutz!
- **screw-up** 실수투성이의 사람 (A person who makes many mistakes)

  [Ex] He's such a screw-up.

Slang

- **fuckup** 실수만 하는 사람, 얼빠진 사람 (A person who messes up; a screw up)

  [Ex] He got fired because he was a fuck-up.

42 Influential Through Manipulation 사기, 수완가, 배후 조종

planner; strategist; contriver; deviser; maneuverer; opportunist

Informal

- **hustler** 사기꾼 (A person who is always working, usually, illegally)

  [Ex] That guy is a hustler, he always balling.

- operator 수완가 (특히 부정직한 방법도 마다치 않는 사람)

  [Ex] Add to all this the fact that he is a very smooth operator.

- **string puller** 배후 조종자 (A person influential through manipulation)

  [Ex] In case anyone was wondering, the streets belong to the people, not the cops and their string-pullers.

- **wheeler-dealer** (사업, 정치에서) 권모술수에 능한 사람, 수완가

  [Ex] One thing that is unclear is exactly how successful a wheeler dealer he became after abandoning the bar.

- wire puller 배후 조종자 (A person who uses private or secret influence for his own ends)

  [Ex] Monroe gave him a piece of paper, and the wire-puller began to make his calculations.

Informative

정보 제공자, 밀고자

Informal

- **CI** 비밀 정보원 (Confidential informant)

  [Ex] Swarek: I got a snitch in the club. / Best: No CIs. Nothing complicated. I want this fast, simple.

- **rat** 밀고자 (Someone who reports misdeeds to an authority; narc; snitch)

  [Ex] We are certainly overrun by the rats in the Labor party.

- **snitch** 밀고자 (A person who informs or reports the misdeeds of someone else)

  [Ex] I don't want to be a lousy snitch. Ryan has been using the color printer for his business a lot.

- tattle tale 수다쟁이, 고자쟁이(talebearer) (A person who frequently reports misbehavior)

  [Ex] My little brother is such a tattle tale.

44 Insignificant or Expendable 쓸모없는, 중요치 않은

Formal

disappointment; failure; born loser; dud; flop; has-been; might-have-been; nobody; castaway; derelict; underachiever;

- **loser** 실패작, 불량품 (A worthless person)

  [Ex] Man, Cass is such a loser.

- **waste of space** 아무짝에도 쓸모없는 사람

  [Ex] These people are a waste of space when it comes to dealing with crime.

Informal

- jive turkey 멍청한[쓸모없는] 인간 (Insignificant or stupid person)

  [Ex] If you don't, we'll. I'd have to say you're just a jive turkey.

- puissant 쓸모없는[시시한, 하찮은] 사람[것], 비열한 사람[것]

  [Ex] You should have heard that sorry puissant lawyer when he called back.

- **sad-ass** 불쌍해 보이는 (Looking very unhappy)

  [Ex] "Alright guys, listen, I know this is sad-ass but···."

- schlep 무능한 사람 (A lowly person)

  [Ex] He's such a schlep.

- **small fry** 별 볼일 없는 사람 (Something or someone unimportant)

  [Ex] Only small fry got caught in the police roundup of gang members.

- zero 인기 없는 사람 (An unpopular person)

  [Ex] I can't believe you hang out with that zero.

Intelligent
똑똑한, 지식인

Formal

doctor; genius; intellectual; Einstein; highbrow; prodigy; scholar;

- **know-it-all** (뭐든 다) 아는 체하는 사람, 똑똑한 체하는 사람

[Ex] He's such a know-it-all when in fact he's so ignorant.

- **rocket scientist** (일반적으로) 머리가 좋은 사람, 수재 (A very clever or intelligent person)

[Ex] It doesn't take a rocket scientist to know what was in her head.

- whiz 수완가, 전문가, 명인, 명수 (A person with skill in a particular subject or trade)

[Ex] She's a real whiz when it comes to math!

Informal

- brainiac 아주 똑똑한 사람, 수재 (A very intelligent person from Steve Wazniac)

[Ex] Think of all the Wall Street brainiacs who insisted there was no credit issue.

- egghead 인텔리, 지식인 (An overly intellectual person; someone who thinks too much)

[Ex] Charles can't order lunch without using an algebraic formula – what an egg head!

- pointy-head 지식인 (Intelligent person)

[Ex] They believed the world was over populated, because some pointy headed scientists told them so.

- sharpie 교활한 사람, 빈틈없는 사람 (A person of sharp intelligence)

[Ex] Any member of the public who had invested once could tell it was clearly being run by a group of sharpies rather than proper bankers.

- **smart ass** 수재, 수완가, 건방진 녀석, 우쭐하는 놈

[Ex] 1. I can't stand smart-asses, but when I pictured one, it wasn't hard to be one. / 2. She's a smart-ass teacher.

46 Know-it-all
잘 아는 체하는 사람

Informal

- **armchair general** (자기) 전문 이외의 일에 잘 아는 체하는 사람

  [Ex] There are enough armchair generals filling our television and radio stations doing that.

- **backseat driver** (자동차에서) 이래라저래라 운전 지시를 하는 승객, 참견하기 좋아하는 사람, 무책임한 비평가 (A person who persists in offering unwanted advice to the person in charge)

  [Ex] Stop being such a backseat driver. You will only make things worse.

- Monday morning quarterback (이미 일이 있고 난 후에) 뒤늦게 따따부따하는 사람

  [Ex] I'm sick and tired of a Monday-morning quarterback like him.

47 Lawyer
변호사

Informal

- **ambulance-chaser** (교통 사고를 쫓아다니는) 3류[악덕] 변호사

  [Ex] Your friend should get one of those ambulance chasers and file a lawsuit.

Lazy

게으른

Formal

idler; good-for-nothing; lounger; shirker; sluggard; wastrel;

- **couch potato** 오랫동안 가만히 앉아 텔레비전만 보는 사람

[Ex] Please don't lie around like a couch potato. Get up and do something productive.

- loafer 게으른 사람 (Lazy person)

[Ex] The Bible promises no loaves to the loafer.

Informal

- **bum** 게으름뱅이, 건달 (A lazy person)

[Ex] Get off your butt, you bum!

- gold-brick (꾀병을 부리는) 게으름뱅이 (A lazy person)

- goof-off 게으름뱅이, 농땡이 치는 사람 (A lazy person)

[Ex] Well, even then, she wasn't a goof-off.

- lazy dog 게으른 사람 (A lazy person)

[Ex] Get out of bed, ya lazy dog!

- lazy-bones 게으른 사람 (A lazy person)

[Ex] You'll be late for school, lazy bones.

- slacker 태만한 사람, 게으름뱅이 (A lazy person)

[Ex] Those people are real slackers.

- slack-jaw 태만한 사람, 게으름뱅이

[Ex] As for social mobility, old slack jaw has made it impossible to buy a house and even more impossible to move if you have one.

- **slouch** 게으른 사람, 잘못하는 사람 (A person with shoulders and head bent to look lazy and unattractive)

[Ex] I'm no slouch but I've struggled with the concept of growth for years.

49 *Male*
남자

Formal

- Mister nice-guy 멋진 남자 (A nice person)

[Ex] But after that there was no more Mister Nice Guy.

Informal

- **dude** 녀석, 놈, (부르는 말로) 당신, 자네 (A male)

[Ex] "Dude!" Randy said. "Are you like on 'roids or something?" ('roids = steroids)

- **wingman** 섹스 상대방을 고르는 데 옆에서 도움을 주는 남자

[Ex] I got this girl's number last night. My wingman kept her friends out of the way.

Man – Young
어린 남자

Informal

- **jock** (고교, 대학의) 힘만 센 운동선수

  [Ex] His biggest worry in high school was staying out of the way of the jocks, until he got bigger than they were.

- **prep** (비싼) 사립고 학생 (A student or graduate of an expensive prep school, a preppy)

  [Ex] Only preps wear Abercrombie and Fitch.

- **preppy** (전형적으로) 비싼 사립학교 학생 같은 청소년

  [Ex] John looked very preppy today.

Marriageable
결혼 상대

Informal

- catch 좋은 결혼 상대자, 횡재한 물건

  [Ex] Yeah, we're both single, lonely people. I mean, she said I was a catch.

52 Mother
엄마, 어머니

- **helicopter parent** 극성 부모 (자녀를 지켜보며 주위를 맴도는 부모. 특히 교육 측면에서 대단한 열의를 보이는 경우를 가리킴. 'Helicopter mother, helicopter mom, helicopter dad'도 같은 의미로 사용됨 / An over-attentive parent. One who hovers over their child as a helicopter hovers.)

  [Ex] We hovered over every school, playground and practice field – "helicopter parents", teachers christened us, a phenomenon that spread to parents of all ages, races and regions.

- **soccer mom** 사커 맘 (자녀를 스포츠, 음악 교습 등의 활동에 데리고 다니느라 여념이 없는 전형적인 중산층 엄마를 가리킴 / A woman who devotes much of her spare time to her children's activities, typically driving them to and from sports events in which they are involved; the stereotypical suburban mother)

  [Ex] She will be a big appeal to all the soccer moms in middle America.

- stage mother 어린 연기자의 어머니 (The mother of a child actor)

  [Ex] So the new gossip is that Linda is becoming a real stage mother, after her daughter has been in only 1 play. She didn't even have a speaking role!

- stage parent 어린 연기자의 부모 (An over-bearing parent of a child actor)

  [Ex] Pushy stage parents are something of a necessity in show business.

- **tiger mom** 자녀 교육에 열성적인 동양계 엄마 (2011년 Amy Chua의 "Battle Hymn of the Tiger Mother"에서 유래. 타이거 마더, 엄격함과 동시에 사랑과 믿음을 바탕으로 아이를 양육하는 엄마로서, 예의 범절 및 상대에 대한 존중을 교육하고 좋은 성적을 얻도록 함)

  [Ex] She also has a tiger-mother in tow, which doesn't help.

- **MILF** 보통 나이에 비해 젊어 보이거나 매력적인 아줌마

  [Ex] Oh, he even told one student that the boy's mother was a MILF.

- sugar mom 돈 많은 중년 여자 (보통 성관계 대가로 자기보다 훨씬 젊은 남자에게 많은 선물과 돈을 안겨 주는 중년 여자를 나타냄)

Nasty

못된, 더러운, 나쁜

Formal

rascal; rogue; snake; vermin; cad(비열한 인간); knave; miscreant; reprobate; scoundrel

Informal

- varmint 말썽꾸러기 (특히 아이 / A misbehaving child)

[Ex] We won't let such varmints interfere with our New Year's feast.

Slang

- **bastard** 놈, 녀석, 싫은 사람[것] (A mean or nasty person)

[Ex] Holden thinks about how much of a moron and a bastard he is.

- **bitch** (일반적으로) 여자(를 낮춘 말)

[Ex] "I just want to roll down the windows and scream to all the girls we pass", she continued. "I've a huge cock in my pussy, bitches. I'm getting fucked by two people I love and you're just driving around looking."

- MOFO (Mother Fucker의 준말 / Short for Mother Fucker)

[Ex] I know who you're talking about, that kid's a mofo.

- **mother fucker** 후레자식 (An extremely strong general insult)

[Ex] You stupid mother fucker.

- pisshead 바보, 병신 (Asshole)

[Ex] Look at the pisshead over there wearing a knitted sweater.

- **prick** 멍청한 놈, 지겨운[싫은] 녀석, 얼간이

[Ex] Does being a rich prick who thinks he can get away with everything qualify as a profession?

- schmuck 멍청이, 얼간이

[Ex] You read in the tabloids every day, some schmuck hits it big and falls to pieces because he wasn't ready for success.

- SOB 개새끼, 개자식 (Acronym for "son of a bitch")

[Ex] He swore that he would be a SOB if he was lying.

New Comer
신참

Informal

- Johnny-come-lately (특히 지나치게 자신만만한) 신참 (A newcomer)

[Ex] She might take offense if some Johnny-come-lately thinks he can do a better job.

Old Person

고참, 한물간 사람, 나이 든 사람

Informal

- has-been 한물간 사람 (A person who was once famous or successful, but is no longer)

  [Ex] That guy used to be so cool! Now he's just some has-been.

- old timer 고참자

  [Ex] There were many of his type among the old timers.

- over the hill 한물간[퇴물이 된] (Middle-aged or older)

  [Ex] Most teenagers think that their parents are over the hill, no matter what their ages are.

Slang

- old-fart 늙은 사람 (An elderly person)

  [Ex] The old fart was driving too slow.

Overweight, Obese, Fat Person 비만, 뚱보

Informal

- chunk 몸이 딱 벌어진 사람

  [Ex] Yo, check out John Kim over there. He's a chunk!

- fat-ass 뚱뚱한 (사람) (An overweight person)

  [Ex] Is this how you spend your free time, fat-ass? Lying half-naked on a bed in black socks at 11:30 in the morning?

- **fatty** 뚱뚱한 사람 (A fat person)

  [Ex] Britain is fast becoming a nation of fatties.

- junk in the trunk 엉덩이가 아주 큰 여자 (A woman with a large rear end)

  [Ex] That chick's got a lot of junk in the trunk.

Police Officer

경찰

Informal

- 5-0 경찰 (The police; Pronounced as "five oh")

  [Ex] 1. 5-0 at the party! / 2. The 5-0 are coming to break up the fight.

- bronze 경찰 (The police)

  [Ex] The bronze are up ahead, slow down.

- cherry-tops (경찰차 안의) 경찰 (Police, usually in cars; From the flashing red light (the same color as red cherries) on police cars.)

  [Ex] Jimmy was doing 90 and got chased by the cherry-tops.

- **cop** 경찰

  [Ex] Damn cop gave me a ticket, I hate him.

Poor, Poor person, Homeless Person 가난한, 집 없는

Formal

- **charity case** 자선사업 대상자, 빈민구호 대상자 (A case for a welfare worker)

  [Ex] I'm going to his formal dance, but he's just a charity case.

- on stamps 가난하여 정부 보조 식품 할인권으로 생활하는 사람

  [Ex] I'm so broke, I'm almost on stamps!

Informal

- **bum** 떠돌이, 부랑자 (A homeless person or beggar)

  [Ex] When he came back from the backpacking trip, he looked like a bum.

- gutter punk (집이 없는) 조무래기, 똘마니, 풋내기

  [Ex] I look like the majority, I dress like them most of the time. No more gutter punk, freak attire.

- trailer park trash (트레일러 파크에 거주하는) 부랑인

  [Ex] I don't want to go to the flea market, it's going to be full of trailer park trash.

Slang

- ass out 돈이 하나도 없는 (Without money; Broke)

  [Ex] I can't go to the show tonight, I'm ass out.

- **out on one's ass** 거리로 쫓겨난 (Having been kicked out of one's residence)

Profession
직업

59-1. Bartender (바텐더)

Formal

- barkeep 술집 주인[판매원], 바텐더 (Bartender)

[Ex] Hey, barkeep, could I get another one?

59-2. Accountant (회계사)

Informal

- bean counter 1. (경멸적) 통계 전문가 2. (관청, 기업의) 경리 담당자, 경리 사원, 숫자[머릿수]
만 따지는 사람 (Derogatory term used in referring to accountants)

[Ex] I would hate to be a bean counter for a living. I would rather be poor and
have a personality.

59-3. Bodyguard (경호원)

Informal

- **bouncer** (극장, 댄스 홀 따위의) 경비원(guard), 경호원(bodyguard)

[Ex] I pushed the girl that slapped me and then the bouncers threw me out.

59-4. Doctor (의사)

- **shrink** 정신과 의사 (A psychologist or psychiatrist)

[Ex] It's like he's on posh drugs, you know, the sort that shrinks for rich-and-famous people give their customers to keep them around, you know?

59-5. Drug Dealer (마약 밀매자)

- **pusher** (마약) 밀매자 (One who sells illegal drugs)

[Ex] We need education, treatment and tough punishment for pushers.

59-6. Expert (전문가)

- spin doctor (정치인, 기관 등의) 공보 비서관, 홍보전문가 (A person (usually involved in Public Relations) who attempt to put a positive "spin", on bad news that surfaces about a client)

[Ex] Yet again, the Government are putting spin doctors ahead of real doctors.

59-7. Official (관리)

Informal

- **brass** 고급장교 (A high-ranking officer)

  [Ex] These top brass deserve to be shot for treason.

- bronze 경찰 (The police)

  [Ex] The bronze are up ahead, slow down.

- cherry-tops (경찰차 안의) 경찰

  [Ex] Jimmy was doing 90 and got chased by the cherry-tops.

- **cop** 경찰

  [Ex] Damn cop gave me a ticket. I hate him.

- **narc** 마약 전담 수사관, 마약 단속 경찰 (A narcotics agent)

  [Ex] Others are often visited by 'narcs' posing as traders.

- **fed** 연방 정부의 관리, (특히 연방 수사국(FBI)의) 수사관, 연방 정부

  [Ex] Don't let the feds find out about your cash business.

59-8. Office worker (사무직원)

Informal

- desk jockey 사무직원

  [Ex] The twins got jobs as desk jockeys at an RV rental place, so they explain rental contracts in both of Canada's national languages.

- **nine-to-fiver** 정시定時 근무자, 월급쟁이 (A person with an office job)

  [Ex] The film begins with Forest Whitaker playing a bored and frustrated nine-to-fiver who feels stuck in his routine.

59-10. Prostitute (매춘부)

Informal

- **escort** (돈을 받고) 사교 모임에 동반해 주는 여자 (고급 콜걸을 의미함)

  [Ex] I hired a fine escort last night – she blew me away.
- hooker 창녀 (A prostitute)

  [Ex] Hookers look for customers near the big hotels.
- whore 창녀

Slang

- ho bag 매춘부 (Prostitute)

  [Ex] I need to track down my ho-bag sister.
- **hoe** 창녀 (A general insult, usually applied to females)

  [Ex] She is such a hoe.
- **skank** 매춘부 (Whore, Prostitute)

  [Ex] They worried he might hook up with a skank and start bringing them around.

59-11. Thief (도둑)

Informal

- **fence** 장물아비, 장물을 팔다

  [Ex] So wait, they're gonna fence all that stuff and then pay us for it?

Promiscuous Female
문란한 여성

Formal

- **sleep around** 여러 남자[여자]와 자다[성관계를 갖다] (To have sex with many people)

  [Ex] He's never at home because he sleeps around so much.

Informal

- **whore** 창녀

Slang

- asshoe 멍청한 창녀, 항문성교를 좋아하는 창녀

  [Ex] Don't be an asshoe!

- fuckbunny 난잡한 젊은 여성

  [Ex] She's such a fuckbunny.

- **garden tool** 난잡한 젊은 여성 (Promiscuous female)

- slag 갈보 (A promiscuous female; UK slang)

  [Ex] She's been slagging around like the girl in that Police song, 'Roxanne.'

- **slut** 1. 난잡하게 놀아먹는 계집, 잡년 2. 지저분하고 게으른 계집 (A promiscuous female)

  [Ex] Stay back, slut!

- **smut** 난잡한 여자 (Promiscuous female)

  [Ex] She's a smut.

- **tart** 바람난 여자, 매춘부 (A person, usually female, that is a show-off or just a stupid bimbo)

  [Ex] That chick with the short skirt is such a tart.

- **tramp** 잡년, 화냥년 (A disreputable female)

  [Ex] Wait, wait, wait, wait, wait. Is your "friend" that top heavy tramp in reception?

Radical

급진적인 사람들

- God Squad (특히 전도에 열심인) 기독교도들

  [Ex] I'm not with the God Squad or anything like that. I am not calling to tell you how horrible you are or get you to change your mind about what you do.

- **tree-hugger** 급진적인 환경 보호 운동가

  [Ex] She's such a tree-hugger that now she's out protesting against blowing your nose on Kleenex.

62 *Repulsive*
역겨운, 혐오스러운

Formal

- **weirdo** 괴짜, 별난 사람 (A weird person)

Informal

- **creep** 싫은 녀석, 불쾌한 사람 (An annoying person)

  [Ex] Tell your brother to go away. He is such a creep.

- **douche bag** 싫은[시시한]놈

  [Ex] "Fuck you, douchebag" Adam said. "If she wanted you to have her phone number, she would have given it to you last week when you showed up."

- maggot 비열한 인간 (Repulsive person)

  [Ex] You were so maggot last night, you fucked the homeless guy.

- **sleaze** 부정직한 사람, 부도덕한 사람 (A vulgar, contemptible, untrustworthy people)

  [Ex] He is a real sleaze. I used to dance and he was there every night. He would drop $10,000 on a girl and then she'd leave with him.

- **sleazebag** 부정직한[부도덕한] 사람 (Sleaze; a bad person)

  [Ex] The banks are just money making corporations run by greedy sleazebags, pretty much like all other corporations.

- slime (더럽고) 끈적끈적한 물질, 점액, 불쾌한 사람

  [Ex] He is a traitorous slime and I utterly despise him and all his misgovernment.

- slimeball 더러운 인간 (A bad person)

  [Ex] The comments I've read also indicate that there are too many people just like these slimeballs who steal too.

- stinker 아주 기분 나쁜 인간, 골칫거리 (A misbehaving person; A fairly childish term)

  [Ex] I think he's an absolute stinker to do that to her.

- stinkpot 악취를 풍기는 것, 역겨운 놈 (Repulsive thing[person]; displeasing thing[person])

  [Ex] Gordon is a stinkpot. He can't catch me.

Retentive

지나치게 깔끔한

- anal (사람이) 지나치게 깔끔한, 신경질적인 (Shortened form of anal retentive)

  [Ex] Quit being so anal!

- **anal retentive** (사람이) 지나치게 깔끔한, 신경질적인

  [Ex] My boyfriend is really anal retentive about his car.

Risk-Taking

무모한

- **cowboy** 무모[무책임]한 사람, 위험한[어려운] 일을 쉽게 떠맡는 사람

  [Ex] The cowboy driving that subway train scared the passengers.

- grandstanding 사람들의 눈길을 끌려는 행위

  [Ex] Opponents of the measure say it's political grandstanding that could prove devastating to the economy.

- high roller (특히 도박에) 돈을 많이 쓰는 사람

  [Ex] Yes, it's true, even high rollers aren't immune to the credit crunch.

- **showboat** 무모하게 과시하다 (To perform or behave in a showy and flamboyant way)

  [Ex] Critics say he has used the post for grandstanding and showboating.

Rural Dweller

촌놈

Informal

- bushpig 촌놈 (An unattractive person from the Bush, i.e. the country-side of Australia)

  [Ex] You bush pig.

- hayseed 시골뜨기 (A person from a rural area; Un-hip, bumpkin)

  [Ex] Anyone living outside of Manhattan is a hayseed.

- hillybilly 시골뜨기 (Rural dweller)

- **redneck** 시골 사람 (모욕적으로 쓰여 교육 수준이 낮고 정치적으로 보수적인 미국 시골 사람을 나타냄)

  [Ex] You people are just a bunch of rednecks groaning and moaning all the time.

- **stick** 벽촌, 촌놈 (A person who lives in a rural area)

  [Ex] That guy is such a stick!

- yokel (무식한) 촌놈, 무지렁이 (A person from a rural area; hick)

  [Ex] As a good yokel I attended our parish Harvest Thanksgiving Mass and Harvest Supper the other day.

66 Ruining the Fun
흥을 깨는

- party pooper 좌중의 흥을 깨는 사람 (A person who "ruins" fun)

  [Ex] Come on, party pooper, bust a move.

- wet blanket 흥을 깨는 사람 (A person that kills fun or humor)

  [Ex] I hate to be a wet blanket, but I thought the show was terrible.

67 Skill, Skilled, Talent, Talented 기술이 좋은, 재능이 좋은, 사부

- **black-belt** 유단자, 특정 분야의 전문가 (A person very skilled in a particular area)

  [Ex] I've got a black belt in cooking.

- **Jedi** 제다이 (영화 Star Wars에 나오는 신비스러운 기사단騎士團의 기사; 우주의 평화와 정의를 지킴. 또는 Jed·i knight / The Jedi are a fictitious order of warrior monks who play an important role in the 'Star Wars' movie series by George Lucas. They were responsible for the maintenance of peace and order in the Galactic Republic, and were skilled in various mental disciplines from domination to psychokinesis.)

  [Ex] The way you talked that cop out of a speeding ticket, man that was jedi.

- **rock star** 아주 매력이 있거나 재능이 있는 사람

  [Ex] You're such a rock star.

Slang

- hot shit 대단한 것, 훌륭한 사람, 거물

  [Ex] That would-be Marilyn Monroe thinks she's hot shit.

Snoopy or Meddlesome
참견, 훈수하는 사람

Formal

- kibitzer (노름을 구경하며) 참견하다, 훈수 두다
- **rubberneck** 고개를 돌려 보다 (차를 타고 지나가면서 사고가 난 곳 등을 보는 것)

  [Ex] The traffic jam was caused by rubber-neckers slowing down for a gawk at the accident.

Informal

- buttinski 말참견하는 사람 (A meddler; someone who intrudes or interferes)

  [Ex] Get out of here, Buttinski. You weren't invited into this talk.

Stingy or Greedy
구두쇠, 욕심쟁이

Informal

- Bogart (돌아가며 피우는 마리화나 등을) 독점하다 (To steal, monopolize or hog)

  [Ex] Don't Bogart my cookies!

- cheapo 구두쇠 (Tightwad)

  [Ex] I will forego the use of paper plates for months till they go on sale for 20 cents off. Some call me a cheapo. I call it pure genius.

- cheapskate 구두쇠 (Tightwad, a stingy person)

  [Ex] You only got me a half pint - you cheapskate!

- money-grubber 악착같이 돈을 긁어모으는 (사람) (A person focused on acquiring money)

  [Ex] Not all Christians are media hogs, hypocrites or moneygrubbers.

- **paper chaser** 돈[이익]만 쫓는 사람 (Someone who runs behind money for profit)

  [Ex] Greg is a paper chaser.

- **penny-pincher** 깍쟁이, 구두쇠 (A frugal person)

  [Ex] Compared to other business barons like Bill Gates and David Geffen, Donald looks like a lousy penny-pincher.

- skin-flint 구두쇠, 수전노 (A mean person who hates spending money)

  [Ex] A lot of this has to do with notorious skin flint show owners Procter & Gamble.

- **tightwad** 구두쇠, 수전노 (A stingy person)

  [Ex] My mom's such a tightwad, she wouldn't spend $30 on a DVD player.

Slang

- tight ass 구두쇠, 인색함, 고지식한 사람 (A stingy person; an uptight person)

  [Ex] Chris is such a total tight ass!

70 *Strange*
괴상한, 이상한

Informal

- **freak** 괴짜, 기형, 변태 성향을 갖고 있는 사람

  [Ex] He is such a freak!

71 *Stupid*
멍청한

Informal

- airbrain[airhead] 바보, 얼간이 (fool)

  [Ex] He's confused again. What an airhead!

- **bimbo** 섹시하지만 멍청한 여자 (An unintelligent female)

  [Ex] Anyone who hangs around with bimbos like Paris Hilton is just asking for trouble.

- birdbrain 새대가리, 멍청이 (An unintelligent person)

  [Ex] That birdbrain delivered the wrong box again.

- **bonehead** 멍청이, 얼간이 (An idiotic or foolish person)

  [Ex] You bonehead!

- buffoon 멍청이, 얼간이 (An idiotic or foolish person)

  [Ex] You stupid buffoon.

- **dimwit** 투미한 사람, 얼간이 (An unintelligent person)

  [Ex] Your new boss is kind of a dimwit, isn't he?

- doink 바보, 멍청이 (A moron; idiot; GOOF. Used in an endearing way)

  [Ex] Man, you are such a doink for believing that!

- doofus 얼간이, 얼뜨기 (An unintelligent person; IDIOT; MORON)

  [Ex] Dave is such a doofus at times.
- fathead 얼간이, 바보 (Fool)

  [Ex] He's such a fathead; he won't listen to anybody.

- **jerk** 순진한 사람, 세상 물정에 어두운 사람, 멍청이, 바보 (A mean person; Idiot)

  [Ex] If you would meet Adam on the street or if you two boys wouldn't have acted like jerks, you would know that Adam is the sweetest, gentlest man in the world.

- knucklehead 얼간이, 멍청이 (An unintelligent person)

  [Ex] What are you doing, ya knucklehead?

- mule head 고집 센 (사람), 완고한 (사람), 다루기 어려운(사람) (Stupid but stubborn (person))

  [Ex] Take yourself back to Belgium, mule head, and resume boasting about your nation's bravery and integrity.

- peabrain 바보, 얼간이 (Fool, idiot)

  [Ex] Oh dear! I see you still haven't read any of the papers pointed out to you, peabrain.

- **retard** 지능 지체자, 천치, 바보 (An unintelligent person)

  [Ex] You're such a retard.

- snapperhead 바보, 멍청이 (An idiot)

  [Ex] Shut up, you snapperhead!

- space cadet (마약 중독자처럼) 멍한 사람

  [Ex] He certainly deserves better than to work with these space cadets.

- **tard** 저능아

  [Ex] You are a real tard.

- thickhead 우둔한 사람 (Stupid person)

  [Ex] The fact that Moses destroyed the table demonstrated only that he had to handle with such thickheads in the only way they would understand.

- thickie 우둔한 사람 (Stupid)

  [Ex] Such thickies should not be allowed anywhere near government.

- dickhead 바보 (Asshole; stupid person; moron)

[Ex] He is such a dickhead.

- dickwad 비열한 놈, 바보, 멍청이 (General insult; jerk; asshole)

[Ex] Magician: Those yokels out there get what they deserve. I give them pure magic, and they respond like a bunch of slack-jawed cattle. / Sam: Yeah, well, maybe they respond that way because you're such a total dickwad.

- **dipshit** 굼벵이, 쓸모없는 사람, 한심한 사람, 재주 없는 사람

[Ex] The guy's a complete dipshit.

- fuck-ass 바보, 멍청이 (Another word for idiot, moron, etc.)

[Ex] You stupid fuck-ass, you broke my shit.

- fuckwit 바보, 얼간이 (An unintelligent person; moron; dim-wit; idiot)

[Ex] Don't trample that dog crap into my house, fuckwit!

Stupid and Clumsy or Socially Inept 멍청하고 사회부적응

Informal

- chucklehead 바보, 모자라는 사람, 멍청이 (An unintelligent person)

  [Ex] Shut up you chucklehead. Boy, Bob sure is a chuckleheaded idiot. He's so stupid he forgot to friggin' shut up his mouth.

- clod 얼간이, 바보 (Someone gullible)

  [Ex] That clod is so gullible, I told him Iraq won the war. Ha.

- **dummy** 바보, 멍청이 (An unintelligent person)

  [Ex] That's not the right answer, you dummy!

- gomer 바보 (Geek, nerd, or weirdo)

  [Ex] What a gomer!

- lummox 재치 없고 둔한 녀석, 굼벵이, 멍청이(lump) (A clumsy person)

  [Ex] Even John Major looked like the model of competence, a man in control compared to this lummox.

- meatball[meathead] 얼뜨기 (Clumsy person)

- schlub 바보, 얼간이 (A clumsy, oafish person)

  [Ex] I can see some poor old schlub filing suit against the company for not working as advertised.

Stupid and Obnoxious
멍청하면서 기분 나쁘게 하는

- doo-doo head 멍청이, 얼간이 (Very stupid person)

  [Ex] Shut up, you doo-doo head!

- **jackass** 멍청이 (A stupid or idiotic person)

  [Ex] Stop being a jackass, Kayla!

Sweet, Nice
달콤한

- peach 훌륭한 사람, 미남, 미인 (A sweet or nice person)

  [Ex] The store manager, Antonio, was a peach of a guy.

Too Talkative

말이 많은, 수다스러운

Formal

informer; busybody; prattler; scandalmonger; tattler; telltale

Informal

- **big mouth** 입이 싼 사람 (A noisy, indiscreet, or boastful person)

  [Ex] If you don't stop that big mouth, you are going to pay for it.

- blabbermouth 입이 싼 사람

  [Ex] There are already too many blabbermouths out there, but they are loud without being interesting except to themselves.

- chatter-box 수다쟁이 (Someone who talks a lot)

  [Ex] Anne is a chatterbox in class, so as punishment she has to do extra homework.

- chinwagger 말이 많은 사람, 수다쟁이 (Someone who talks a lot)

  [Ex] That guy wouldn't shut up about how his Viking character died in Dungeons and Dragons. What a chinwagger!

- fat mouth (행동은 하지 않고) 말만 많은 사람 (Very talkative person)

  [Ex] But you've got a big fat mouth, and a cavernous aircraft hanger size empty skull.

- gabber 수다쟁이 (Very talkative person)

  [Ex] Talk-show gabber Joy Behar got the chance to go toe-to-toe Wednesday with a leading Democrat presidential hopeful Senator.

- gas bag 말이 많은 사람, 떠버리 (A person who makes many empty statements)

  [Ex] Rush Limbaugh may be a gasbag, but not everything he says is wrong.

- loudmouth 떠버리, 말이 많은 사람

  [Ex] He is such a loud mouth that you can't trust him with any secrets.

- windbag 수다쟁이, 떠버리 (A talkative person who says nothing of substance)

  [Ex] It's good to expose windbags as windbags in front of a lot of people.

Uncool Person, Jerk, Asshole 나쁜 자식, 재수 없는 놈, 멍청한 놈

Informal

- buffoon 익살꾼, 교양 없는 사람, 바보 (A ludicrous or bumbling person; a fool)

  [Ex] This is the ideal opportunity to sack these two overpaid buffoons.

- chicken head 바보, 멍청이 (Jerk)

  [Ex] For instance, calling a girl a "Chicken head" is an unflattering term, yet anyone unfamiliar with it would have no clue what the meaning is.

- **hooker** 창녀 (A general insult)

  [Ex] You stupid hooker!

- rat 쥐새끼 같은[비열한] 놈 (A criminal; a bad person)

  [Ex] He's a little rat, isn't he?

- **scumbag** 쓰레기 같은 인간, 더러운 놈

  [Ex] Some scumbags even take up two parking spaces or double park.

- **son of a gun** 나쁜 자식 (A bad person)

  [Ex] He's an arrogant son of a gun, but that confidence will pass on to the players.

Slang

- **ass** 고집불통

  [Ex] Don't be such an ass.

- ass clown 사회성이 없고 둔감한 사람 (비하하여 일컫는 말)

  [Ex] Those people in the personnel office are such ass-clowns.

- asswipe 1. 화장지(의 대용품) 2. 빌어먹을 놈, 얼간이, 알랑쇠

  [Ex] It didn't help much that Karl Wellingham was a Major League, Grade-A asswipe.

- bugger 녀석, 놈(chap), 싫은 녀석

  [Ex] That bugger stole my car!

- cock 혼자 우쭐대는 사람, 독불장군

  [Ex] A cock would say things like, "what would you guys do without me?"

- cocksucker 더러운 인간 (보통 남자에 대한 대단히 심한 욕)

  [Ex] Man, my English teacher is a cocksucker.

- **cunt** 1. (성교 대상으로서의) 여자, 계집 2. (경멸적) 계집

  [Ex] My ex-girlfriend is a fucking cunt.

- **dick** 새끼, 자식, 놈 (A general insult; jerk; asshole)

  [Ex] Wilfred: That motorcycle dick is ruining the neighborhood. You need to put that asshole in his place. / Ryan: What's the point of a confrontation? I'd just get my ass kicked.

- dick wad 비열한 놈, 바보, 멍청이 (A stupid person)

  [Ex] Don't be such a dick wad.

- **faggot** (경멸적) 자식, 새끼 (A general insult, meaning homosexual)

  [Ex] That guy is such a faggot.

- **fuck** 비열한 녀석 (A really stupid person)

  [Ex] You stupid fuck!

- **fucker** 바보 같은 놈, 싫은 사람, 녀석, 놈

- fuckhead 바보, 얼간이 (특히 남성 / A general insult; jerk)

  [Ex] That stupid fuckhead pulled in front of me.

- **jackass** 멍청이 (A stupid or idiotic person)

  [Ex] Stop being a jackass, Kayla!

- **jerk** 바보, 멍청이 (A mean person; Idiot)

  [Ex] That jerk just called me a dirty name.

- **piece of shit** 기분이 나쁜 새끼, 형편없는 새끼 (Very displeasing person)

  [Ex] You useless piece of shit!

- **prick** 멍청한 놈, 지겨운[싫은] 녀석, 얼간이

  [Ex] He is just a rich prick who thinks he can get away with everything.

- schlong 싫은 녀석, 지겨운 녀석 (Displeasing person; dick)

  [Ex] You are such a schlong!

- **shit fucker** 병신, 바보 (A person who is being an idiot or a stupid ass)

  [Ex] You such a shit fucker.

- **snatch** 여자 (여자의 비속어 / Derogatory term for a disliked female; bitch)

  [Ex] She is such a snatch!

- **son of a bitch** 나쁜 자식 (A bad person)

- **twat** 등신, 멍청이 (A displeasing person; idiot)

  [Ex] "Oh, you sneaky little twat." she hissed.

- wank 잘난 체하는 남자 (A smug, self-involved person, usually male)

  [Ex] What a wank.

- wanker 재수 없는 새끼 (특히 남자를 가리키는 욕)

  [Ex] You are such a wanker!

Unintelligent

멍청한

Informal

- blithering idiot 순진한 멍청이

  [Ex] The man is a blithering idiot, addicted to debt.

- blockhead 바보, 멍청이, 돌대가리 (A silly, unintelligent or foolish person)

  [Ex] They're a bunch of blockheads who would have been criminals if they didn't graduate from high school.

- **blond** 멍청한 금발 미녀

  [Ex] Geeze, how could I forget that? I'm such a blond!

- bubblehead 멍청이, 얼간이

  [Ex] I am so fed up with having to pay for the incompetence of bubbleheads.

- **bumbass** 바보, 멍청이 (One who has both lazy and retarded qualities)

  [Ex] Why don't you stop watching television and study a little bit for once, you bumbass.

- dumb-bell 얼간이, 바보 (An unintelligent person)

  [Ex] That person can't do anything right; what a dumbbell!

- **dumbhead** 얼간이, 바보 (An unintelligent person)

  [Ex] I just wonder which dumbhead in the government came up with this idea.

- jughead 바보 (A fool)

  [Ex] That jughead sent our baggage to the wrong hotel.

- lamebrain 바보, 멍청이, 얼간이 (A total idiot)

  [Ex] Scott Whitson is a lamebrain.

- nimrod 바보, 얼간이

  [Ex] The guy next door to my cousin is a total nimrod.

- nincompoop 멍청이 (Idiot)

  [Ex] Being the stubborn nincompoop that I am···.

- nitwit 바보, 멍청이 (A very unintelligent person; moron; imbecile)

  [Ex] Jay is such a nitwit.

영어 표현에도 등급이 있다!

- rattlebrain 머리가 텅 빈 사람 (An empty-headed man)

  [Ex] O, Augustine, you are a sad rattle-brain!

- twerp 천한 놈, 바보 (A fool; a twit)

  [Ex] Now you've broken it, you twerp!

- twit 얼간이, 멍청이, 바보 (A foolish or annoying person)

  [Ex] I would assume the two twits trying their best to look like tough guys are your brothers.

Slang

- **ass** 바보, 멍청이 (Idiot, Fool)

- **asshoe** 멍청한 창녀, 항문성교를 좋아하는 창녀 (A dumb prostitute)

  [Ex] She's an asshoe!

- ding-a-ling 바보, 얼간이, 괴짜, 미치광이, 별난 사람

  [Ex] He shit the sheets. He's a real ding-a-ling.

- dingbat 바보, 멍청이

  [Ex] Tiffany is the biggest dingbat I know!

- ding-head 멍청이, 얼간이 (A person acting stupid)

  [Ex] All those ding-heads are causing trouble around this neighborhood.

- ditz 바보, 얼간이, 괴짜, 별난 사람 (An unintelligent female)

  [Ex] Kim and Cher are such ditzes!

- dope 얼간이, 바보 (An unintelligent person)

  [Ex] Why do you have to be such a dope?

- **dumb bastard** 바보, 멍청이 (A stupid person)

  [Ex] If I ever get my hands on that son-of-a-bitch who drives that snowplow, I swear I will castrate the dumb bastard.

- dumb cluck 바보, 멍청이 (A stupid person)

  [Ex] The other whore is the mother of harlots, you dumb cluck.

- **dumb fuck** 바보, 멍청이 (A stupid person)

  [Ex] Don't be such a dumb-fuck.

- **dumbass** 얼간이, 바보 (A very unintelligent person)

  [Ex] What kind of dumb-ass talks back to the teacher?

78 Unreliable

신뢰할 수 없는

Informal

- **fly-by-night** 빨리 한몫 잡을 생각만 하는, 금전적으로 믿을 수 없는, (빚에 몰려) 야반도주 하는 사람, 믿을 수 없는 사람 (An unreliable organization, especially a business)

  [Ex] Health care and education are too important for politicians to use for their own fly by night political ambitions.

79 Useless

쓸모없는

Informal

- punk 쓸모없는 사람, 조무래기, 똘마니, 풋내기

  [Ex] Your kid is a real punk.

Very Rich

엄청난 부자

- jillionaire 엄청난 부자 (An extremely wealthy person)

  [Ex] Stop being a frickin' jillionaire!

Young Person

젊은 사람

- grommet 신참 서퍼 (A young, typically pre-pubescent surfer; 1960s slang)

  [Ex] Wally's brother Beav, is a grommet down at Huntington Beach.

- **shorty** 젊은 여자 (A young female. Origin: hip-hop slang; a person)

  [Ex] What's up, shorty?

- whipper-snapper 건방진 애송이 (Arrogant young person)

  [Ex] Why, I was using those slang words when you were nothing but a whipper-snapper!

Chapter 6

Types of Things
사물의 이름, 형태, 관련 기타 표현들

이번 장에서는 미국 성인들이 여러 가지 물건들 대해 어떤 표현들을 사용하는지 정리했습니다. 참고로 마약류에 관련된 속어들을 많이 나오는데, 이는 1960년대 이후 'Recreational Drug'의 사용이 미국 젊은이들 사이에 하나의 문화적인 현상으로 인식되면서 큰 사회적인 문제가 되었고 현재도 많은 논란이 되고 있는 문제이기 때문입니다. 관련 속어들을 알아는 두어야 하지만 직접 언급은 최대한 삼가야 합니다.

1 *Alcohol*

술

Informal

- boilermaker 물 대신 맥주를 입가심으로 마시면서 드는 위스키, 폭탄주

  [Ex] The waitress brings them two boilermakers.

- **booze** 알코올, 술 (Alcohol)

  [Ex] I've never seen her pass up free booze in my life.

- **brew** 맥주 (Beer)

  [Ex] Would you like to come in for a brew?

- hair of the dog 해장술, 숙취일 때 마시는 술

  [Ex] That's some hangover you've got there, Bob. Here, drink this. It's a hair of the dog that bit you.

- hooch (아주 독한) 술 (특히 밀주 / Liquor, especially home-made liquor. e.g. moonshine.)

  [Ex] Pass the hooch.

- **poison** (강한) 술, 독주 (익살 / One's favorite type of alcohol)

  [Ex] What's your poison?

Alcohol – Mix
술 - 혼합

Informal

- **spike** (남의 음료·음식에 몰래 술, 독약 등을) 타다[섞다]

  [Ex] We spiked the punch at the high-school dance.

Alcohol - To Drink Alcohol
술을 마시다

Informal

- **bar hop** 여러 술집을 돌아다니며 술을 마시다 (To visit several bars during a single outing)

  [Ex] We're going bar hopping later. Want to come?

- **tie one on** 고주망태가 되다 (To get drunk)

  [Ex] I really tied one on last night.

Big
큰 것

- **whopper** 엄청 큰 것 (Something big)

[Ex] Weatherman: With these unstable pressure systems, I predict a whopper of a storm is coming our way.

Broken Things
고장 난 것

- bum 고장, 엉망 (Out-of-order; malfunctioning)
- kludge 조잡한 물건, 어설픈 대책

Car, Motorcycle or Other Vehicle 자동차 관련

Informal

- Beamer BMW 자동차 (A BMW automobile)

  [Ex] Suspect tried to boost Witman's Beamer.

- **call shotgun** (10대 사이에서) 차[트럭]의 조수석에 먼저 타려고 하다 (To claim the (front) seat next to the driver in an automobile. Derives from the "old west" when stagecoaches routinely had an armed guard (typically with a shotgun) seated next to the driver on top.)

  [Ex] (Group of people) / Steve: I can give you guys a lift if you want. / Bob: I call shotgun! / Andy: Darn Bob, you already sat in front last time!

- Chevy Chevrolet 자동차의 애칭

  [Ex] Hank sure has a nice Chevy.

- **fender-bender** (자동차의) 가벼운 사고

  [Ex] I've already had a fender-bender this morning, which is not a good sign for the way things are likely to turn out today.

- louie 좌회전 (Left-hand turn. One typically "does", "makes" or "hangs" a louie)

  [Ex] Hang a louie at the next light.

- **pit stop** 1. 피트 스톱 (급유, 타이어 교체 등을 위한 정차) 2. (장기 여행 중의 휴식, 식사 등을 위한) 정차 (A break in travelling, usually for food or use of a bathroom)

  [Ex] Everybody is hungry, so they take a pit stop at a country grill.

- reggie 우회전 (Right-hand turn; One either "does" or "makes" a reggie)

  [Ex] Do a reggie at the stop sign.

- **shotgun** (승용차·트럭의) 조수석 (The passenger seat in a vehicle.)

  [Ex] 1. I get shotgun! / 2. I get to sit shotgun.

7 *Clothes*
복장 관련

Informal

- birth control glasses (군에서 지급해 주는) 못생긴 안경 (The brown-framed prescription eye-glasses issued to new recruits in the U.S. Military, and perceived as notoriously unattractive.)

  [Ex] Adam noticed he also had braces to go with his birth-control glasses. This kid had better hope to make a lot of money if he ever wanted to get laid.

- **daisy dukes** 길이가 아주 짧은 데님 반바지 (Extremely short denim shorts, as worn by the character Daisy on the television program "The Dukes of Hazard".)

  [Ex] She had on some Daisy Dukes.

- **duds** 의류, 옷 (Clothes)

  [Ex] Nice duds.

8 *Clothes - Fly, Zipper*
지퍼 관련

Formal

- **fly** 바지 지퍼 (The zipper on bottom-wear)

  [Ex] The fly of your jeans is open.

Informal

- barn door 바지 앞의 지퍼 (The fly[zipper] on one's pants)

  [Ex] Your barn door is open.

- close[shut] one's barn door 바지 앞 지퍼를 올리다 (Close one's zipper[fly] on the pants)

252 영어 표현에도 등급이 있다!

9 Drug
약물

9-1. Drug (약물 - 일반)

Informal

- **dope** 마약 (Drugs, especially marijuana)

  [Ex] He takes dope; in fact he's high on dope now.

- **LSD** 엘에스디 (강력한 환각제 / Lysergic acid diethylamide)

  [Ex] Chronic LSD use leads to schizo-affective disorder.

- hard stuff 중독성이 강한 마약 (Hard drug)

  [Ex] I've seen too many girls who would fuck a rancid dick for a hit and I never wanted to be that girl. So I've stayed away from the hard stuff too.

Slang

- acid 환각제, LSD (The hallucinogenic LSD; Lysergic acid diethylamide)

  [Ex] Do you think he could sell me some acid?

- dime bag 10달러 분량의 마약 ($10 of an illegal drug; From "dime" + "bag")

  [Ex] Dealer: How much you need? / Client: Just a dime bag.

9-2. Cocaine (약물 - 일반)

Slang

- **coke** 코카인(cocaine), 마약 [코카인]에 취하게 하다 (coke up)

- **crack** 크랙, 정제 코카인 (흡연용 / The freebase form of cocaine that can be smoked)

- eight ball 1/8 온스의 코카인 (A quantity of cocaine or crystal that weighs an eighth of an ounce, hence an "eight ball", which is equivalent to 3.5 grams.)

- **meth** 필로폰 (methamphetamine)

  [Ex] A new way to produce methamphetamine, unseen here a year ago, is becoming the preferred way for users to get a quick high and is fueling an increase in meth-related police activity after several years of decline.

- nose candy 코카인 (Cocaine)

- powder 코카인 (Cocaine)

- rock 코카인, 끽연용 결정結晶, 헤로인 (A piece of crack cocaine)

  [Ex] If she has gone back two or three times, she either spend the money on rock or she enjoyed it.

- snow 코카인 (Cocaine)

- speedball 코카인과 헤로인 섞은 것 (A mixture of cocaine and heroin, usually injected)

  [Ex] He woke up in hospital after speedballing.

- X 엑스터시 (Ecstasy, a particular street drug)

9-3. Marijuana (대마초)

Slang

- bud 마리화나 (Marijuana)

  [Ex] That is some indica big buds! some good shit!

- colitas 마리화나 봉오리 (Marijuana buds)

  [Ex] Warm smell of colitas, rising up through the air. -- "Hotel California", The Eagles.

- **ganja** 마리화나 (Marijuana)

- **grass** 마리화나 (Marijuana)

- **green** 마리화나 (Marijuana: Marijuana is green in color.)

- green bud 마리화나 (Marijuana)

- **joint** 마리화나 담배 (Marijuana cigarette, usually rolled by hand)

- Mary Jane 마리화나 (Marijuana)

- pot 마리화나 (Marijuana)

[Ex] "I smoke pot every now and then." Sarah said. "Is that a problem?" "If you bring it into the house with you, it might be." Shelly warned before Rachelle could speak.

- weed 마리화나 (Marijuana)

[Ex] Narrator: In fact, it was a box of Oscar's legally obtained medical marijuana ⋯. Primo bud. Real sticky weed. -- "Prison Break-In", Arrested Development (TV, 2005), Season 3 Episode 7

9-4. To Do Drugs (마약을 하다)

Informal

- get high (마리화나나 환각제를 통해) 몽롱한 기분을 느끼다
- hit 마약 1회분, 마리화나 한 대, 술 한잔, (약물 따위에) 취하기, 황홀, 도취
- spike up 뭔가 하기 전에 약물을 하다 (To get ready by consuming a drug)

Slang

- bang 마약 주사를 놓다 (To inject drugs intravenously)

- do a line (흡입하려고 가늘게 만들어 놓은) 코카인 한 줄을 흡입하다 (To inhale cocaine)

[Ex] The weird woman is doing a line of coke.

- get a fix 마약을 한판 하다 (To ingest a drug)
- powder one's nose 코카인을 (코로) 흡입하다 (To snort cocaine)
- shoot up (정맥에) 마약을 주사하다 (To inject a drug)
- smoke crack[dope] 마약을 하다 (To do drugs)

9-5. To Smoke Marijuana (마리화나를 피우다)

Essential Things

결론, 요점, 핵심

Formal

cases; core; foundation; key point; last word; main idea; main thing; what it's all about; whole story; the goods; essence; fundamentals; sum and substance;

- **bottom line** 최종 결과, 결론, 요점, 핵심, 중요한 것

  [Ex] What's the bottom line?

- brass tacks 기본[실질]적인 내용들 (Important details)

  [Ex] Let's get down to brass tacks. We've wasted too much time chatting.

- **clincher** (논쟁, 시합 등을 매듭짓는) 결정적인 사실, 결정타 (Sure thing)

  [Ex] DNA fingerprinting has proved the clincher in this investigation.

- crux (문제나 쟁점의) 가장 중요한 부분 (The basic, central, or essential point or feature)

  [Ex] The crux of her argument was that the roadways needed repair before anything else could be accomplished.

- **guts** 요지, 핵심 내용 (The essence of something)

  [Ex] I don't recommend that guide book since it has no guts.

- lowdown 실정, 진상 (The story or truth)

  [Ex] All the reporters hoped to be the first to get the lowdown on the celebrity's marriage plans.

- meat and potatoes 핵심, 요체 (The essence)

  [Ex] Issues like this are the newspaper's meat and potatoes.

- **name of the game** 가장 중요한 점, 불가결한 것, 본질, (본래의) 목적; 당연한 일

  [Ex] Self-interest and preservation is the name of the game.

- **nitty-gritty** (쟁점, 상황의) 핵심 (The essence or core of something; the details; a nutshell)

  [Ex] So, let's get down to the nitty-gritty.

- **nuts and bolts** 기본, 요점, ~에 대한 기초적인 사실, ~의 실제적인 상세함

  [Ex] Committee is a more effective way to deal with the nuts and bolts.

- **where the rubber meets the road** 실력[진가]이 시험되는 장場

  [Ex] Talking about prognosis is where the rubber meets the road.

11 Et Cetera
기타 등등

Informal

- and stuff ~같은 (시시한) 것

  [Ex] Do you find yourself watching TV and stuff?

- yadda yadda yadda 시시한 소리, 그렇고 그런 소리 (이미 알거나 지루한 내용이라서 그만 줄이는 말)

  [Ex] He said he was having problems and yadda-yadda-yadda.

12 Everything
모든 것, 전체

Informal

- everything but the kitchen sink (필요 이상일 정도로) 많은 것들, 생각나는 모든 물건

  [Ex] However, he said that the Bill covered almost everything but the kitchen sink.

13 *Fake*
가짜, 모조품, 짝퉁

Informal

- **bootleg** 불법으로 제작[판매]하는 것, 밀조품, 불법 복사품, 해적판

  [Ex] Person A: He got those shoes at Payless. Person B: Yeah, that's bootleg.

- **knock off** (유명 메이커 의류 등의) 모조품, 가짜 (A forgery)

  [Ex] Deangelo: Is that a Chinatown knock-off? / Jim: That's "Toys 'r' Us" I think. / Deangelo: No, that's definitely a knock-off.

14 *Gun*
총기

Informal

- **ammo** 탄약 (Ammunition)

  [Ex] Ammo's flooding us, man. What are we gonna do?

- **pack heat** (학교 등에서) 총기를 휴대하다 (To carry a firearm)

  [Ex] Watch out, that dude's packing heat.

Hopeless Things

희망이 없음

Formal

chance in a million; no way; not a ghost of a chance; poor prospect

Informal

- cat's chance in hell 전혀 희망이 없는 (Hopeless)

  [Ex] Otherwise there is not a cat's chance in hell of house prices going up.

- Chinaman's chance in hell 가능성이 전무한 (No chance at all)

  [Ex] The evil elf Kucinich hasn't got a Chinaman's chance of winning the nomination.

- dog's chance 아주 희박한 가망성 (No chance at all)

  [Ex] He hasn't a dog's chance of passing the exam.

- **fat chance** 가망 없음, 매우 희박한 가망성 (Little or no chance)

  [Ex] Fat chance of getting a raise this year.

- snowball's chance 가망성이 전혀 없는 일 ('Snowball's chance in hell'의 준말)

  [Ex] As we know from bitter experience, there is not a snowball's chance of getting them back.

16 *List*
목록

- **a-list** 최고 부류[대열](에 속하는 인사들) (A metaphorical list of the most popular people)

  [Ex] *The practice of hiring celebrities is so common that there's even an industry price list for A listers. Shah ukh Khan, India's biggest star, is quoted at $750,000, while movie heartthrob Salman Khan lists at about half that price.*

- **bucket list** 죽기 전에 꼭 해야 할 일이나 하고 싶은 일들에 대한 리스트

  [Ex] *"She had what I call a 'bucket list', and that was the last thing on it."* Marjorie Carpenter said Tuesday.

- D-list 아주 등급이 낮은 유명인 (A very minor celebrity)

  [Ex] *That actress is a D-list.*

Slang

- shit list 블랙리스트 (A list of people one is angry with)

  [Ex] *Congratulations! You just made my shit list.*

Movie
영화

Informal

- flick 영화 (한 편), 영화 (A movie)

  [Ex] A: What did you do on your date last night? / B: We had some dinner and caught a flick.

Slang

- chick flick (여성 관객을 겨냥한) 여자들 영화

  [Ex] My girlfriend couldn't go out tonight because she's watching chick flicks with her friends.

- dick flick (남자 관객 대상의) 남성 위주 폭력 영화

  [Ex] Don't invite any girls to go with us; it's strictly a dick flick.

Names for Things You Can't Remember the Name of
물건의 이름을 모를 때

Formal

appliance; contraption; invention; thing; utensil; apparatus; contrivance;

- doohickey 장치, 물건, 거시기(이름이 확실하지 않을 때의 대용어)

[Ex] Hey, could you hand me that do-hickey over there?

- **you know what** 그것 말이야, 있지 그거

[Ex] You know what, I would like to go there with him.

Slang

- **crap** 쓸모없는 물건 (물건의 이름을 기억하지 못할 때 사용)

[Ex] Stop buying all that crap you don't need.

- shit (부정문에서) 무無, 아주 조금 (Anything; Used in the negative to mean "nothing")

[Ex] There ain't shit going on.

19 *Novel*
소설

Informal

- fanfic 팬픽, 영화나 TV 쇼의 팬이 쓴 이야기 ("fan" + "fiction")

  [Ex] He's really into Star Trek fanfic.

- who-done-it[whodunit] 추리 소설, 스릴러 영화

  [Ex] This riveting mystery is a "whodunit" at its best.

20 *Problem – Easy*
쉬운 문제

Informal

- **no-brainer** 손쉬운 일, 간단한 일 (An easy-to-solve problem)

  [Ex] They would have my vote if the motion came up right now. Since you've been warned, it's a no-brainer.

Problem - Hard, Confusing, Difficult 어려운 문제

Informal

- **can of worms** 뜻밖의 (복잡하고 까다로운) 여러 가지 문제[상황]의 불씨[소지]

  [Ex] Taking that girl home turned out to be a can of worms.

- doozy 아주 어렵고 특별한 문제 (Something very complicated or difficult)

  [Ex] "How do you get yourself involved in these messes?" Peg asked. / "Come on, Mom. How many messes, exactly, do I get myself involved in?" / "OK. Not many", Peg smiled. "But this one appears to be a doozy."

- mumbo jumbo (실은 아무 의미도 없으면서) 복잡하기만 한 말

  [Ex] I may not believe in the mumbo jumbo but I do enjoy and feel enriched by my heritage and culture.

- **rocket science** 고도의 지능이 요구되는 일 (Something very difficult; Used in the negative)

  [Ex] Look, changing the oil may be messy, but it's not rocket science.

- **snag** 암초[뜻하지 않은 장애] (A problem, especially one causing a delay)

  [Ex] There is just one small snag - where is the money coming from?

Slang

- hard-ass 까다로운 문제 (A stubborn person or problem)

  [Ex] Hopefully you don't take such a hard-ass approach as this.

Sanitary Paper

위생용품

Informal

- maxi pad 생리대
- TP 화장실 휴지 (Acronym for "toilet paper")

  [Ex] *We're out of TP.*

Useless or Worthless Things

쓸모없는 것, 가치 없는 것

Formal

junk; rubbish; shoddy goods; trash; garbage;

- drop in the bucket 아주 적은 양, 간에 기별도 안 감, 새 발의 피

  [Ex] *It's just a drop in the bucket compared to how many are killed each year.*

- **small potatoes** 하찮은 것[사람], 소액 (Something insignificant)

  [Ex] *A: You've been spending too much on that account. / B: It's small potatoes.*

- **lemon** (제대로 되지 않아) 쓸모없는 것, 불량품, 특히 고장 난 차

  [Ex] That used car I bought last week is a total lemon.

- Mickey Mouse 중요하지 않은, 작은, 질 낮은

  [Ex] Who's in charge of this Mickey Mouse operation, anyway?

- no biggie 중요하지 않은 것 (Not a big deal)

  [Ex] It's no biggie and easily remedied.

- **crap** 똥, 쓸모없는 것 (Worthless junk and[or] pointless things)

  [Ex] You are a serious piece of crap.

- dogshit 개똥, 쓸모없는 것 (Worthless, inferior; an unimportant thing)

  [Ex] Unfortunately 59.9% of all Americans are dumber than dogshit and will probably put her in office.

- **piece of crap** 품질이 형편없는 것, 기분이 나쁜 것

  [Ex] I read all 110 pages of the piece of crap, last night.

- **piece of shit** 품질이 형편없는 것, 기분이 나쁜 것 (Poor quality; displeasing)

  [Ex] I can't believe you're still driving that piece of shit car!

- piss-ant 무가치한 것 (Small, insignificant, worthless and irritating)

  [Ex] This piss-ant science project is going to get me no more than a C.

- **shit** 쓸모없는 것; 조악한 물건 (Something not worth mentioning)

  [Ex] I'm tired of his shit.

Viscous Things
끈적거리는 것

Formal

blob; clump; hunk; wad

Informal

- glop (기분 나쁘게) 질척거리는 것 (Any unpleasant sticky thing)

  [Ex] I'll probably remember it and laugh whenever I find a massive glop of bird's leavings on my windshield.

- **goo** (불쾌하게) 찐득찐득한 것 (Any thick, sticky substance)

  [Ex] When he wanted food, all he could find was blue goo.

- goop 끈적끈적 들러붙는 것 (Viscous thing)

  [Ex] Catfish is also a scavenger, cleaning the goop up off the bottoms of ponds.

- guck 미끌미끌한 것 (Slimy matter; gunk)

  [Ex] Eww, I just stepped in some guck. Yuck!

- **gunk** 끈적끈적[찐득찐득]한 것, 오물 (Any sticky or greasy substance)

  [Ex] Those bolts have gunk all over them.

- schmutz 오물, 더러움, 얼룩 (An unpleasant, unidentified substance)

  [Ex] Damn, I got schmutz on my shirt!

- **yuck** 역겨운 것 (A gross substance)

  [Ex] It's as if a whole load of yuck was just built up on my shoulders and now it's gone.

Slang

- jizz 정액, 정체를 알 수 없는 끈적끈적한 물질 (A slimy substance, especially when unidentified)

  [Ex] Get that jizz off me!

Chapter 7

The Use and Abuse
of Power
힘, 권력의 사용, 남용

권력, 권한, 힘의 사용과 남용은 인간관계의 핵심이며, 언어 사용 방법, 즉 어떤 표현을 사용하느냐에 따라 이 인간관계가 규정되기도 합니다. 당연히 미국 성인들이 자주 사용하는 표현들에도 다양한 형태의 갈등 관계를 보여주는 informal 표현들, slang들이 많이 있습니다. 이 장에는 이들 중에서 자주 사용되는 표현들을 정리하였습니다.

Abandon
버리다

- **stand up** (특히 연인 사이에서) ~를 바람 맞히다

  [Ex] *She stood me up!*

- ass out 모임에 빠지다, 접근을 못하게 되다

  [Ex] *Everyone knows she's gonna ass out tonight.*
- **bitch out** 겁이나 (어떤 일에서) 빠지다 (To back out of an agreement for any reason)

  [Ex] *He promised to go with me to the party but at the last minute he bitched out.*

Annoy
괴롭히다

[Informal]
- **get on one's nerve** 신경을 건드리다 (To make someone nervous)

  [Ex] *The noise outside is really getting on my nerves.*
- **get under one's skin** ~를 괴롭히다 (To annoy)

  [Ex] *That movie was both creepy and scary, and really gets under the skin.*

영어 표현에도 등급이 있다!

3 *Coerce or Intimidate*

강제로 시키다, 위협하다

Formal

bully; force; scare into; threaten; push around; compel; constrain; terrorize; urge

Informal

- buffalo 강요하다 (To intimidate or coerce, as by a display of confidence or authority)

  [Ex] The director shouts a lot, but don't let him buffalo you.

- build a fire under someone 강요하다, 압력을 넣다 (To coerce)

  [Ex] He built a fire under me for his own interests.

- **bulldoze** ~을 억지로 밀어붙이다, 강행하다 (To coerce or intimidate)

  [Ex] You best shut up before I bulldoze your mouth until you can't speak anymore.

- **crack the whip** 채찍을 휘두르다, 사람들을 볶아대다

  [Ex] Man, my old lady is really cracking the whip on me to get the lawn mowed.

- **do a number on** ~을 해치우다, 면목을 잃게 하다, 철저히 비판하다 (To mistreat)

  [Ex] Sun and pollution can really do a number on your skin.

- **get tough with** 엄한 조치를 취하다, 엄하게 다루다

  [Ex] She does not easily get tough with other people when they did something wrong.

- **have someone by the balls** ~의 약점을 잡다 (To have somebody at one's mercy)

  [Ex] Jane has her boyfriend by the balls at last.

- knock heads together 강경한 수단으로 싸움을 말리다

  [Ex] I welcome the Minister's trying to knock heads together to find a solution.

- **play hardball** 강경 자세를 취하다 (To be uncooperative during negotiation)

  [Ex] If Reagan is gonna play hardball, so will I.

- **pull strings** (~에게 유리하도록) 영향력을 행사하다

  [Ex] I had to pull a few strings, but I ended up getting us box seats.

- **put the heat on** ~에 강한 압박을 가하다, ~의 행동에 눈을 부라리다, ~을 엄하게 다루다[단속하다] (To coerce or intimidate)

  [Ex] The man put the heat on his colleagues' behavior.

- put the screws on (~를 상대로) 바짝 나사를 죄다[압박을 가하다]

  [Ex] Everybody is putting the screw on and the poor guys who are caught in the middle are these small businesses.

- put the smack down ~을 호되게 질책하다, ~을 실각시키다 (To regulate, often by force)

  [Ex] The party started to get out of hand, so we had to put the smack down.

- **put the squeeze on** (~을 하라고) ~에게 압박[압력]을 가하다

  [Ex] The credit crunch, strong Euro and rising fuel costs all put the squeeze on travel this year.

- **railroad** (서둘러, 강압적으로 무엇을 하도록) 몰아붙이다 (To force or bully)

  [Ex] The bill was railroaded through the House.

- **rubber stamp** (법률, 계획 등을) 잘 살펴보지도 않고 인가하다

  [Ex] I can't believe the board just rubber stamped that measure.

- shanghai (어떤 일을) 속여서 하게 하다 (To trick someone into taking a job; to trick someone into joining the crew of a ship)

  [Ex] We were shanghaied into buying worthless securities.

- **steamroll** 힘으로 강제하다, 힘으로 밀어붙이다 (To coerce and intimidate)

  [Ex] Then, after steamrolling back into power in November's midterm elections, Democrats officially gained control of Congress this week.

- **strong-arm** 강압적인, 강권을 쓰는 (Coercing or intimidating)

  [Ex] My government will retain strong armed forces, including the nuclear deterrent.

- **turn up the heat** 압력을 높이다, 강압적으로 하다 (To apply great or increased pressure)

  [Ex] Local tribal chiefs have turned up the heat on Al-Qaeda by joining U.S.

- **twist one's arm** 강압적으로 시키다 (To coerce; intimidate)

  [Ex] So it's not only that he tried to twist arms to get faulty intelligence forward, but he actually exerted retribution on people.

4 *Die*
죽다

Formal

die; pass away; perish; be taken up to the heaven; be with angels; decease; depart this life; go the way of all flesh

Informal

- **bite the dust** 1. 헛물을 켜다, 실패[패배]하다 2. 죽다 (To die; to be utterly defeated)

  [Ex] And it's not just the small foreign companies that are biting the dust.

- **buy the farm** 살해되다, 죽다 (To die, especially in combat)

  [Ex] They knew that if their father were to buy the farm, they would have to sell the house.

- cash in one's chips 가게를 걷어치우다, 죽다 (To die; kick the bucket; perish; depart this life)

  [Ex] In that terrible accident you might cash in your chips right before your wedding ceremony.

- conk out 멈춰 서버리다 (To stop functioning)

  [Ex] The old guy looks as if he's going to conk out any minute.

- croak 죽다 (To die)

  [Ex] Apparently, he croaked when they got to the hospital.

- **go belly up** 죽다, 살해되다 (To fail; to die)

  [Ex] The CSIs looked for something that made the victim go belly up.

- kick off 죽다 (To die)

  [Ex] He kicked off last night.

- **kick the bucket** 죽다 (To die)

  [Ex] She kicked the bucket.

- push up daisies 죽다 (To be dead)

  [Ex] He's pushing up daisies.

- **turn up one's toes** 죽다 (To die)

  [Ex] I hope my husband could give up smoking before I turn up my toes.

Dismiss, Fire, Eject or Send Away

묵살하다, 해고하다, 제거하다, 내보내다

Formal

get rid of; lay off; discharge; give notice to; repudiate

Informal

- bench (선수를) 벤치에 앉혀 놓다, 벤치로 물러나게 하다

[Ex] They benched him for the rest of the game because they thought he was injured.

- **boot** ~을 해고하다, 쫓아내다 (To fire; get rid of; throw out; expel)

[Ex] He got booted from the club.

- **brush off** ~을 무시하다, 외면하다

[Ex] Ever since Jessica found a new boyfriend she's been brushing off her ex, Tony.

- **can** 해고하다, 끝나게 하다, 버리다, 중지시키다 (To fire or get rid of someone)

[Ex] They won't can me; I'm the only one who knows what's going on in this place.

- chuck out 쫓아내다 (To send away)

[Ex] They just say that they are a minority, and that they will be chucked out and forgotten.

- **dump** ~을 해고하다, (애인)을 버리다, (계약)을 해지하다

[Ex] How can you dump me for another man?

- **give someone axe** 해고하다, 쫓아버리다 (To Dismiss, fire, eject or send away)

[Ex] Kate, 39, was unanimously given the axe by judges after a disastrous fall during rehearsals on Friday left her with a suspected broken rib.

- give someone his/her marching orders 해고하다, 쫓아버리다

[Ex] Fabiano was given his marching orders for spitting.

- give someone his/her walking papers 해고하다, 쫓아버리다

[Ex] The coach has been given his walking papers after the team lost again on Saturday.

- **give someone the boot** 해고하다, 쫓아버리다 (To Dismiss, fire, eject or send away)

  [Ex] The Washington Post reports the entire staff of the "Forecast Earth" environmental program was given the boot.

- give someone the chop 해고하다, 쫓아버리다 (To Dismiss, fire, eject or send away)

  [Ex] The whole department has been given the chop.

- give someone the chuck 해고하다, 쫓아버리다 (To Dismiss, fire, eject or send away)

  [Ex] No one has rights to give a person the chuck.

- give someone the gate 해고하다, 쫓아버리다 (To Dismiss, fire, eject or send away)

  [Ex] The guy was a pest, so I gave him the gate.

- give someone the heave-ho 해고하다, 쫓아버리다 (To Dismiss, fire, eject or send away)

  [Ex] The nightclub bouncer gave a drunk customer the heave-ho.

- give someone the push 해고하다, 쫓아버리다 (To Dismiss, fire, eject or send away)

  [Ex] He decided to give Sam the push.

- **give someone the sack** 해고하다, 쫓아버리다 (To Dismiss, fire, eject or send away)

  [Ex] The low paid are fearful of speaking out and fear being given the sack.

- give someone the shaft 해고하다, 쫓아버리다 (To Dismiss, fire, eject or send away)

  [Ex] In any case, it's a mighty cocky thing to give them the shaft like that.

- give someone the shove 해고하다, 쫓아버리다 (To Dismiss, fire, eject or send away)

  [Ex] The Irishman was given the shove after bosses got wind he had applied to the BBC.

- **kiss goodbye** ~와 작별을 하다 ('무엇을 잃게 되거나 하지 못하게 될 것을 받아들인다'는 뜻 / To give up hope of getting something that you want very much)

  [Ex] We can kiss goodbye to arms limitation treaties and arms inspections as well.

- **pink slip** 해고 통지서 (Notice of termination from a job)

  [Ex] He got the pink slip for neglecting his duty.

- **sack** 해고하다, 파면하다 (To dismiss from a job; fire)

  [Ex] Four hundred workers face the sack.

- send somebody packing 해고하다, 퇴짜 놓다 (To dismiss from a job; fire)

  [Ex] Just hours before he was sent packing, however, the 33-year-old told the AP he was being victimized.

- send somebody to the showers 해고하다, 퇴짜 놓다 (To dismiss from a job; fire)

  [Ex] I had to send Jane to the showers.

- **show somebody the door[gate]** 쫓아내다, 해고하다 (To dismiss from a job; fire)

  [Ex] In the private sector, if you screw up, you are shown the door.

- **sideline** 열외로 취급하다

[Ex] *There could be no better description of the efforts to sideline climate-change skeptics.*

- throw somebody out on his/her ass 내쫓다, 해고하다 (To dismiss; to fire)

[Ex] *The shop keeper threw the beggars out on their ass.*

- throw somebody out on his/her ear 내쫓다, 해고하다 (To dismiss; to fire)

[Ex] *It is no wonder that the council was thrown out on its ear by the electorate.*

- toss somebody out 쫓아내다, 해고하다 (To dismiss; to fire)

[Ex] *No one wants to see people tossed out of jobs.*

- turn somebody out 내쫓다, 해고하다 (To dismiss; to fire)

[Ex] *If you won't go yourself, I shall turn you out.*

6 *Flatter*

아첨하다

Formal

compliment; court; fawn on; flatter; praise; wheedle; rub the right way; sweet talk; work on; adulate; blandish

Slang

- **ass-kiss** 아첨하다 (To seek favor through flattery; to be a sycophant or toady)

  [Ex] They just want their asses kissed.

- **kiss one's ass** 아첨하다 (To seek favor through flattery; to be a sycophant or toady)

  [Ex] He's always kissing his boss's ass.

- **lick (one's) ass** 남에게 굴복하다, 아부[아첨]하다

  [Ex] He would lick his supervisor's ass to get that promotion.

- **suck up (to one)** 아부하다, 아첨하다

  [Ex] Britain could have joined years ago instead of sucking up to the good old USA as usual.

Have, Take, Get

얻다, 갖다, 잡다

Informal

- **snatch** 와락 붙잡다, 잡아채다, 잡아 뺏다 (To obtain quickly)

  [Ex] The thief snatched away the purse in a lady's hand.

- **sneak** 몰래 챙기다[가져가다] (To acquire discretely)

  [Ex] I sneaked a cake when they were out of the room.

Ignore

무시하다

Informal

- **blow off** 무시하다, 퇴짜 놓다 (To ignore)

  [Ex] She has better thing to do that night so she will blow off the boring plans.

- **tune out** 상관[주의]하지 않다, ~에 귀를 기울이지 않다 (To ignore)

  [Ex] They tune us out when we tell them to wait. They see the other side of the coin as being interesting.

영어 표현에도 등급이 있다!

Insult

모욕하다, 경멸하다

Informal

- **dis** 경멸하다 (To insult)

  [Ex] *That was a really big dis.*

- smack 공격적인 언행, 비난 (Offensive speech about another person)

  [Ex] *I hear you've been talking smack about me.*

Interfere or Intrude
참견하다, 방해하다

Formal

barge in; burst in; encroach; interlope; intervene

Informal

- **bug** ~을 괴롭히다, 방해하다, 귀찮게 굴다 (To pester)

  [Ex] Don't bug me, I really need to concentrate!

- **butt in** ~에 참견하다, 주제넘게 나서다 (To meddle in another person's private business)

  [Ex] John told his brother not to butt in when he was talking to his girlfriend.

- hack into 해킹하다 (To use computer skills to gain unauthorized access to files or networks)

  [Ex] Systems are always being designed to try to stop people hacking into them.

- **mess with** ~에 쓸데없이 참견하다, 간섭하다, 귀찮게 하다 (To annoy)

  [Ex] Why are you messing with him?

- **poke one's nose into** 남의 일에 간섭하다 (To interfere or intrude)

  [Ex] Although we must take our responsibilities seriously, we should not poke our noses into people's lives.

- **put one's two cents in** 자기 의견을 말하다 (To state one's opinion)

  [Ex] Please allow me to put my two cents worth in on this issue.

- shove one's oar in 쓸데없는 참견을 하다, 공연히 덥적거리다 (To interfere; to interlude)

  [Ex] Don't shove your oar in other people's affairs.

- **stick one's nose into** ~에 참견하다, 간섭하다

  [Ex] Don't stick your nose into other people's business.

영어 표현에도 등급이 있다!

Kill

죽이다, 처형하다, 살해하다

Formal

destroy; execute; finish; kill; put to death; annihilate; dispatch, eradicate; exterminate; slay

Informal

- axe 해고하다 (To terminate from a job; fire)

  [Ex] Aston Martin plans to axe up to 600 jobs.

- blow someone away 사살하다, 압도하다, ~에 완승하다 (To kill, usually with a firearm)

  [Ex] She is going to blow him away!

- **do away with** 1. ~를 죽이다 2. 자살하다 (To kill)

  [Ex] We must do away with all inefficient practices.

- gun somebody down ~를 쏘아 쓰러뜨리다[죽이다]

  [Ex] In other areas, refugees were gunned down as they tried to flee.

- hose ~을 속이다, 속여 빼앗다, ~을 죽이다, 해치우다 (To seriously injure or kill)

  [Ex] Let's hose these assholes!

- knock off 죽이다 (To kill)

  [Ex] The gangster knocked off his rival.

- **liquidate** (사람·물건)을 치우다, 없애다, 죽이다; 제거하다 (To kill another human being)

  [Ex] After the protection money was not delivered, Capone ordered Frank Nitti to liquidate the malefactor.

- mow down (사람들을 여러 명) 살육하다 (To kill in large numbers, esp. by gunfire)

  [Ex] The demonstrators were mown down by the soldiers.

- **neutralize** 죽이다, 말살하다 (To kill and put something out of its misery)

  [Ex] I'm so going to neutralize that baby kitten.

- **rub out** ~를 죽이다[살해하다] (To kill)

  [Ex] It urged Latino gang members to rub out a suspected witness against Gotti who was being held in prison.

- snuff somebody out 죽이다 (To kill)

[Ex] Another day, another dead teenager, their life snuffed out in a mindless act of violence that defies belief in our supposedly civilized society.

- **terminate** 죽이다 (To kill)

[Ex] She terminated the President of USA with extreme prejudice.

- wipe out 말살하다 (To destroy)

[Ex] Whole villages were wiped out by the earthquake.

- zap 사정없이 제압하다, 망가트리다, 죽이다

[Ex] When I stuck a pen in my power supply, it zapped the hard disk.

12 *Lead*

지휘하다, 앞장서다, 결정권을 갖다

Formal

chair; direct; lead; take control; spearhead; be in the driver's seat; boss

Informal

- **call the shots** (상황을) 지휘[통제]하다 (To be the leader)

  [Ex] This is my party, I call the shots!

- **carry the ball** (어떤 일을) 책임지고 하다 (To lead)

  [Ex] My co-worker was sick, so I had to carry the ball.

- **have the final say** 최종 결정권(발언권)을 갖다 (To be the ultimate decision-maker)

  [Ex] The idea that the Secretary of State has the final say is completely unfounded.

- **have the last word** 최종 결정권(발언권)을 갖다 (To be the ultimate decision-maker)

  [Ex] Diplomacy, not speeches or votes, will continue to have the last word in peacemaking.

- **rule the roost** (무리 사이에서) 가장 강한 영향력을 행사하다, 지배권을 쥐다

  [Ex] Today the country's nationalists rule the roost and hand out the jobs.

- **wear the pants** (아내가) 남편을 깔고 뭉개다, 내주장하다 (To be in charge)

  [Ex] He obviously likes his wife being the one wearing the pants.

13 Leave

떠나가다, 사퇴하다

Informal

- bounce 떠나가다 (To depart)

  [Ex] I am getting a bit tired of this party, let's bounce.

- **bow out** 떠나다, 퇴직[퇴장]하다, 사임[용퇴]하다 (To leave, resign, withdraw)

  [Ex] Man, I think I'm gonna bow out soon and get to bed.

14 Make Believe

믿게 하다

Informal

- **sell** (아이디어[서비스, 후보자 등]을 받아들이도록) 납득시키다 (To convince)

  [Ex] I sold my boss on letting me work from home once a week.

Make Someone's Life Difficult 곤란하게 만들다, 골칫거리가 되다, 괴롭히다, 탄압하다

Formal

cause concern to; harass; torment; badger; plague; vex;

- **crack down on** ~에 단호한 조치를 취하다, ~을 엄히 단속하다, 탄압하다

[Ex] The crack down on drug abuse means that fewer addictions will occur.

- **get on one's back** 남을 괴롭히다 (To cause difficulty or make trouble for someone)

[Ex] My mom is always on my back to study.

- give somebody a bad[hard] time ~에게 어려움을 가져오다, ~에게 어려움을 주다

[Ex] My boyfriend always gives me a hard time.

- **rub somebody's nose in it** 남의 언동[실패]을 야단치다, 벌주다, 남에게 잔소리를 퍼붓다

[Ex] When Bob failed his exam, his brother rubbed his nose in it.

Informal

- bust one's ball 남을 아주 곤란하게 만들다, 혼을 내주다

[Ex] I got my balls busted last night by my wife nagging me.

- **bust one's butt** 남을 아주 곤란하게 만들다, 혼을 내주다 (To make someone's life difficult)

[Ex] I told her that I have told them that if they misbehave in church I will take them outside and bust their butts.

Slang

- fuck one over 먹이[밥]로 삼다 (To take advantage of)

[Ex] I'm pretty sure the mechanic fucked me over.

- piss on somebody[something] ~를 괴롭히다 (To annoy)

[Ex] They throw verbal abuse at him. They humiliate him by pissing on him.

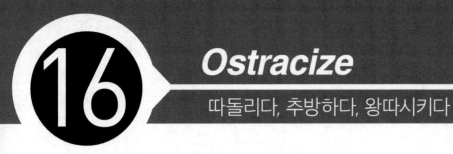

Ostracize

따돌리다, 추방하다, 왕따시키다

Formal

avoid; blackball; boycott; exclude; shut out; excommunicate

Informal

- freeze somebody out (일부러 쌀쌀맞게 굴거나 곤란하게 하여) ~를 (~에서) 몰아내다[(~을) 못하게 하다], 따돌리다

  [Ex] The American proposal to freeze out Russia looks dead.

- **give somebody the cold shoulder** 매몰스럽게 굴다

  [Ex] He was given the cold shoulder in the team.

- put in the dog house 면목을 잃다, 난처한 입장에 빠지다

  [Ex] We are put in the dog house if we are not as clean as another country.

Slang

- **put on the crap[shit]** 면목을 잃다, 난처한 입장에 빠지다

17 Remind
상기시키다, 들먹이다

Formal

- **rub in** (기억하고 싶지 않은 일을) 자꾸 들먹이다[상기시키다]

  [Ex] Louise: What? I only know two restaurants. And they have cloth napkins. / Bob: Don't rub it in.

18 Steal
훔치다

Informal

- clean somebody out (남)에게서 (돈을) 빼앗다 (도박·불경기 따위가 사람을 빈털터리로 만들다 / To take all of a person's money)

  [Ex] He was completely cleaned out gambling.

19 *Support*

도와주다

back; defend; sponsor; stand behind; support; shore up; throw support behind; advocate for; endorse; stand behind; subsidize

Informal

- **chip in** 돈을 추렴하다, 제 몫을 내다, 기부하다, 돕다 (To be helpful; take part in)

  [Ex] Yo, can't you see I'm carrying this really heavy box. Come on, chip in!

- **go to bat for** ~를 도와주다, ~의 편이 되다 (To take someone's side)

  [Ex] I tried to go to bat for Bill, but he said he didn't want any help.

- go to the mat for (~와의 언쟁에서 ~의) 편[역성]을 들다

  [Ex] We went to the mat for him because he'd helped us in the past.

- **have one's back** 뒤를 봐주다 (To look out for one's interests or well-being)

  [Ex] Nobody has my back.

- in someone's corner ~의 편에 서서 (In someone's side or support)

  [Ex] He is always in my corner.

- **play ball** 기꺼이 협조하다 (To cooperate)

  [Ex] Aren't you tired of doing what everyone else want you to do? Maybe it's time you quit playing ball with them and just play ball with me.

- put one's money on ~의 성공을 장담하다, 확신하다 (To believe in)

  [Ex] He'll be there tonight. I'd put money on it.

- **stick up for** ~을 변호하다, 옹호하다(defend), (권리 따위)를 지키다 (To support of defend)

  [Ex] He won't be sticking up for something he doesn't believe in.

20 *Tolerate*

용인하다

Informal

- **slack** 기회, 여유 (To tolerate)

  [Ex] Give him some slack – he's just a kid.

Chapter 8

Deceit and Treachery
사기, 속임, 배반, 배신

Native speaker들은 거짓말, 속임, 배반 등에도 다양한 표현들을 사용하고 있습니다. 이번 장은 이와 관련된 표현들을 정리하였습니다. 특히 친밀한 사이의 대화 중에 사용되는 '거짓말 관련' 표현들은 꼭 기억해 놓아야 합니다.

Betrayal

배신, 배반

1-1. Betray a Secret or Expose Betrayal (비밀을 폭로하다, 비밀을 불다)

Formal

betray; inform; uncover; unmask; blurt out; double-cross; let slip; break faith; disclose

Informal

- **blow** (비밀을) 불다[들통나게 하다] (To expose; to betray a secret)

  [Ex] The man blew the secret agent's cover.

- blow something wide open (비밀을) 만천하에 폭로하다

  [Ex] But today we can blow that secret wide open. We can barely bring ourselves to tell you this.

- blow the lid off (비밀을) 불다[들통나게 하다]

  [Ex] The self-admitted steroid user blew the lid off of baseball's performance-enhancing drug era by naming names.

- **blow the whistle on** (비밀을) 불다[들통나게 하다]

  [Ex] Companies should protect employees who blow the whistle on dishonest workmates and work practices.

- **finger** (경찰에 범인을) 찌르다 (To identify to the authorities the perpetrator of a crime)

  [Ex] A white male in his twenties was fingered as the perpetrator.

- fink 일러바치다, 배신하다 (To inform on another person or group to authorities)

  [Ex] Did she fink on me?.

- **point one's finger at** 밀고하다 (To inform on another person or group to authorities)

  [Ex] Please do not point a finger at others purely on a speculative basis.

- **pull the rug out from under** 배신하다 (To betray a person)

  [Ex] Then, the Government pull the rug out from under local authorities and withdraw the funding.

영어 표현에도 등급이 있다!

- **put the finger on** (범인)을 경찰에 밀고하다

  [Ex] I put the finger on my neighbor who stole my car.

- sell down the river 남을 속이다, 배신하다 (To betray a person)

  [Ex] He has been sold down the river by the people who were supposed to protect him.

- **sell out** (~을 위해) 신념[원칙]을 버리다, 배신하다 (To betray a person)

  [Ex] They will sell out on you in a minute.

- **snitch** 일러바치다 (To betray a person)

  [Ex] It was no one else but his friend who snitched on him to the police about his crime.

- **spill one's guts out** 비밀을 불다 (To give something away; to tell secret information)

  [Ex] The criminal spilled his guts out to the investigator.

- **spill the beans** (비밀을) 무심코 말해 버리다

  [Ex] I spilled the beans and told Jackie I loved her.

- **stab in the back** (자기를 믿는) ~의 뒤통수를 치다[~를 배신하다] (To betray a person)

  [Ex] I can't believe I trusted you with my secrets, then you stabbed me in the back.

- **tip somebody off** 밀고하다, 비밀을 알려 주다

  [Ex] He was arrested two days later after a friend tipped off the FBI.

- **turn somebody in** 밀고하다 (To give something away; to tell secret information)

  [Ex] They have a unit that is designed to track down people who have escaped, but she says that somebody turned her in.

1-2. Discover Betrayal (배신을 발견하다, 범행 현장에서 잡다)

Formal

catch in the act;

- **catch red-handed** 범행 현장에서 잡다 (To catch someone doing something illegal)

  [Ex] Four of the men were caught red handed as a result of a covert surveillance operation.

- **catch somebody with his/her pants down** 범행 현장에서 잡다

  [Ex] He lied about being in Paris courtesy of the Sausis and was caught with his pants down. (courtesy of ~ : ~ 덕분으로)

- catch with a hand in the cookie jar 범행 현장에서 잡다

[Ex] Instead, when caught with our hands in the cookie jar, the first thing we do is look for someone or something to blame.

- catch with a smoking gun 범행 현장에서 잡다

[Ex] It is the individual who has to be caught with the smoking gun in his hand before that person can be removed from government.

- **have somebody cold** 불법을 행하는 현장에서 잡다

[Ex] We were told at SHAPE that so far as interception of communications was concerned, "The Yugoslavs had us cold."

- **nail** (거짓 따위를) 들추어내다, (부정 따위를) 찾아내다

[Ex] I want to nail that myth, which is quite wrong.

<u>1-3.</u> Betray by Reneging or Abandoning
(배신하다, 저버리다, 교묘히 빠져나가다)

Formal

abandon; be a Judas; bite the hand that feeds one; desert; knife in the back; stab in the back; bail; dump; jilt; leave high and dry; sell out; abdicate

Informal

- blow off (약속 따위를) 어기다, 배신하다

[Ex] Last week they blew off Lizzie McGuire star Hilary Duff because they said she wanted too much money for a sequel.

- cop out 1. (약속 따위를) 어기다, 배신하다 2. (책임 따위를) 회피하다

[Ex] Saying you're sick just because you want to avoid a big test that you're pre-pared but scared for is a cop out.

- **ditch** 1. ~을 버리다, 처분하다 2. ~와 관계를 끊다 (To leave behind)

[Ex] My friends ditched me at the library.

- **give something a miss** ~을 포기하다 (To forgo something)

[Ex] I think I'll give badminton a miss tonight.

- **go AWOL** 탈영하다, 무단결근[외출]하다 (To go missing without permission or explanation)

[Ex] The guitarist went AWOL in the middle of the recording.

- **opt out** 탈퇴하다 (To choose not to take part in something)

  [Ex] I may opt out of the organization.

- **walk out on somebody** ~를 버리다 (To abandon)

  [Ex] The husband walked out on his family one day and never returned.

- weasel out 처벌을 교묘히 면하다 (To escape punishment)

  [Ex] They can manipulate words to weasel their way out of anything.

- **wiggle out of** (교묘히) 빠져나가다 (To escape from)

  [Ex] He used his cleverness to wiggle out of doing work.

- **worm out of** 교묘히 면하다 (To escape punishment)

  [Ex] I'd like to see him worm out of this charge.

1-4. Betray by Shifting Blame (다른 사람에게 떠넘기다)

Formal

scapegoat; make a fall guy; use as a whipping boy; victimize

Informal

- leave somebody holding the baby (어려운 문제나 상황을) 다른 사람에게 떠넘기다

  [Ex] He changed to another job and we were left holding the baby.

- **leave somebody in a lurch** (어려운 문제나 상황을) 다른 사람에게 떠넘기다

  [Ex] It's moral and human's duty not to leave a person in the lurch.

- **offload** (자기가 원치 않는 것을) 없애다, 다른 사람에게 떠넘기다

  [Ex] The government cannot continually offload social problems onto businesses and expect them to pay.

Defraud, Cheat
속이다, 사기 치다

Formal

deceive; pull the wool over somebody's eyes; bamboozle; cheat

Informal

- **con** 사기의, 속이는 (To swindle or scam)

  [Ex] She believed the con artist's story hook, line, and sinker.

- **fleece** 바가지를 씌우다 (To rip off; to take advantage of)

  [Ex] She claims he fleeced her out of thousands of pounds.

- **rip off** ~에게 바가지를 씌우다 (To steal from or con someone)

  [Ex] This hamburger is a rip-off! I want my money back.

- **screw** (사람에게서 특히 많은 돈을) 우려[뜯어]내다 (To deceive; to cheat)

  [Ex] The taxpayer feels like they're getting screwed by the banks in every way.

- sell somebody bill of goods 야바위를 치다 (To play a trick upon a person)

  [Ex] He takes no responsibility for that and simply tries to sell us a bill of goods.

- send somebody to the cleaners 빈털터리를 만들다 (To cheat; to deceive)

  [Ex] They were sent to the cleaners.

- **sting** (사기꾼의) 교묘한 사기 (Fraud, cheating)

  [Ex] It was a sting operation and the target was knocked out.

- take somebody to the cleaners (속여서) 빈털터리로 만들다 (To cheat; to deceive)

  [Ex] Here, they realized, is a sucker they can really take to the cleaners.

3 **Insult**
모욕

Informal

- backhanded compliment 빈정대는 투의 칭찬

  [Ex] In a backhanded compliment she said he looked very good for his age.

4 *Lies*
거짓말

Formal

fib; garbage; hogwash; hokum; hot air; hype; moonshine; poppycock; puffery; rot; rubbish; whopper; lie; deceit; falsehood; equivocation;

- applesauce 허튼소리 (Nonsense)

[Ex] The sky is falling? That's just applesauce!

- **beat around the bush** 돌려서 말하다, 변죽을 울리다

[Ex] A: So, are you really a musician? / B: Well, you see, I've written some songs and uh, a friend of a friend knows this guy who'll can get a record deal and…. /B: Come on, stop beating around the bush.

- bilge 부질없는 이야기[생각], 허튼소리 (Lies)

[Ex] What are you on about? You're talking bilge.

- blow smoke 허풍을 떨다, 쓸데없는 이야기를 하다

[Ex] He was talking big about how he knew math, but when I talked to his math teacher it turned out that he was just blowing smoke.

Informal

- crock 거짓말, 허풍, 실없는 소리, 난센스, 도움이 안 되는 것

[Ex] True beauty is on the inside? What a crock!

- **trash** 거짓말, 난센스 (Nonsense; full of lies)

[Ex] Now he can't stand them and is always talking trash.

- tripe 허튼 소리, 거짓말 (Nonsense; full of lies)

[Ex] Actually , Milo, your article is a load of tripe.

Slang

- b.s. 허튼소리, 거짓말 (Bullshit의 두음문자 / Lies; words or actions meant to be deceptive)

[Ex] That's a bunch of b.s.!

- bucket of shit 허풍, 거짓말 (Lies)

  [Ex] This is a bucket of shit.

- **bullshit** 허튼수작, 거짓말(lie), 허풍, 과장 (Nonsense or completely untrue)

  [Ex] That is nothing but bullshit. I do not believe a word of it.

- claptrap 쓸데없는 말 (Pretentious, pompous, nonsensical and or empty language.)

  [Ex] I've had enough of your claptrap.

- **crap** 허튼소리 (Nonsense; full of lies)

  [Ex] I guess it's just a load of crap what everyone says about her.

- crock of shit 거짓말, 허풍, 실없는 소리 (Something that is false, misleading, full of lies, etc.)

  [Ex] The assertion that your car is exceptional is a crock of shit.

- **horseshit** 1. 실없는 소리, 거짓말, 허풍 (경멸[혐오감] 따위를 나타내어) 헛소리 마, 바보 같으니
  2. 허튼소리를 하다

  [Ex] Don't you realize that's horseshit?

- load of shit 쓰레기 같은 거짓말 (Bullshit)

  [Ex] 10 inches?? You're joking. That's nothing but a load of shit.

- **pile of crap** 거짓말, 말도 안 되는 소리 (Nonsense; full of lies)

  [Ex] What he says is a pile of crap.

- **pile of shit** 거짓말, 말도 안 되는 소리 (Nonsense; full of lies)

  [Ex] Unfortunately, the culmination of 11 works of study was a big pile of shit.

Nonsense

허튼소리

Informal

- **baloney** 무의미, 잠꼬대 같은 소리, 허황된 말 (Nonsense)

  [Ex] Baloney!

- horesfeathers 난센스, 허튼소리 (Nonsense)

  [Ex] Oh man, you are talking complete horsefeathers.

6 *Dishonest*
정직하지 못하다

Formal

dishonest; deceive; lie; con; fib; stretch the truth

Informal

- prank (농담으로 하는) 장난 (A childish trick)

  [Ex] What started off as a prank evolved into some serious crimes.

- **pull one's leg** 놀리다, 농담하다 (To kid)

  [Ex] Are you pulling my leg?

- **full of baloney** 실없는 소리, 허튼소리, 엉터리, 거짓말 (To be dishonest, full of lies)

  [Ex] Ibrahim, you are full of baloney.

Slang

- **full of bullshit** 실없는 소리, 허튼소리, 엉터리, 거짓말 (To be dishonest, full of lies)

  [Ex] We just concluded that this guy was full of bullshit.

- **full of crap** 실없는 소리, 허튼소리, 엉터리, 거짓말 (To be dishonest, full of lies)

  [Ex] This guy is utterly full of crap.

- **shit** 겉치레, 겉치레만의 이야기, 거짓말 (To attempt to deceive; lie to)

  [Ex] That watch is yours? You're shitting me!

- sling the crap[shit] 거짓말하다 (To lie)

Deceive
속이다, 기만하다

deceive; mislead; double-cross; outwit; two-time; trick

- bamboozle 속이다 (To deceive using underhanded methods; dupe; hoodwink)

  [Ex] The card cheat bamboozled me out of my money!

- **fake out** 속이다, 기만하다

  [Ex] David Copperfield faked out a bunch of teenage robbers by using magic on them.

- feed somebody a line (환심을 사기 위해) 남에게 허풍 떨다, 거짓말하다, 아첨하다

  [Ex] Those who oppose us are fed a line to create an effect.

- fox 속이다 (To deceive)

  [Ex] I must admit I'm completely foxed.

- give somebody a line 속이다 (To deceive)

  [Ex] I am sick to watch John gives people a line.

- hoodwink 속이다 (To deceive by underhanded methods)

  [Ex] The car salesman hoodwinked me into buying a lemon.

- **phish** 사기성 이메일 (이메일을 통해 합법적이고 믿을 만한 기업 행세를 하며 사용자를 속여 개인 정보를 넘겨받아 이를 신원 도용에 사용하는 것)

  [Ex] Tax officials have asking workers who receive phishing emails to report them immediately.

- **Ponzi scheme** 폰지형型 이자利子 사기 방식 (피라미드식 이식利殖 사기 수법)

  [Ex] The US and UK economies are officially sanctioned Ponzi schemes which are now unraveling.

- pork 속이다, 이용해 먹다 (To take advantage of)

  [Ex] I had to cover Bob's work shift last night. He completely porked me!

- pull a fast one ~을 속여 넘기다, 속임수로 이기다

[Ex] That motherfucker tried to pull a fast one on me. There was no way the car was worth that much.

- **scam** 사기 (A fraudulent business scheme; swindle)

[Ex] My parents lost their retirement in some internet scam.

- **screw** (사람에게서 특히 많은 돈을) 우려[뜯어]내다 (To deceive; to cheat)

[Ex] He screws people over to take their money.

- **shenanigans** 1. 허튼소리(nonsense), 장난 2. 속임, 사기, 기만(deceit) (Trickery; misbehavior)

[Ex] Our entrepreneurs are the best, despite the shenanigans of a venal government.

- smoke and mirrors 교묘한 속임(수) (Something deceptive)

[Ex] It turns out the presentation was rigged. The whole thing was smoke and mirrors.

- snooker 속이다, 기만하다 (To deceive; to take advantage of; cheat; swindle)

[Ex] We got snookered. I saw you doing it and you saw me doing it and the next thing we know, it's our freaking job.

Slang

- **fuck** 속이다, 이용해 먹다 (To take advantage of; cheat; trick)

[Ex] Are you trying to fuck with me?

- fuck over ~을 이용해 먹다 (To take advantage of)

[Ex] The company promised me a big pay-off but they really fucked me over.

- take it in the ass 속다, 이용당하다

[Ex] We really took it in the ass on that deal.

Exaggerate Something's Importance 과장하다, 요란 떨다

8

Formal

exaggerate; overemphasize; blow out of proportion; make a big thing of; make a mountain out of a molehill; magnify; overestimate; aggrandize; hyperbolize; inflate

Informal

- ballyhoo 괜한 소란, 야단법석

  [Ex] They announced, amid much ballyhoo, that they had made a breakthrough.

- **blow up** 과장하다 (To make exaggerated claims)

  [Ex] The whole affair was blown up out of all proportion.

- **hype** (대대적으로 과장된) 광고를 하다 (To advertise or praise it a lot)

  [Ex] I just hope whatever is announced lives up to the hype.

- **lay it on thick** 심하게 과장하다

  [Ex] Man, he sure did lay it on thick when he tried to get his girlfriend to come home from the party early.

- **make a federal case** 어떤 일을 마치 연방(대)법원에서 재판해야 할 정도로 중요한 것처럼 취급하다 (Exaggerate the importance of)

  [Ex] I think it's totally wrong to make a federal case against this.

- **name drop** (친하지도 않은) 저명인사의 이름을 마치 친구인 양 팔고 다니다

  [Ex] I'm going to name drop a little bit and I hope I don't come off sounding like a snob.

- **spread it on thick** 과장하다, 허풍 치다 (In speech or writing, to be overly effusive)

  [Ex] Tom spread it on thick to sell more products.

- **make a big deal** 유난을 떨다 (Exaggerate the importance of)

  [Ex] This is hardly the first time NASA has made a big deal over a next-generation spaceship.

- make a big production 유난을 떨다 (Exaggerate the importance of)

  [Ex] Arthur Godfrey made a big production out of making tea years ago on his radio program.

9 Falsify

위조하다, 조작하다

Formal

alter; tamper; fake; fabricate; falsify

Informal

- **cook the books** 회계 장부를 속이다

  [Ex] He was arrested for cooking the books.

- **doctor** (문서 따위를) 위조[조작]하다, ~을 속이다

  [Ex] He was accused of doctoring the figures.

- fudge 속이다, (비용 등을) 부풀리다, 과장하다, 우유부단하다, 꾀부리다, (약속 등을) 어기다[지키지 않다] (To falsify)

  [Ex] Politicians are often very clever at fudging the issue.

10 *Steal*

훔치다

Formal

steal; take; nab; sneak; pilfer; purloin; take advantage of; cheat; trick

Informal

- **boot-leg** 불법으로 제작[판매]하는 것, 밀조품, 불법 복사 품, 해적판

  [Ex] Ahhh, I remember those great nights where I used to get BOOTLEG copies of music on Napster 3.

- **cabbage** (~을) 훔치다, 슬쩍하다 (To steal; to borrow without asking)

  [Ex] I cabbaged my roommate's beer from the fridge last night.

- **carp** 훔치다 (To Steal, to take something without permission)

  [Ex] While the cashiers back was turned, I carped a hat from the rack.

- **clean somebody out** (남)에게서 (돈을) 빼앗다, (도박·불경기 따위가 사람)을 빈털터리로 만들다 (To take all of a person's money)

  [Ex] The Ponzi scheme I invested in cleaned me out.

- **cop** ~을 훔치다 (To steal or walk out of a place with)

  [Ex] I went to the dealership and copped me a pimped-out Suburban for 40 G. (G: grand = 1,000 dollars)

- **cop a feel** (몸을) 몰래 더듬다 (To unwantedly grope a person; "feel up")

  [Ex] I was having fun dancing with that guy until he tried to cop a feel.

- **filch** 좀도둑질을 하다 (To steal something small or of little value)

  [Ex] To filch from friends and relatives is the mark of a coward.

- **heist** (상점, 은행에서 금품을) 강탈하다, 강도짓을 하다

  [Ex] He heisted that convenience store.

- **hoist** 훔치다 (To steal)

  [Ex] So we hoisted a series of cold drinks in the John Snow on Broadwick Street.

- **lift** ~을 훔치다 (To steal)

  [Ex] She lifted a CD from the store.

- **loot** 약탈하다, 훔치다, 횡령하다 (To rob)

  [Ex] We looted the bank.

- nick ~을 기만하다, 속이다, ~에게서 (~을) 사취하다 (To steal something)

  [Ex] Sorry, I nicked your seat.

- pinch ~을 훔치다 (To steal)

  [Ex] Someone has pinched my bag.

- **rip off** ~에게 바가지를 씌우다, 바가지, 속여 빼앗다 (To steal from, or con someone)

  [Ex] Premier League tickets are a rip off.

- skank 훔치다 (To steal)

  [Ex] He skanked my pencil.

- smash and grab (가게의) 진열장을 깨고 물건을 탈취하는 행위

  [Ex] Police broke up a number of smash and grab gangs last year.

- snag 훔치다 (To steal)

  [Ex] He snagged the money from his mom's wallet.

- sneak 좀도둑질하다 (To acquire discretely)

  [Ex] I sneaked a cake when they were out of the room.

- snitch 훔치다 (To steal)

  [Ex] People who shouted about being "staunch", hard core "cons", turned out to be snitching thing for England.

- **scalp** 암표를 팔다 (To sell tickets to an event for more than their list price)

  [Ex] He was trying to pick up some cash scalping tickets.

Words Intended To Confuse 혼란하게 만드는 말

Formal

double-speak; gibberish; equivocation

Informal

- eyewash 허풍, 거짓 약속 (False promise; words intended to confuse)

  [Ex] I did not realize that that was nothing more than political hyperbole and eyewash.

- gobbledygook (특히 공문서에 쓰이는 복잡하고) 이해할 수 없는 말들 (Nonsense)

  [Ex] Sure you get points for using pseudo-scientific gobbledygook, but it's all quite meaningless.

- **mumbo jumbo** (실은 아무 의미도 없으면서) 복잡하기만 한 말, 허튼소리

  [Ex] The doctor was just talking a lot of medical mumbo jumbo.

- **red herring** (중요한 것에서) 관심을 딴 데로 돌리는 것

  [Ex] Some people say that using ethanol as a fuel is just a red herring distracting people from the real issues of oil dependency and that what we really need is a complete replacement for fossil based fuels.

Chapter 9

Confrontation and Competition
대립, 경쟁

대결, 싸움, 논쟁 등은 많은 informal 표현 및 slang들을 만들어 냈습니다. 이번 장에서는 대결, 싸움, 경쟁 등과 관련된 표현들을 정리합니다. 물리적, 신체적인 대결뿐만 아니라, 언어를 사용한 대립, 논쟁, 경쟁에서는 아무래도 감정을 가감 없이 보여줘야 하기 때문에 속어적인 표현들이 많습니다. 하지만 실제로 사용할 때는 주의해야만 합니다.

1 *Arrest*
구속하다, 체포하다

Informal

- **bust** 단속하다, (경찰이) 급습하다, 가택 수색을 하다 (To arrest; to be incarcerated)

  [Ex] He got busted for drugs.

- nab (특히 현행범을) 잡다, 체포하다 (To arrest)

  [Ex] I got nabbed the other night!

- **nail** (도둑 따위)를 붙잡다 (To arrest)

  [Ex] The police haven't been able to nail the killer.

- nick (범인)을 체포하다, ~을 훔치다 (To arrest)

  [Ex] The police nicked him climbing over the fence of the house he'd broken into.

2 *Attack*

공격하다

2-1. Attack In a Group (여럿이 공격하다)

Informal

- gang up on ~을 집단으로 공격하다

  [Ex] The girls had promised not to gang up on Adam but they had broken that vow the night before.

2-2. Attack Physically (신체적인 힘을 사용하여 공격하다)

Informal

- **beat down** ~을 때려눕히다, 타도하다

  [Ex] Mr. Smith beat down that dude who came up on his porch asking for money.

- hose ~을 죽이다, 해치우다 (To attack and kill somebody, usually using a firearm)

  [Ex] Let's hose these assholes!

2-3. Attack Verbally (말로 공격하다)

Formal

abuse; blame; criticize; slander; berate; censure; reprove; vilify

- **bad mouth** 험담, 헐뜯기, 중상 (To say bad things about another person)

  [Ex] Why did he want to bad mouth me?

- bawl somebody out ~에게 호통치다 (To cry loudly)

  [Ex] Someone in the audience bawled out 'Not him again!'

- bite somebody's head off ~에게 호통치다

  [Ex] My first writing experience I remember was biting the head off a paper guy.

- give somebody an earful 잔소리를 늘어놓다 (To give excessive or animated talk)

  [Ex] He gave me an earful about his boss.

- **give somebody a piece of one's mind** 생각한 바를 거리낌 없이 말하다, 따끔하게 한 마디 하다

  [Ex] She gave a piece of her mind to the students that lived in the dormitory, cause she was a dormitory leader.

- give somebody flak 꾸중을 하다 (To criticize)

  [Ex] My boss gave me flak for coming late.

- **haul somebody over the coals** 엄하게 야단치다 (To reprimand angrily)

  [Ex] He should be hauled over the coals & fined for running the team down like that.

- **jump all over somebody** 호되게 꾸짖다 (To reprimand angrily)

  [Ex] Next time, before jumping all over others, check your facts.

- **rake somebody over the coals** 심하게 질책하다, 비난하다 (To reprimand angrily)

  [Ex] That guy was really raked over the coals after the boss found out about his mistake.

- snap somebody's head off 심하게 꾸짖다 (To reprimand angrily)

  [Ex] You just snap my head off every time I open my mouth! If being with me is so distasteful to you, you can leave.

- tell somebody where to get off 화를 내며 꾸짖다 (To reprimand angrily)

  [Ex] Someone should tell the banks and their overpaid bosses where to get off.

Slang

- chew one's ass off 비난하다 (To attack verbally)

  [Ex] Mom's gonna chew your ass off if she catches you drinking her liquor.

- give somebody the dickens ~를 화를 내며 꾸짖다 (To reprimand angrily)

2-4. Verbally Attacked (말로 공격을 받다)

Informal

- **catch[get] hell** 크게 혼나다, 심한 꾸중을 듣다

[Ex] Man, my pop found out I skipped yesterday and I caught hell.

2-5. Attack Physically or Verbally (물리적으로 또는 말로 공격하다)

Formal

assail; assault; attack; pounce upon; beset

Informal

- **bash** ~을 세게 때리다, 때려 부수다 (To hit somebody a solid blow)

[Ex] Why do you have to bash my beliefs?

- **give somebody (holy, merry) hell** 공격하다 (To attack)

[Ex] I also remember him giving hell to people who he felt had not supported him correctly after one of those sessions.

- let loose on[at] 공격하다 (To attack)

[Ex] You can almost hear his inner child stamping up and down, just itching to be let loose on it.

- take a swipe at ~을 겨누어 배트를 휘두르다, ~을 공격하다 (To attack unexpectedly)

[Ex] He took a swipe at Democrats, arguing that they are living in the past.

- whale into somebody 맹렬히 공격하다 (To attack)

[Ex] I was so angry, I simply whaled into him.

Slang

- cut somebody a new asshole[one] 공격하다, 비난하다 (To attack)

[Ex] The teacher is cutting students a new asshole for no reason.

- rip[tear] somebody a new asshole[one] 공격하다, 비난하다 (To attack)

2-6. Attack Unexpectedly (갑자기 공격하다)

Formal

ambush; launch a surprise attack; launch a preemptive strike;

- **blindside** 1. 상대방이 못 보는 쪽에서 공격하다 2. 기습하다

[Ex] Americans were frightened, confused, outraged, baffled, stunned, and sorrowful after this "blindside attack".

- **blitz** ~을 기습하다, ~을 전격적으로 하다, ~을 괴멸시키다 (To defeat utterly; to destroy; to be hit suddenly and without warning by multiple sources. Origin: From the German term "blitzkreig" which describes a sudden and unexpected attack.)

[Ex] None of them would leave me alone - it was a total blitz!

Informal

- blow someone out of the water ~을 기습하다

[Ex] If he isn't careful, he could be blown out of the water.

- bushwhack 매복하다

[Ex] Afghan officials say Taliban fighters who bushwhacked two convoys carrying members of the same family have killed at least 30 people.

- jump down somebody's throat 갑자기 공격하다 (To attack unexpectedly)

[Ex] You have to be pretty thick-skinned to blog; you don't know who is out there ready to jump down your throat.

- **sucker punch** 불시의 타격 (To attack sneakily)

[Ex] We were caught by a sucker punch.

③ Complain
불평하다

Formal

bleat; carp; cavil(트집을 잡다); grumble; make a fuss; moan; snivel; dissent; find fault; object

Informal

- **beef** 불평, 불만, 말다툼, 싸움 (A complaint or disagreement)

   [Ex] He has a beef with anyone who tells him otherwise.

- **bitch** ~에게 불평[우는소리]을 하다 (불평, 불만, 불쾌한 것, 까다로운 것)

   [Ex] She's always bitching about people she hates.

- bitch and moan 언제나 불평만 해대다 (To complain all the time)

   [Ex] The guy bitches and moans, or doesn't participate because he does not want to part of the group.

- bitch session 사람들이 모여서 불평[불만]을 해대는 비공식적인 모임

   [Ex] Where's Jim? Is he holding a bitch session again with other workers?

4 *Defeat*

무찌르다, 이기다, 극복하다

<u>4-1.</u> Defeat In a Fight or Competition (전투, 경쟁에서 무찌르다[이기다])

Formal

beat; defeat; overthrow; crush; demolish; wipe out; vanquish;

- clobber 완패시키다 (To defeat)

[Ex] Long-distance travelers and especially those travelling business class will be clobbered.

- **do number on** ~을 해치우다, 면목을 잃게 하다, 철저히 비판하다 (To defeat)

[Ex] Sun and pollution can really do a number on your skin.

- make mincemeat of (싸움·언쟁·시합 등에서) ~를 묵사발을 만들다

[Ex] I can imagine a defense lawyer making mincemeat of him if we ever put him up in court.

- maul (사람을 공격하여 살을 찢는) 상처를 입히다 (To strike heavily)

[Ex] There was a savage mauling of six people by three pit bulls.

- **pulverize** 완전히 쳐부수다, 분쇄하다 (To destroy completely)

[Ex] In less than a month, however, American warplanes were flying over Afghanistan, pulverizing Taliban and Al Qaeda positions.

- stomp 짓밟다 (To defeat)

[Ex] Some see the change as a perfect example of government stomping on ethnic tradition.

- **take down** 공격하다, 체포하다 (To defeat)

[Ex] Troops went to the war to take down terrorists.

- thrash 때려눕히다 (To defeat)

[Ex] In August 1939, Zhukov had thrashed the Japanese on the border of Mongolia and Manchuria.

- **kick (one's) ass** 누군가를 혼내주다 (To be victorious)

  [Ex] Our football team kicked their ass this weekend!

- **kick one's butt** 누군가를 혼내주다 (To defeat)

  [Ex] I will kick his butt in front of many people.

- knock the socks off somebody 완전히 패배시키다 (To defeat completely)

  [Ex] The fall of the company's stocks knocked their socks off.

- lick (경기·전쟁에서) ~을 무찌르다, 이기다, 극복하다 (To beat someone up)

  [Ex] I'll give you a lickin' after school!

- shellack 얻어맞다, 큰 점수 차로 지다

  [Ex] The team from everywhere took a real shellacking.

- smoke 물리치다 (To defeat)

  [Ex] She said she wasn't planning to go full out but she smoked us in speed and endurance.

- whip 패배시키다 (To defeat)

  [Ex] We whipped them in semifinals.

- whip somebody's ass 때려눕히다 (To defeat)

  [Ex] Cuban intelligence has "whipped the asses of American intelligence for decades", Noriega said.

- whomp 결정적으로 패배시키다 (To beat severely)

  [Ex] The Seahawks are gonna whomp the Lancers!

- wreck 완전히 패배시키다 (To defeat badly)

  [Ex] Dude, I just got wrecked at video games.

4-2. Defeat in Competition (경쟁에서 이기다)

- shut out 영패시키다, 완봉승을 거두다 (To defeat impressively)

  [Ex] The Dodgers shut out the Giants 3 to 0.

- slaughter (시합 등에서) 완승[압승]을 거두다 (To defeat impressively)

  [Ex] At least a slaughter like that makes it easier to admit defeat.

- slay (전쟁·싸움에서) 죽이다 (To defeat; to kill)

  [Ex] He sees no purpose or justification in slaying his friends, tutors and mentors.
- **sweep** (스포츠 경기에서) 완승을 거두다[휩쓸다] (To defeat)

  [Ex] She made a clean sweep of all women's tennis titles.

4-3. Defeat Physically (물리적으로 패배시키다)

Formal

  defeat; beat up; knock around; trounce

Informal

- bash somebody up ~를 강타하다 (To defeat physically, hit strongly)

  [Ex] I was threatened with a knife, bashed up and robbed.
- beat somebody to a pulp 묵사발이 되도록 패다 (To beat somebody up)

  [Ex] Only three days ago a senior reporter from my network was beaten to a pulp by the police.
- **beat the (living) daylights out of** 정신을 잃을 정도로 때리다 (To beat somebody up)

  [Ex] Just as they are about to rape her, Adam miraculously appears and beats the living daylights out of the two guys.
- lambast ~을 세게 치다, 매질하다, ~을 엄하게 꾸짖다, 호되게 비난하다

  [Ex] I really need to lambast someone.
- **rough up** ~를 두들겨 패다 (To hurt)

  [Ex] The Chinese police had reportedly roughed up photographers and a British television crew.
- wallop 세게 치다 (To beat somebody up)

  [Ex] Once, she walloped me over the head with a frying pan.

Slang

- beat[kick, knock] the crap[shit] out of somebody 흠씬 때리다, 실컷 패다
- **fuck somebody up** ~의 신세를 조지다, 심하게 상처를 주다 (To severely injure (a person) or damage or ruin (a thing))

  [Ex] He really fucked that guy up!

4-4. Defeat Physically or Verbally (물리적으로 또는 말로 패배시키다)

Informal

- have somebody's head on a plate 때리다, 괴롭히다 (To beat up; to harass or annoy)

  [Ex] I'm afraid if anyone hurt my child I would want their head on a plate.

- skin somebody alive ~을 몹시 꾸짖다[벌주다], ~을 완전히 해치우다

  [Ex] It is like she has been skinned alive, he told a reporter.

Slang

- beat[break, bust] somebody's ass[ball, bun, butt] 흠씬 패다

⑤ *Be Defeated*
패하다, 굴복하다

Formal

be beaten; be defeated; give in; surrender; give up; succumb; suffer; defeat; yield

informal

- bend over (for somebody) 굴복[복종]하다 (To submit)

  [Ex] Gas prices are going up again! Bend over, SUV drivers!

- **bite it** (수수께끼·질문 따위에서) 패배를 자인하다 (To be defeated)

  [Ex] The principal wants to see you in her office. Get ready to bite it.

- **buckle under** (압력에 못 이기고) 허물어지다 (To succumb to pressure)

  [Ex] But this evening they seem to have buckled under pressure from the public.

- **cave in** 굴복하다 (To succumb to pressure)

  [Ex] The President is unlikely to cave in to demands for a public inquiry.

- **cry uncle** 항복하다, 패배를 인정하다, 자비를 청하다 (To beg for mercy)

  [Ex] I'm going to make my examination cry uncle.

- get owned 지다, 패배하다 (To lose; to be defeated)

  [Ex] Oh man! I got owned!

- **give over** 포기하다, 항복하다 (To surrender)

  [Ex] You have no choice but to give yourself over to the police.

- **knuckle under** 항복하다, 압력에 굴복하다 (To give in to pressure)

  [Ex] He figured there was absolutely no way he was getting out of this one without getting whacked around. Even so, he had absolutely no intention of knuckling under to this maggot.

- **say uncle** 항복하다, 패배를 인정하다 (To accept defeat; to cry uncle)

  [Ex] If you say uncle, I'll let go of you.

- **take a beating** 대패[참패]하다 (To be defeated)

  [Ex] Our team took a beating in our last match.

- take a licking 지다, 패배하다, 얻어맞다 (To suffer a defeat or a beating)

   [Ex] Just like the saying "takes a licking and keeps on ticking", you could play with them for hours and they wouldn't break.

- throw in the sponge 패배를 인정하다 (To quit; to surrender)

   [Ex] Don't give up now. It's too soon to throw in the sponge.

- **throw in the towel** 패배를 인정하다 (To quit; to surrender)

   [Ex] Most people throw in the towel when they break down and eat a candy bar, go a few days without exercising, or buy a pack of cigarettes.

6 *Fail*

실패하다

Informal

- eat it 실패하다, 패하다 (To fail)

[Ex] Oh, man, Tony Hawks did a triple flip & landed on his face – he totally ate it!

Slang

- **fuck up** ~을 개판으로 만들다[조지다]

[Ex] I completely fucked up my exams.

Fight, Quarrel or Argue

싸우다, 대결하다, 논쟁하다, 언쟁하다

Formal

argument; battle; brawl; clash; combat; controversy; disagreement; feud; bicker; scuffle; fracas; contention; fray; melee; duel; spar; have a shootout; assault; attack; challenge; fight; cross swords

Informal

- bust-up 심한 언쟁 (To attack; beat up)

  [Ex] Sue and Tony had a bust-up and aren't speaking to each other.

- duke it out 끝장날 때까지 싸우다 (To fight with somebody using your hands tightly closed)

  [Ex] In the end, duking it out is the only way of settling the question of who is really superior.

- **dustup** 소동, 싸움, 주먹다짐, 논쟁 (A disagreement or fight)

  [Ex] There were failed attempts at college, minor dustups with the law and trouble with drugs and alcohol.

- **face-off** 대결 (To fight)

  [Ex] Both teams are ready to face off.

- **free-for-all** 난투극, 난장판 (Chaos; a chaotic situation lacking rules or control)

  [Ex] The picnic turned into a free-for-all after midnight.

- get physical 싸움을 시작하다 (To start a fight)

  [Ex] Are you going to cooperate or do we have to get physical?

- **go at it** 결연히[필사적으로] 싸우다 (To start a fight)

  [Ex] These guys were really angry and went at it.

- gun for somebody ~을 죽이려고[해치려고] 찾아다니다

  [Ex] I've heard that the sheriff is gunning for me, so I'm getting out of town.

- mix it up (~와) 다투다[문제를 일으키다] (To fight physically)

  [Ex] He's bored with life and always trying to mix it up.

- **pissing contest** (주도권, 우위를 잡기 위한) 싸움, 말다툼

  [Ex] The mayor and the sheriff are engaged in a pissing contest.

- roughhouse 난투를 벌이다, 시끄럽게 놀다, 야단법석을 떨다 (To play roughly)

[Ex] The conductor of the car reported that a crowd of students was having a roughhouse on the car.

- ruckus 야단법석, 대소동 (A great deal of noise, argument or confusion; A fight)

[Ex] A yearly night of glamour and ruckus, the Source Awards are entertainment at its superstar-studded finest.

- rumble 갱들의 싸움(gang fight) (A brawl; a fight)

[Ex] There is a rumble tomorrow in the park.

- run-in 언쟁, 싸움 (A fight)

[Ex] I had a run-in with a boss.

- slug-fest 심한 타격전, 난타전 (A fight)

[Ex] It will be a tough brawl, a slug-fest, but the Clintons are known for their brass knuckles.

- spat 싸움, 승강이 (A fight)

[Ex] Now, there is a spat between the Deputy Prime Minister and his boss.

- square off (~와) 싸우다[싸울 준비를 하다] (To start a fight)

[Ex] In my mind, I was imagining them squaring off like WWF wrestlers.

8 *Have, Take, Get*
잡다, 획득하다, 얻다

Informal

- cop ~을 잡다, 획득하다, ~을 체포하다 (To get, receive, purchase, steal or have)

[Ex] *Yo, I'm about to cop a drink, want one?*

9

Hit Violently

세게 때리다, 세게 치다

Formal

hit; punch; strike; cuff; swat; thump; smite

Informal

- give a thumper 세게 때리다 (To strike someone with great force)

  [Ex] I just gave him a thumper.

- slug (주먹으로) ~을 강타하다, (공을) 세게 치다, 싸우다 (To strike someone with great force)

  [Ex] I slugged him in the face.

- bang ~을 쾅[탕]하고 닫다, ~을 찰싹 때리다 (To hit; punch; slap)

  [Ex] If he keeps saying that, watch me walk over and bang him.

- bang out 때려눕히다 (To hit or cause bodily injury)

  [Ex] If you don't shut up, I'm going to bang you out.

- **beat the hell out of** 심하게 때리다 (To beat violently)

  [Ex] "It's not surprising that they would say there's no right to beat the hell out of the officer", Bodensteiner said.

- belt (혁대 따위로) ~을 후려치다 (To strike a strong blow with a belt or one's fist)

  [Ex] I will belt you upside your head if you look at my lady's teats one more time!

- bop (주먹, 막대기 따위로) ~을 때리다, 치다 (To hit; strike)

  [Ex] Son, you know you shouldn't bop your brother. A bop in the head is not nice!

- **bust** (주먹으로) ~을 치다, 때리다 (To punch or hit)

  [Ex] If you don't shut up, I'm going to bust you in the mouth.

- bust on ~을 마구 때리다 (To hit; attack)

  [Ex] The bouncers busted on some drunk guy last night.

- **clobber** ~을 사정없이 때리다, 때려눕히다 (To strike with great force)

  [Ex] His car got clobbered by a freight train.

- clonk ~을 치다 (To hit with a dull thudding force)

  [Ex] Yar··· you clonked me in the din. (din; head)

- clout (특히 손으로) 세게 때리다 (To hit someone)

   [Ex] I got clouted by that guy.

- clunk 쿵하고 치다, 때리다 (To hit)

   [Ex] But there are times when the clunking fist needs to stop clunking and do something more appropriate and probably gentler.

- conk 머리를 세게 때리다 (To hit)

   [Ex] I really wanted to go up and conk her on the head, but the secret service probably wouldn't have liked it.

- hit someone where it counts 급소를 때리다 (To hit the most hurting place)

   [Ex] On the stroke of half-time, they were hit where it counts.

- kapow 때리다, 치다, 세게 때리는 소리 (To hit; The sound of hitting hard)

   [Ex] KAPOW! Batman has socked it to Spider-Man in the box office battle.

- kick someone where it counts 급소를 차다 (To kick the most hurting place)

   [Ex] Perhaps he will give the commission a kick where it counts.

- knock (one's) socks off ~에게 큰 영향을 미치다, 타격을 주다, 깜짝 놀라게 하다

   [Ex] Wait 'til you hear this idea. It'll knock your socks off!

- pow 세게 때리다, 세게 때리는 소리 (To hit; The sound of hitting hard)

   [Ex] POW! They really did have muscle.

- put the smack down 세게 때리다 (To hit hard)

   [Ex] It's time to put the smack down with this England team.

- **slug** 세게 때리다 (To hit; to punch)

   [Ex] The two boxers slugged it out.

- **smack** 탁 소리가 나게 치다 (To hit; to slap)

   [Ex] He got smacked right in the jaw.

- smack down 업어메치다 (To beat with physical violence)

   [Ex] Frank got smacked down by that 350 pound bouncer.

- sock it to somebody 세게 치다, 강타하다 (To hit)

   [Ex] If you really sock it to her, you're going to alienate every Hispanic voter in the country.

- **thud** 쿵하고 내리치다 (To hit)

   [Ex] A rock thrown in the air thuds on the sand and echoes underground.

- **thump** 내리치다 (To hit)

   [Ex] I'll thump you if you say that again.

- thunk 둔탁한 소리를 내며 치다, 때리다 (To hit)

   [Ex] The noise of the ball thunking off the middle of his bat booms around the nets.

- thwack 탁 때리다 (To hit)

[Ex] Every day without exception, people are to be seen enjoying thwacking a ball through the croquet hoops.

- wallop 세게 치다 (To punch)

[Ex] Once, she walloped me over the head with a frying pan.

- whack 세게 치다 (To punch)

[Ex] James whacked the ball over the net.

- wham 치다, 때리다 (To hit; To punch)

[Ex] He backed up and a car whammed into him.

- whap 치다, 때리다 (To punch)

[Ex] A friend of mine once crossed the line when teasing me and fast as lightning, I whapped him under the kneecaps with my walking stick.

- whump 때리다, 치다 (To punch)

[Ex] At the time of writing, the postal responses hadn't whumped onto her door-mat yet.

- zonk 한 방 때리다, 기절시키다, 때려눕히다 (To punch)

Slang

- **beat one's ass** 심하게 때리다 (To beat somebody up; To kick one's ass)
- **beat the shit out of** 심하게 때리다 (To beat severely)

[Ex] Some sick twist beat the shit out of her.

- **kick one's ass** 심하게 때리다, 혼내주다 (To beat severely)

[Ex] Next time I hear something like that, I'm gonna kick their ass.

10 *Knock Down*

때려눕히다

Formal

bring down; knock down; level; prostrate; strike down

Informal

- deck ~을 때려눕히다 (To knock down)

  [Ex] Johnny decked Tim, and he fell to the floor his face bleeding.

- flatten 때려눕히다 (To crush an object down from a greater size to a smaller one)

  [Ex] I'll flatten you if you do that again!

- floor (특히 스포츠 경기에서) 때려눕히다

  [Ex] He floored his opponent in the match.

- lay somebody flat 때려눕히다 (To knock somebody down)

  [Ex] The bomb laid the tall building flat.

Knock Unconscious

때려서 실신시키다

Formal

knock senseless; knock unconscious

[Informal]

- knock somebody out 때려눕혀 정신을 잃게 하다 (To knock unconscious)

  [Ex] I was knocked out for an instant.

- knock somebody's lights out 때려눕혀 정신을 잃게 하다 (To knock unconscious)

  [Ex] In the dark, the man flourished the bat and knocked the boy's light out.

- punch somebody's lights out 때려눕혀 정신을 잃게 하다 (To knock unconscious)

  [Ex] The man at the bar became so verbally aggressive that after a while I threatened to punch his lights out.

Slang

- coldcock (주먹이나 몽둥이로) 실신할 정도로 때리다

  [Ex] The SOB coldcocked me - I never saw it coming.

12 *Punish*
벌을 주다

Informal

- **kick ones' ass** 벌을 주다, 혼내 주다

  [Ex] *You will kick his ass with your improved serve.*

- **slap on the wrist** 가벼운 꾸지람(에 불과한 것) (A light punishment)

  [Ex] *The judge gave the defendant a slap on the wrist.*

Reject, Ignore

거절하다, 내쫓다, 무시하다

Formal

- **brush off** ~를 딱 못 본 척하다 (To reject; to ignore)

  [Ex] They wandered inside, casually brushing off the sales person.

- cut somebody dead ~를 딱 못 본 척하다 (To reject; to ignore)

  [Ex] I asked her about it in the meeting and she just cut me dead.

- give the elbow (교제하던 사람을) 차다[퇴짜 놓다] (To reject; ignore)

  [Ex] He thinks he was given the elbow because he was too nice.

- **turn a blind eye** ~을 못 본 체하다 (To ignore a misdeed)

  [Ex] Football culture has traditionally turned a blind eye to wrongdoing.

Informal

- 86 제거하다, 내쫓다, 서비스를 거부하다

  [Ex] I was 86ed from the bar last night.

- **dis** ~을 경멸[멸시]하다, 업신여기다, 깔보다 (An insult or instance of disrespect)

  [Ex] Are you dissing me?

- give the shaft 업신여기다, 멸시하다 (To reject:, ignore)

  [Ex] I think what happened to Paris Hilton was deserved because basically she was giving the court the shaft and she and her mother acted ridiculous.

Seek Revenge

복수하다

Formal

seek revenge; take an eye for an eye; pay back; settle with; avenge; redress; retaliate; vindicate;

- **even the score** (자기에게 해를 입히거나 속임수를 쓴 자에게) 복수하다[응징하다]

[Ex] He tried to even the score but did consider what the full outcome might be.

- fix somebody's wagon 보복하다, 앙갚음을 하다 (To seek revenge)

[Ex] If you ever do that again, I'll fix your wagon!

- **get even** ~에 복수하다 (To seek revenge)

[Ex] I'll get even with you for this, just you wait.

- get one's own back ~에게 복수하다, 보복하다 (To seek revenge)

[Ex] One of the marks of infantilism is a kneejerk desire to get one's own back, even at the expense of harming oneself.

- get square with ~와 대등해지다, ~에 앙갚음하다, 보복하다 (To seek revenge)

[Ex] I will get square with you tomorrow.

- **settle the score** 복수하다, 보복하다 (To seek revenge)

[Ex] Now he wants to settle the score, and seeks revenge accordingly, but things have changed since he left the neighborhood.

- **settle accounts** 복수하다, 보복하다 (To seek revenge)

[Ex] Hence the hit men keep on arriving on our shores to settle accounts by violent means.

Chapter 10

Progress & Decline
진전과 퇴보

Progress는 American way of life의 일부입니다. 따라서 앞으로 나아가고, 또는 퇴보하는 것에 관한 표현들이 많이 발달해 있는 것 또한 미국 영어의 특색입니다. 이번 장은 진전과 퇴보에 관련된 표현들을 정리했습니다. 대부분의 informal expression, slang들은 간단한 단어의 조합들로 이루어져 있지만, 그 단어들이 원래 갖는 의미에서 변형되어 완전히 새로운 의미를 갖게 된 것들이 많으므로 반드시 새로운 의미를 확인해야만 합니다.

1 *Begin*
시작하다

1-1. An Attempt (시도)

Formal

attack; attempt; trial; try; fling; stab;

- **go** 시도 (Attempt)

[Ex] I doubt if he'll listen to advice from me, but I'll give it a go.

- **shot** 시도 (An attempt)

[Ex] It is a long shot certainly, but maybe not impossible.

- take for a spin 시운전하다

[Ex] 1. Chris: There it is, Meg. What do you say we take it for a spin? / 2. Let's take this baby for a spin! (baby: 자동차를 의미)

Informal

- crack 시도[도전](의 기회) (An attempt)

[Ex] She hopes to have another crack at the world record this year.

- lick at 시도하다 (To have a go at)

1-2. Start (시작하다)

Formal

begin; get underway; launch; start; take off; get the ball rolling; kick off; commence; embark; inaugurate; initiate; lay the foundation for; set about

- buckle down ~에 온 힘을 쏟다, ~에 착수하다

  [Ex] Hoping to avoid the axe, the guys buckle down to impress the higher ups.

- **get a move on** (명령문으로 쓰여) 빨리해[서둘러] (To start a task; to move quickly)

  [Ex] She had to get a move on if she wants to go home before midnight.

- get cracking 즉시[서둘러] 일을 시작하다 (To start a task)

  [Ex] There's a lot to be done, so let's get cracking.

- **get going** ~하기 시작하다 (begin; To start a task)

  [Ex] Come on, you guys, let's get going!

- **get in on the ground floor** (계획·프로젝트 등에) 처음부터 관여하다 (To start a task)

  [Ex] It's great to get in on the ground floor of a new narrative series, especially one as promising and swashbuckling as this.

- **get moving** 빨리 시작하다[떠나다, 움직이다] (To start a task)

  [Ex] Let's get the project moving, guys, we have just two days.

- get one's foot in the door 기회를 얻다, 잽싸게 끼어들다, 발을 들여놓다

  [Ex] In fact it is a struggle for many young people even to get their foot in the door.

- **get one's teeth into** ~에 열중하다, ~에 달려들어 시작하다 (To start a task)

  [Ex] It was a project for me to prove myself; something for me to get my teeth into.

- get the show on the road (활동·여정을) 시작하다 (To start)

  [Ex] Let's get this show on the road!

- **get-go** 시작, 개시, 최초 (The beginning)

  [Ex] He has been guilty from the get-go.

- **have a go at something** ~을 해보다 (To give it a shot or try; take a chance)

  [Ex] "Have a go" said one soccer player to the next referring to taking a shot at goal.

- have one's foot in the door (입회가 어려운 클럽 따위에) 들어갈 기회를 얻다, 잽싸게 끼어들다 (To reach the initial stage in accomplishing something)

  [Ex] Then England will surely have one foot in the door for the World Cup next year.

- **kick-off** (활동의) 시작, 개시 (The beginning)

  [Ex] Kick-off meeting.

- knuckle down (~을) 열심히 하기 시작하다 (To start a task)

  [Ex] He managed to knuckle down to his lessons long enough to pass his examination.

- sink one's teeth into ~에 기세 좋게 달려들다 (To start a task)

  [Ex] Both are highly recommended – I can't wait to sink my teeth into this book.

- **tee off** 시작하다 (To begin)

  [Ex] What time does the party tee off tonight?

1-3. Exert Effort (노력을 기울이다)

Formal

do one's best; exert oneself; stick with it; drive on; plug away; persevere; persist;

- **all-nighter** (집회, 공연 따위) 철야 시합, (상점)철야 영업소, 밤샘

  [Ex] I had to pull an all-nighter before the final.

- bang up job 기대에 넘는 성과를 내다

  [Ex] She did a bang up job on the proposal.

- do one's damndest 사력을 다하다 (To exert one's effort)

  [Ex] We must also do our damndest to make sure it never happens again.

- do the full monty 벌거숭이가 되다, 갈 데까지[끝까지] 가다

  [Ex] What did you have in mind, a patch-up job or the full monty?

- do the heavy lifting 어려운 일을 하다 (중량 운동을 하는 것에서 파생)

  [Ex] The idea of the group apprenticeship is a positive one, because it does the heavy lifting for the small employer.

- **give all the way** 최고의 노력을 하다 (To exert one's best effort)

  [Ex] Give all the way to the end and you'll be paid off.

- **give it all one's got** 전력[혼신의 힘]을 다하다 (To do one's best effort)

  [Ex] Whatever you do, you must give it all you've got.

- **give it one's best shot** 전력[혼신의 힘]을 다하다 (To do one's best effort)

  [Ex] I gave it my best shot, but couldn't stand her demands.

- give one's left[or right] nut to do ~하기 위해서라면 뭐든지 하다

  [Ex] I know you'd give a nut to have me again but you'll just have to wait.

- **go the distance** 끝까지 해내다 (To endeavor to be successful)

  [Ex] This is going to be a long, hard project. I hope I can go the distance.

- **go the extra mile** (~을 위해) 특별히 애를 쓰다

  [Ex] Those who go the extra mile will get rewarded someday.

- **go the limit** 끝까지 노력하다 (To do one's best effort)

 [Ex] Let's do everything we can. Let's go the limit.

- **go the whole nine yards** 끝까지 열심히 하다, 할 수 있는 것은 다하다

 [Ex] She went the whole nine yards with a wedding dress.

- **haul ass** 힘들어서 어떤 일을 하다, 서둘러 움직이다 (To work very hard; To hurry)

 [Ex] I had just forty-eight hours to haul ass across the country.

- **keep on trucking** 버티다, 끈기를 갖고 하다 (To persist)

 [Ex] Really hope to see ya, all right. Love ya. Just – no, that – miss ya. You know what? You just keep on truckin'.

- knock oneself out 전력을 다하다, 녹초가 되다 (To exert one's best effort)

 [Ex] Stella knocked herself out by working so much.

- **make a full-court press** 전방 압박을 하다, 전력을 다하다 (To exert effort)

 [Ex] Clearly, we've made a full court press on trying to find him.

- **nail** ~을 완벽하게 하다, 해치우다

 [Ex] She really nailed me in the divorce settlement. I lost almost everything of value to her lawyer.

- **nose to the grindstone** 쉬지 않고 죽어라 일하다

 [Ex] The only way to get ahead is to work hard. Just keep your nose to the grindstone.

- pour it on (상대의 실패·약점 따위를 이용해) 전력을 기울이다 (To exert one's best effort)

 [Ex] She was really pouring it on, making sure he knew she was available.

- **pull an all-nighter** 밤을 새서 하다 (To work overnight)

 [Ex] If you're the college type, you've likely pulled an all-nighter.

- pull a gallstone 괄목할 성과를 이루다 (To accomplish something remarkable)

 [Ex] That guy without the leg just won the gold medal! He really pulled a gall-stone!

- **slave away** 힘들게 일하다, 노예처럼 일하다 (To work extremely hard)

 [Ex] I've slaved away fixing my broken cars in 30 degree weather.

- slog (시간이 오래 걸리는 힘든[지루한] 일을) 열심히 하다, 힘겹게 걷다

 [Ex] It's a hard slog, but somebody has to do it.

- split a gut 지독하게 노력하다 (To exert effort)

 [Ex] He split a gut to pass through the exam.

- **sweat it out** 열심히 (땀 흘려) 일을 해내다 (To exert effort)

 [Ex] With the Olympics only a month away, the athletes are sweating it out in last-minute training.

- **tough it out** 어려움을 참고 견디어 내다 (To exert effort)

[Ex] Even though it was harsh and dangerous he still toughed it out and accomplished what he intended to.

Informal

- suck it up 닥치고 참다 (To deal with something displeasing without complaining)

[Ex] You just suck it up and you do it, period.

- **suck it up and take it** 닥치고 참아라

[Ex] "So you're saying we have to suck it up and take it?" Rachelle asked.

Slang

- **break one's ass** 뼈 빠지게 일하다 (To work very hard)

[Ex] If you want to succeed, break your ass on one thing.

- **break one's balls** X 빠지게 일하다 (To work very hard)

[Ex] Jimmy always breaks his balls to keep in shape.

- **bust one's ass** 전력을 다하다, 대단한 노력을 기울이다 (To work very hard)

[Ex] Dude, you'd better bust ass if you wanna finish that on time!

- **bust one's balls** 전력을 다하다, 대단한 노력을 기울이다, X 빠지게 일하다

[Ex] I busted my balls making him understand me but he acted wrong anyway.

- **work (one's) ass off** 매우 열심히 일하다 (To work hard)

[Ex] Louise: You've been working your you-know-what off? I've been working my ass off! Night and day training! / Bob: Louise, take it easy.

② *Improve*
개선하다, 개량하다

2-1. Get Back On Track (제자리를 찾다, 재기하다)

Formal

change; come around; improve; make strides; revamp; come to heel; get back on track; amend

Informal

- **back in the saddle** 다시 일하는, 제자리로 돌아온

  [Ex] I stopped running while my ankle was healing, but now I'm back in the saddle.

- **back on (one's) feet** 다시 일어나서, 재기하여 (Doing better after an unfavorable event)

  [Ex] Things were bad after I lost my job, but I'm back on my feet again.

- **do a 180** 왔던 방향으로 되돌아가다, 처음으로 다시 가다

  [Ex] But since then, he's "done a 180" on the issue.

- get on the ball 빈틈없이 하다, 주의 깊게 하다 (To become focused)

  [Ex] If you don't get on the ball, you'll be fired.

- **shape up** 태도를 개선하다, 더 열심히 일하다 (To improve your work or your behavior)

  [Ex] You'd better get rid of that attitude and shape up, young man.

- **sing a different tune** 견해[의견, 태도 등]를 바꾸다 (To change one's opinion[attitude])

  [Ex] They seem to sing a different tune on some occasions.

- **toe the mark[line]** 규칙에 따르다

  [Ex] John finally got fired. He just couldn't learn to toe the line.

- clean up one's shit 개과천선하다 (To improve one's behavior or performance)

  [Ex] He cleaned up his shit.

- get off one's ass 일을 시작하다

  [Ex] Get off your asses and do something.

- get one's ass in gear 꾸물거리지 말고 당장 움직이다 (To stop wasting time; to start a task)

  [Ex] We'd better get their asses in gear and get a production photo out SOON or the phony photos will just keep coming.

- get one's head out of one's ass[butt] 멍청한 행동을 그만하다

  [Ex] Because it was very famous lecture, she got her head out of her ass.

- get one's shit together 다시 집중하다, 인생을 제대로 정리하다

  [Ex] I told my son if he doesn't get his shit together soon that he's got to move out.

2-2. Enhance (증가시키다, 증강하다)

Formal

add bells and whistles; enrich; optimize; refine; upgrade; augment; elevate; enhance; garnish; refurbish; renovate

Informal

- amp up (출력을) 높이다, 증가시키다, 흥분시키다 (To increase)

  [Ex] Meanwhile, in the ice rink, Rhona Martin, our one real contender, was amping up Britain's curling team.

- glam 미화[치장]하다, 매력적으로 보이게 하다 (To glamorize)

  [Ex] I glammed up to be introduced to a new friend.

- gussy up (옷을 멋지게) 차려입다 (To decorate something to make it look attractive)

  [Ex] She gussied herself up for the big party.

- **jack up** (특히 가격을) 대폭 인상하다 (To increase sharply)

  [Ex] Jack up the oil prices.

- **kick it up a notch** 한 단계 높이다 (To increase the intensity of something)

  [Ex] It's the second week of Wimbledon and it's time to kick it up a notch.

- posh up 향상시키다 (To enhance)

[Ex] Women don't like men who don't want to posh themselves up, sartorially speaking.

- **rev up** 활성화되다, 힘이 붙다, 활기를 띠다 (To increase the speed at which something operates)

[Ex] Exercise is not likely to rev up your metabolism.

- **soup up** (자동차, 컴퓨터 등의) 성능을 높이다

[Ex] You can drive around, soup up your vehicles, win prize money from various races and even move into nicer dwellings eventually.

- **spiff up** 몸치장을 하다, 모양을 내다, 멋을 부리다 (To dress up)

[Ex] We went home to get spiffed up for the party.

- **step up** ~을 증가시키다[강화하다] (To increase the rate, level, amount, etc. of something)

[Ex] Security has been stepped up at the airport since the bomb scare.

- vamp it up 섹시함을 강조하다 (To increase the sexiness)

[Ex] They vamped it up in skin tight trousers, oversized hoop earrings, bandanas and baring toned midriffs.

2-3. Make Good Progress (좋은 진전을 보이다)

Formal

advance; cover ground; forge ahead; gain ground; make headway; make strides; press forward

Informal

- **churn out** 대량 생산하다 (Mass production, to have large scale of manufacturing)

[Ex] Asian factories will be churning out more large panels for LCD TVs.

- come up roses 썩 잘돼 가다 (To make good progress)

[Ex] She's had an unhappy time recently but everything seems to be coming up roses for her now.

- **go great guns** (사람이) 척척 잘해 나가다, (일이) 대성공이다 (To be successful)

[Ex] You can go great guns in order to impress your boss, beat the competition or notch up another success.

- go like gangbusters 성황을 이루다 (To make good progress)

  [Ex] Our sales have went off the new year like gangbusters.

- **kick in** 효과가 나타나기 시작하다 (To begin taking effect)

  [Ex] I think that Advil is finally starting to kick in.

- make short work of ~을 재빨리 이기다[해치우다]

  [Ex] I'm sure you can make short work of what I gave you this morning.

3 *Succeed*
성공하다

3-1. Succeed (성공하다)

Formal

be successful; become rich; carry off; do well; bear fruit; flourish; score

Informal

- bring off 성공하다 (To succeed)

  [Ex] I'm glad we brought off the plan without a hitch.

- call it Christmas 문제에 대한 좋은 해결책으로 하다 (A good solution to a problem)

  [Ex] We'll just get some beer and call it Christmas.

- **cinch** 확실한 일, 쉬운 일 (To be sure to succeed)

  [Ex] When asked to put his index finger on his nose by the police officer, Cristian said, "That's a cinch!"

- **deliver (the goods)** 약속을 이행하다, 기대[요구]에 부응하다

  [Ex] She always delivers on her promises.

- **do the trick** 효과가 있다 (To be effective)

  [Ex] Just give him 10 dollars. That'll do the trick.

- **get somewhere** 조금[약간] 진전을 보다 (To make some progress)

  [Ex] Do you think it still takes money to get somewhere in life?

- have (got) it made 성공시키다 (To be in a situation in which success is guaranteed)

  [Ex] I admire your enthusiasm and dedication, which have made it possible.

- **hit the jackpot** 대박을 터뜨리다 (To have a stroke of luck; have sudden luck)

  [Ex] Many gamblers try to hit the jackpot in Las Vegas.

- make a go of it 성공시키다, 잘해 나가다; ~을 잘하다 (To succeed)

  [Ex] I knew we could make a go of it and be happy.

- make the grade 필요한 수준에 이르다, 성공하다

[Ex] There are critics who say the military has reduced their standards ⋯ taking recruits who wouldn't normally make the grade.

- nail (특히 스포츠에서) ~을 이뤄 내다 (To succeed; accomplish)

[Ex] He nailed a victory in the semi-finals.

- **on the roll** 일이 잘 진행되는 (To be successful)

[Ex] I'm gonna play bingo all night. I'm lucky - I'm on the roll!

- strike it lucky 행운을 만나다 (To be lucky to do; to have a luck)

[Ex] We certainly struck it lucky with the weather - it's beautiful today.

- **strike oil** 큰 벼락부자가 되다 (To become very rich quickly)

[Ex] They really struck oil with that investment.

- **turn the trick** 목적을 이루다, 일이 잘 되다 (To accomplish a goal; succeed)

[Ex] With Nagy's encouragement, Fleiss joined Adams's staff, turning tricks for a year and a half and learning the business.

- work like a charm 기적같이 이뤄지다[성공하다]

[Ex] Economically, the policy worked like a charm.

- **wrap something up** (합의·회의 등을) 마무리 짓다 (To finish)

[Ex] That just about wraps it up for today.

3-2. Succeed through Perseverance (어려움을 딛고 성공하다)

Formal

bring about; bring off; overcome; rebound;

- **bounce back** (타격·패배·병 따위에서) 곧 회복하다 (To recover quickly from adversity)

[Ex] Ben: Aiden got in a car accident a few months ago. Really banged him up. / Sara: How's he doing now? / Ben: Well, he was able to bounce back pretty good.

- **pull off** (힘든 것을) 해내다[성사시키다] (To achieve)

[Ex] This is becoming an increasingly difficult task to pull off.

- win out[through] (어려움에도 불구하고) 성공하다[해내다]

[Ex] It won't be easy but we'll win through in the end.

3-3. In a Promising Situation (조짐이 좋은)

Formal

having complete control

Informal

- **cooking (with gas)** 일이 잘 풀리는

  [Ex] Everything was cooking well with gas.

- in the catbird seat 유리한 입장에 있다 (In a privileged position)

  [Ex] With prices falling dramatically, buyers seem to be in the catbird seat.

- in whack 정상(상태)에 (In good working condition; The opposite of "out of whack")

  [Ex] KJ: Hey man, my car is all out of whack. / GP: Don't worry. I can get it in whack.

- on the top of heap 높은 직위에, 유리한 위치에 (On a top position)

  [Ex] Joe Gideon is on the top of the heap, one of the most successful directors and choreographers in musical theatre.

- up to scratch 표준에 달하여[기대에 부응하여] (Of acceptable quality; in good condition)

  [Ex] Some first-rate services are provided, but too many are not up to scratch.

- up to snuff 표준에 달하여[기대에 부응하여]

  [Ex] I don't think this batch of macaroni and cheese is quite up to snuff.

3-4. A Certainty (성공이 확실함)

Formal

certainty; certitude

Informal

- ace in the hole 따로 떼어 둔, 으뜸 패, 비장의 무기 (만일에 대비한 것)

  [Ex] On top of this experience, Mr Salway has another ace in the hole.

- **cinch** 확실한 일, 쉬운 일 (A sure thing)

  [Ex] When asked to put his index finger on his nose by the police officer, Cristian said, "That's a cinch!"

- **shoo-in** 쉽게 우승할 사람 (A certainty; in a competition, the probable winner)

  [Ex] His expressive and high soprano voice made him a shoo-in as the little prince.

- **slam dunk** 성공이 확실한 것, 확실한 것 (A sure thing)

  [Ex] This will be a slam dunk.

- **sure bet** 틀림없음, 확실함 (A certainty)

  [Ex] He is a sure bet for the presidential nominations.

- **sure shot** 틀림없음, 확실함 (A certainty)

  [Ex] Ledger is considered by many a sure shot for an Oscar.

- **sure thing** 틀림없음, 확실함 (A certainty)

  [Ex] The reelection of the president is by no means a sure thing.

3-5. A Success (성공)

Formal

accomplishment; big hit; grand slam; consummation

Informal

- **killing** 대성공 (An impressive success; to generally be high performing or do a task well)

  [Ex] He makes a killing selling umbrellas when it rains.

- knockout 성공 (A success)

  [Ex] Visually, this movie is a knockout.

- **smash** (노래, 영화, 연극의) 엄청난 히트[대성공]

  [Ex] That movie was a huge smash!

4 *Stall*

지지부진, 교착상태

4-1. Make Minimal Progress (그럭저럭 되어가다)

Formal

struggle; make do

Informal

- **get along** (일이) 되어가다, (with) 진척되다 (To make a reasonable progress)

  [Ex] I manage to get along, one way or another.

- **jerry rig** 임시방편으로 처치하다

  [Ex] I jerry rigged the water pump. It should last the night.

- **muddle through** 그럭저럭[어떻게 하다 보니] 해내다

  [Ex] They may be able to muddle through the next five years like this.

- **squeak by[through]** 간신히 성공하다, 겨우 곤경에서 벗어나다[헤어나다]

  [Ex] Those tactics may be good at squeaking by in an election, but they are very bad if you want to lead one nation.

4-2. Postpone (연기하다, 미루다)

Formal

delay; hold over; put on hold

- hang fire 행동[진척]을[이] 미루다[미뤄지다] (To delay or to be delayed)

  [Ex] The project had hung fire for several years for lack of funds.

- let it ride (간섭 말고) 되는 대로 내버려 두다 (Let it as it goes)

  [Ex] Why not let it ride out its time? On a free vote, the forum decided unanimously that it would adjourn.

- **mothball** (계획을) 보류하다

  [Ex] The original proposal had been mothballed years ago.

- **on the back burner** ~을 일시 보류하다 (Of low priority; Contrast with "on the front burner")

  [Ex] Since we've found out the auditors are coming, the invoices are on the back burner.

- put something on ice 보류하다, 연기하다 (To postpone)

  [Ex] Nevertheless, it was put on ice pending the outcome of that investigation.

- **put something on the back burner** 뒷전으로 미루다

  [Ex] That must be another government policy put on the back burner.

- **shelve** (계획을) 보류하다

  [Ex] The government has shelved the idea until at least next year.

- **sleep on something** ~에 대해 하룻밤 동안 생각해보다

  [Ex] I will have to sleep on it some more.

4-3. Waste Time (시간을 낭비하다, 빈둥거리다)

be idle; dawdle; kill time

- **beat a dead horse** 이미 끝난[쓸모없게 된] 일을 다시 문제 삼다, 헛수고하다

  [Ex] Sorry to beat the dead horse, but I really need to talk to you about this again.

- dilly dally 꾸물거리다 (To mess around or waste time; Typically used by the very elderly)

  [Ex] He doesn't dilly dally, he doesn't mince words, he simply gets big things done.

- **fool around** (할 일을 안 하고) 노닥거리다 (To waste time)

  [Ex] He fooled around all through school.

- goof around(off) 시간을 허비하다 (To waste time)

  [Ex] At first blush, it may seem like children just goofing around, but it is much more serious than that.

- loaf 빈둥거리다, 놀며 지내다 (To take so much time, procrastinating or being lazy)

  [Ex] Man, you're loafing.

- **mess around** 1. 빈둥대다 2. 느긋하게 즐기다 (To waste time; To delay)

  [Ex] Quit messing around and come down stairs. We need to leave soon.

- tool about[around] 빈둥거리다 (To waste time, mess around)

  [Ex] "I'm going to get a car like this!" Allie declared. The car small, like Allie (and like Leslie), and it was cute like Allie (and like Leslie). Adam could see Allie tooling around L.A. in one.

Slang

- crap around 농땡이 부리다 (To waste time)

  [Ex] Time has passed away while I have been crapping around doing this and that.

- dick around 빈둥거리며 돌아다니다.

  [Ex] I don't even think I got anything done all Tuesday, I just skipped class and dicked around.

- fart around 빈둥거리다 (To waste time; to mess around)

  [Ex] With her heavy workload, one could never accuse Katy Perry of farting around.

- **fuck around** 빈둥거리다 (To waste time; to mess around)

  [Ex] He just fucks around on the computer all day.

- jack around (일부러) ~의 시간을 허비하다.

  [Ex] Let's go. We're being jacked around here.

- piss around 멍청하게 시간을 보내다[허비하다] (To waste time; Also piss about)

  [Ex] American submarines are pissing around under our polar ice cap looking for Russians.

- screw around 시간을 낭비하다 (To waste time)

  [Ex] I feel so useless when I screw around.

- screw the pooch 헛되게 시간을 보내다

  [Ex] Q: How did you do on the exam. / A: I totally screwed the pooch.

5 *Deteriorate*
악화시키다

5-1. Mishandle or Meddle With (잘못 처리하다)

Formal

abuse; harm; meddle; fumble; gum up(껌 같은 것을 붙여 작동을 못하게 하다)

Informal

- diddle around with something 만지작거리며 시간을 낭비하다

  [Ex] All they did at the mall was diddle around.

- **fiddle with** (마음에 들지 않아서 자꾸 이리저리 바꾸며) 만지작[주물럭]거리다 (To mess with)

  [Ex] I've been fiddling with this thing all day, and it still doesn't work.

- **mess around with something** ~을 (함부로) 만지작거리다[손대다], ~를 가지고 놀며[수리하며, 만지작거리며] 시간을 보내다 (To mess with; to not take a task seriously)

  [Ex] Those mobsters don't mess around, so don't try to make any jokes.

- screw around with something 망치다, 엉망으로 만들다

  [Ex] These people are screwing around with nature in order to push a political agenda.

Slang

- dick around with something ~을 (함부로) 만지작거리다[손대다], ~를 가지고 놀며[수리하며, 만지작거리며] 시간을 보내다

  [Ex] We finished the treasure hunt while the other team was still dicking around with the map.

- fart around with something ~을 (함부로) 만지작거리다[손대다], ~를 가지고 놀며[수리하며, 만지작거리며] 시간을 보내다

  [Ex] All we do in America is fart around with computers all day.

　영어 표현에도 등급이 있다!

- **fuck around with something** ~을 (함부로) 만지작거리다[손대다], ~를 가지고 놀며[수리하며, 만지작거리며] 시간을 보내다

  [Ex] Don't fuck around with sharp knives!

- **fuck with** ~을 (함부로) 만지작거리다[손대다], ~를 가지고 놀며[수리하며, 만지작거리며] 시간을 보내다

  [Ex] You better not be saying what I think you're saying. I'm not the kind of guy you want to fuck with.

5-2. Backtrack or Worsen (원점으로 돌아가다, 퇴보하다, 악화되다)

Formal

backpedal; retreat; get worse; go downhill; sink

Informal

- **go back to square one** 다시 원점으로 돌아가다 (To backtrack to the start)

  [Ex] The plan of building a garbage disposal facility went back to square one due to opposition from the residents.

- **go back to the drawing board** 다시 원점으로 돌아가다 (To backtrack to the start)

  [Ex] I think that the proposal should go back to the drawing board.

- **go south** (주가 따위가) 하향하다 (To take a turn for the worse)

  [Ex] His health has gone south.

- hit the skids 내리막이 되다, 파멸[영락]하다 (To suffer from failure)

  [Ex] An arrogant, shallow chef hits the skids when his cooking empire is usurped by a mean-spirited rival.

Slang

- **the shit hit the fan** 난장판이 되다, 난리 나다 (Something bad happened)

  [Ex] When my parents got home, the shit hit the fan.

5-3. Ruin (망치다, 파괴하다)

bring down; ruin; waste; wreck;

- **blow it** 실수하다, 얼빠진 짓을 하다 (To botch; destroy)

  [Ex] He's had his chance and blown it big time.

- **bust** ~을 부수다, ~을 못 쓰게 만들다 (To cause a crowd to disperse; break up)

  [Ex] The cops busted the party.

- **fry** 부수다, 망가트리다, 파괴하다

  [Ex] Yeah, I spilled some coke into my monitor and fried it.

- muck up (하고 싶던 일 등을) 망치다 (To ruin; mess up)

  [Ex] Are you suggesting that they actually haven't mucked up the economy this time?

- trash 망가트리다, 못 쓰게 만들다 (To ruin; destroy; mess up)

  [Ex] The band was famous for trashing hotel rooms.

- **waste** 망가트리다 (To destroy)

  [Ex] She wasted her car when she got in that wreck.

- wipe out ~을 완전히 파괴하다[없애 버리다] (To destroy)

  [Ex] The entire town was wiped out.

- bork 망가트리다, 부수다 (To break; ruin; destroy)

  [Ex] I think I borked your computer.

- scrog 망치다, 고장 내다 (To damage or ruin; Also spelled skrog)

  [Ex] The data tapes got scrogged in transit.

- **fuck something up** ~을 개판으로 만들다[조지다]

  [Ex] Thanks for fucking up my car.

- **fuck up** 부수다, 망가트리다, 파괴하다

  [Ex] I'm disappointed that he fucked up the work.

영어 표현에도 등급이 있다!

6 *Hit Obstacle*

장애를 만나다

6-1. Blunder or Make a Mistake (망치다, 실수하다)

Formal

be wrong; stumble; blunder;

- **blow it** 실수하다, 얼빠진 짓을 하다 (To completely fail a task)

  [Ex] I guess I blew it because I got cold feet.

- drop the ball (책임지고 있는 일을) 실수로 망치다

  [Ex] I could use some help. I don't want to drop the ball on this one.

- louse up ~을 엉망으로 만들다[잡치다] (To mess something up)

  [Ex] The Government appointed her, but she is lousing up the Government's efforts to promote energy saving.

- make a muck of ~을 더럽히다, 망쳐놓다 (To make a mistake)

  [Ex] The disgraceful incident made a muck of his honor.

- make a pig's ear of ~을 엉망으로 하다[만들다] (To make a mistake)

  [Ex] I totally agree that the US and UK have made a pig's ear of their economies.

- **mess up** (~을) 엉망으로 만들다[다 망치다] (To severely injure)

  [Ex] If you cancel now, you'll mess up all my arrangements.

- **miss the boat** (기회를 살리기에는) 이젠 너무 늦다, 호기를 놓치다

  [Ex] In fact, if they are not careful, they are going to miss the boat.

- **muck up** ~을 엉망으로 하다[망치다] (To ruin; mess up)

  [Ex] And, while they remain in power, they are mucking up the nation's finances.

- put one's foot in it (부주의로 말미암아) 어려운 처지에 빠지게 되다, 실수하다

  [Ex] Looks like he's really put his foot in it this time.

Informal

- ball up 혼란하게 하다, (계획 따위)를 망치다 (To mess something up)

  [Ex] You ball up another contract, and you are finished!

- cock up 실수하다, 엉망으로 만들다 (To mess something up. Used primarily in England)

  [Ex] It's my ass on the line and I don't want a cock up!

- **screw up** ~을 엉망으로 하다[망치다] (To err; mess up)

  [Ex] They screwed up that paint job.

Slang

- **fuck up** 실수하다, 엉망으로 만들다 (To mess something up)

  [Ex] My parents' divorce really fucked me up.

6-2. Malfunction (오작동하다, 결함을 보이다)

Formal

work improperly; misbehave; flaw; impairment

Informal

- **bug** 버그 (컴퓨터 프로그램의 결함, 작동 오류 / A fault in a computer system)

  [Ex] There's a few bugs to work out in the system.

- **glitch** 작은 문제 (A flaw)

  [Ex] A glitch in the computer is stopping the printer from working.

- **go haywire** (일이) 잘못되다[걷잡을 수 없게 되다] (To malfunction)

  [Ex] My computer went haywire.

- **hitch** 장애, 지체, 고장, 중단 (Snag; trouble)

  [Ex] I'm glad we brought off the plan without a hitch!

- crap out 실패하다, 망쳐 놓다, 못 쓰게 되다 (To stop operating properly)

[Ex] Freaking controller crapped out.

6-3. Cause Problems for Oneself
(자멸하다, 자신에게 문제를 일으키다, 자기 발목을 잡다)

Formal

destroy one's own future; ruin one's prospects;
- **ask for trouble** 사서 고생하다, 공연한 짓을 하다

[Ex] That is asking for trouble, and the proposal must be rejected.

Informal

- **cut one's own throat** 1. 자기 목을 찌르다 2. 자멸을 초래하다, 자살하다

[Ex] They don't want to cut their own throats by adopting measures that would kill off capital flows to their companies.

- **shoot oneself in the foot** 자신에게 문제를 일으키다 (To cause problems for oneself)

[Ex] It is clear that the industry shot itself in the foot with this.

- step on one's cock 위험을 자초하다 (To cause problems for oneself)

6-4. Moderate to Difficult Problems (약간 어려운 문제)

Formal

brain twister; stumper; dilemma; predicament; quandary;

- **fly in the ointment** 옥의 티, 어려운 문제나 단점

  [Ex] One fly in the ointment is who pays for it.

- **hot potato** 뜨거운 감자, 난감한 문제

  [Ex] The abortion issue in the USA is a political hot potato.

Informal

- **pain in the ass** 아주 어려운 문제, 골칫거리 (An extremely difficult or unpleasant problem)

  [Ex] That violent student is the school's pain in the ass.

- **pain in the neck** 아주 어려운 문제, 골칫거리

  [Ex] That guy is a pain in the neck with his constant demands.

- **pain in the rear (end)** 아주 어려운 문제, 골칫거리

  [Ex] Montgommery was one sweet pain in the rear end.

Slang

- ball-buster 어려운 문제 (Difficult problem)

  [Ex] But he has to show that he can be a ball-buster.

- bastard 아주 어려운 문제 (Very difficult problem)

  [Ex] This problem is a bastard!

- mind-fucker 아주 어렵거나 기분 나쁜 문제 (An extremely difficult or unpleasant problem)

  [Ex] Oh, those are just the mind-fuckers.

- pisser 굉장히 어려운[불쾌한] 것 (An extremely difficult or unpleasant problem)

  [Ex] So it's a pisser that Anthony's probably not going to win, then.

6-5. Easily Resolved Problems (쉽게 해결되는 문제)

Formal

   kid-stuff; no-brainer;

- **hiccup** (약간의) 문제

  [Ex] It is just another little hiccup that the system needs to be aware of.

- picnic 쉽게 풀리는 문제 (A problem as easy as picnic)

  [Ex] Learning to swim is not a picnic.

- **piece of cake** 식은 죽 먹기 (Something easy)

  [Ex] The test was a piece of cake.

- **waltz** 어려움 없이 해내다[완료하다] (To do something in a relaxed and confident way)

  [Ex] The recruits have waltzed through their training.

6-6. Errors (실수)

Formal

  slip; faux pas; lapse

Informal

- balls-up 엉망으로 한[망친] 것 (Errors)

  [Ex] I made a real balls-up of my exams.

- **blooper** (사람들 앞에서 범하는 당황스러운) 실수

  [Ex] Check out the DVD for behind-the-scenes commentary, deleted scenes, and a blooper reel.

- goof up 어리석은 실수를 하다 (To make a mistake)

  [Ex] Am I worried that someone might goof up and get hurt? Of course.

- **screw-up** 실패, 실수, 실책 (A mistake)

  [Ex] It was a huge screw-up.

- slip up 실수를 하다 (To make a mistake; Usually written either slip-up or slipup)

  [Ex] Magnifying oversights and seeing slipups as proof of catastrophe, they unleash hostility, anger, despondency, or jealousy.

Slang

- **boner** 어리석은 실수 (A clumsy error)

  [Ex] So from then on Jimmie was ace-high with them, because he had admitted the boner instead of trying to lie out of it.

- nip slip 옷이 잘못되어 은밀한 부위가 노출됨

[Ex] Photos of nip slips when I was 13 or 14, places where my pussy lips were visible, some out of focus shots. Most of them would fall plainly in the category of child pornography.

6-7. Unexpected Difficulties (뜻밖의 어려움)

Formal

brake; catch; Catch-22; trap; twist; hazard; pitfall; snare; stumbling block

Informal

- kicker (때로 the ~) (뜻밖의) 문제점, 불리한 점[상황], 의외의 결말[전개], (계약서 따위의) 부당 조항 부분 (A pitfall; a previously hidden or concealed difficulty or problem)

[Ex] And, for a kicker, I can tell them you've slept with me, a fourteen year old, and you'll get statutory rape on top of it.

- snag 암초, 뜻하지 않은 장애 (A problem, especially one causing a delay.)

[Ex] There is just one small snag. Where is money coming from?

6-8. Unfair Situation (부당한 상황, 차별)

Formal

discrimination; inequity

Informal

- bad rap (오심으로 인한) 억울한 죄, 부당한 형벌, 부당한 비난 (False accusation)

[Ex] He gets a bad rap, but he's a cool dude.

- raw deal 부당한 대우, 가혹한 처사 (Unfair or unjust treatment; a bad deal)

[Ex] Homosexuals have had a pretty raw deal from most of the churches.

6-9. Problematic Situation (문제 상황, 곤경, 난처한 상황)

Formal

dilemma; plight; predicament; quandary

- cook someone's goose 큰 문제에 빠지다 (마치 남의 집 오리를 죽인 것처럼)

[Ex] Thompson will cook his own goose if he lets this ridiculous nonsense go ahead.

- **hot spot** 분쟁 지대 (Area in trouble)

[Ex] We must urgently address the problem, specifically the hot spots.

- **hot water** 곤경, 고생 (A trouble)

[Ex] He did his best but he was in hot water.

- pinch 위기, 유사시 (Problematic situation)

[Ex] Lots of people who have lost their jobs are starting to feel the pinch.

- **tight spot** 난처한 입장, 궁지 (A difficult situation; a troublesome situation)

[Ex] If dad had another stroke, then he's in a tight spot.

- **tough spot** 곤란한 위치 (Problematic situation)

[Ex] I mean, it's sad to see what's happened to this company, and obviously, their workers are in a tough spot.

Informal

- deep doo-doo 아주 난처하게 됨, 곤경에 빠짐 (Serious trouble)

[Ex] "We're in deep doo-doo now." said Bush the Elder as the election returns came in.

Slang

- **deep shit** 몹시 골치 아픈 일 (To be in trouble)

[Ex] I shot the wrong asshole, now I'm in deep shit!

6-10. Risky Situation (위험한 상황)

Formal

shot in the dark; spin of the roulette wheel;

- **close call** 위기일발, 구사일생

[Ex] Jerry experienced a close call when he was sailing on his boat and a strong gale knocked down his mast and missed his head by a hair.

- **close shave** 위기일발, 구사일생(Close call; Risky situation)

[Ex] The car almost hit me. That was a close shave.

- clutch 위기, 절박한 경우

[Ex] Big-time players deliver in the clutch.

- crapshoot 위험하여 예측 불가능한 일, 불확실한 일, (주사위) 도박

[Ex] That team has been up and down lately but I got a good feeling about to-night. At the least it's a crapshoot.

- high-wire act 줄타기, 아슬아슬한 행동 (Very risky act)

[Ex] It is a high wire act because so many things are at stake.

- **hot seat** 곤경에 빠져 (Being in trouble)

[Ex] He saved me when I was on the hot seat.

- iffy proposition 불확실한 제안 (Risky proposal)

[Ex] Spring hiking in the Whites is an iffy proposition.

- **narrow shave** 간신히, 아주 근소한 차이 (Close call)

[Ex] I was nearly dead. It was a narrow shave.

- **narrow squeak** 아슬아슬하게 모면함

[Ex] They have already had some narrow squeaks and some embarrassing defeats.

- **near miss** 위기일발(의 상황) (Close call)

[Ex] Due to an air controller's ineptitude, the two flights to LAX were in a near miss situation.

- when the chips are down 막상 일이 닥치면

[Ex] I'm not sure what I'll do when the chips are down.

- **when the going gets tough** 상황이 힘들어지면

[Ex] Amateurs fall by the wayside when the going gets tough.

6-11. Take a Risk (위험을 무릅쓰다, 무모한 짓을 하다)

Formal

dare; gamble; play with fire; skate on thin ice; leap before looking

Informal

- bet the farm 전 재산을 걸다, 큰 도박을 하다, 절대 확신하다 (To risk everything)

  [Ex] Mike bluffed with his ace high, and bet the farm losing everything.

- **fly by the seat-of-one's pants** (계기에 의존하지 않고) 직감으로[손으로 더듬어] 조종하다

  [Ex] You're not told what to do, so for the first month you're flying by the seat of your pants.

- **go for broke** (~에) 전부를 걸다 (To risk everything in some endeavor)

  [Ex] She goes for broke and wins big time.

- **go for it** 단호히 목적을 추구하다, 사생결단으로 덤비다 (To risk everything in some endeavor)

  [Ex] Sink or swim, let's go for it.

- **push one's luck** 행운이 계속되기를 기대하다, 운을 너무 믿고 덤비다

  [Ex] You didn't get caught last time, but don't push your luck!

- put one's ass on the line 위태로운[위험한] 상황에 있다 (To take a huge risk)

  [Ex She put her ass on the line prior to the debate.

- **stick one's neck out** 무모한 짓을 하다, 위험을 자초하다[자초하는 짓을 하다]

  [Ex] But I wouldn't expect any politician to stick his neck out by supporting this.

7 *Fail*
실패하다

7-1. Fall Short (역부족이다, 미치지 못하다)

Formal

come to nothing; fall short; run dry; abate; fade; taper off; wane;

- peter out 점차 작아지다[조용해지다 등]

  [Ex] *The campaign petered out for lack of support.*

- poop out (일, 기능을 못하고) 나가떨어지다 (To collapse; to stop functioning)

  [Ex] *My computer finally pooped out.*

- **run on empty** 연료를 다 쓰다, 힘을 잃다, 역부족이다

  [Ex] *I think his energy and mental reserves are almost running on empty.*

- **run out of gas / steam** (일이) 진척이 안 되다, 멈추다 (To stop functioning)

  [Ex] *I say to the national Republican Party, that message has run out of gas here in Tennessee.*

7-2. Fail (실패하다)

Formal

be defeated; go wrong; back the wrong horse; flounder; miscarry;

- can't cut the mustard (요구) 기준에 미달하다, 기대에 부응하지 못하다

  [Ex] *Those evangelists would not be convincing if they couldn't cut the mustard.*

- fall down on the job 일을 제대로 하지 않다 (To fail)

  [Ex] *It appears that the Secretary of State is falling down on the job and needs some reinforcement.*

- **fall flat** 완전히 실패하다[아무런 호응을 못 얻다] (To fail completely)

[Ex] The new play fell flat and closed in a week.

- **fall flat on one's face** 완전히 실패하다 (To fail completely)

[Ex] He fell flat on his face to reform the policies.

- fall off the wagon (금주를 그만두고) 다시 술을 마시기 시작하다, (일반적으로) 금욕을 깨다, 절제를 잃다 (To resume drinking alcohol or doing Things - drugs after a period of sobriety)

[Ex] I had this other thought, that was: what better way to distract myself than to fall off the wagon?

Informal

- **crater** 떨어지다, 실패하다 (To fall as if from a great height, hit the ground with a significant impact, and end up below ground level. Used figuratively to describe a severe downturn in popularity, reputation, value, etc.)

[Ex] My stock portfolio cratered during the tech sector implosion a few years back.

- **fall on one' ass** 엉덩방아 찧다, 실패하다 (To fail completely)

[Ex] The ruling party fell on its ass to gain the popularity from the citizens.

- fizzle out 흐지부지되다 (To fail or to end in a weak or disappointing way)

[Ex] It is estimated today that nearly half of all first-time marriages will fizzle out.

- **flop** 완전히 실패하다 (To fail miserably)

[Ex] The film flopped badly at the box office.

- **go west** 죽다, 못쓰게 되다, (돈 등이) 없어지다 (To fail)

[Ex] The number of times that a marriage went west was no particular surprise.

- not get to first base (사업, 관계 등에서) 1단계를 넘지 못하다[순조롭게 출발하지 못하다]

[Ex] If that doesn't happen, we haven't even got to first base.

- **screw** ~을 엉망으로 하다[망치다] (To err; mess up)

[Ex] He screwed that interview.

- **tank** 완전히 망하다 (To decline and fail suddenly, come to an end)

[Ex] His regime will tank soon.

Slang

- crap out 실패하다, 망쳐 놓다, 못쓰게 되다 (When something stops operating properly)

[Ex] Freaking controller crapped out.

7-3. Fail Utterly and Completely (완전히 망하다, 완전히 실패하다)

Formal

come to nothing; go out of business; crash; hit bottom; come to naught

Informal

- blow something sky-high 완전히 망치다, 실패하다 (To destroy or ruin)

  [Ex] One word in the wrong quarter and this whole thing might blow sky-high.

- choke something off (긴장하거나 해서) 망치다[실패하다] (To stop in midstream)

  [Ex] It would damage British industry, choke off foreign investment and destroy jobs.

- crash and burn 잡쳐 버리다 (To have a spectacular failure or fall from grace)

  [Ex] Dude, if you don't stop doing crack, you're going to crash and burn.

- deep-six (계획 등을) 포기하다 (To abandon; to get rid of; to ignore)

  [Ex] I'm sick and tired of the deal we made. It's time to deep-six that shit.

- **go belly up** 완전히 망하다 (To die; to be ruined financially)

  [Ex] Did you hear his business went belly up?

- go down in flames 파멸하다, 못 쓰게 되다 (To fail completely)

  [Ex] I suspect the American auto industry will never learn, and will go down in flames because of it.

- go down like a lead balloon 파멸하다, 못 쓰게 되다 (To fail completely)

  [Ex] I tried it yesterday and it went down like a lead balloon.

- **go down the drain** 헛수고[수포]로 돌아가다, 못 쓰게 되다, (회사가) 도산[파산]하다

  [Ex] Years of work went down the drain.

- go down the tubes 못 쓰게 되다, 도산倒産하다 (To fail)

  [Ex] The country was going down the tubes economically.

- go over like a lead balloon 완전히 망하다 (To fail completely)

  [Ex] Their experiment went over like a lead balloon.

- **go up in flames** 꺼져 없어지다 (To fail completely)

  [Ex] If anything happens again, his whole career could go up in flames.

- **go up in smoke** (계획, 희망 등이) 연기처럼 사라지다[수포로 돌아가다] (To fail)

  [Ex] His career went up in smoke after a steroids scandal.

- pack it in 일[활동]을 그만두다 (To close down work for the moment)

  [Ex] Hey boss, I'm going to pack it in.

- **pull the plug on** ~의 생명 유지 장치를 떼다, ~을 죽이다, 제거하다

  [Ex] Now computer suppliers are threatening to pull the plug on the business.

- **scratch** (행사, 경기 참가 등을[에서]) 취소[제외]하다 (To cancel; to get rid of; to give up on)

  [Ex] The horse was scratched from the race because of injury.

- scupper 실패하게 하다, 좌절시키다 (To put an end to)

  [Ex] In my view that is a tactic designed to scupper the proposal.

- take a dive 일부러 져주다 (To purposely lose a fight; to fail)

  [Ex] The boxer was paid to take a dive.

- torpedo 그르치다, 망치다 (To destroy any endeavor with a stealthy, powerful attack)

  [Ex] Her comments had torpedoed the deal.

7-4. Cause to End (멈추다, 정지하다)

Formal

end; finish; shut down; call it a day; call it quits

Informal

- bite the big one 죽다 (To die or to get killed)

  [Ex] Do you think Joe will bite the big one?

- go tits-up 죽다, 작동을 멈추다 (To die or stop functioning)

  [Ex] The motor on my boat went tits-up today.

7-5. A Failure (실패)

Formal

collapse; defeat; loss; sinking ship; total loss; bomb; fiasco; flop; loser; mess;

misadventure; rout(완패, 괴멸)

- **crash** 1. 멈춤, 작동 정지, 고장 2. 멈추다, 고장 나다 (To shut down; cease to work, applied to a computer or program)

 [Ex] My computer crashed.

- end of the line 한계, 종말 (The very end; the definite end)

 [Ex] It was the end of the line for the urban farming experiment.

- **epic fail** 크나큰 실패 (A large failure)

 [Ex] Your post was lovely, but that particular statement was an epic fail.

- kiss of death 죽음의 키스, (언뜻 도움이 될 듯하나) 종국에 파멸을 가져오는 것

 [Ex] Her praise of my idea is the kiss of death.

- **meltdown** 원자로의 용융, 심각한 위기 (A serious failure in a system)

 [Ex] This financial meltdown is like watching ice cream melt on a hot summer day.

- **bust-up** 실패, (일의) 망침 (A failure)

 [Ex] Well it was only a matter of time before a bust up like this happened.

- clunker 심각한 실수 (A person, speech, product or other item that is a complete flop.)

 [Ex] Though Cruise appeared in the box-office clunker "Lions for Lambs", his track record is undeniable: He's finished first seven times.

- curtains 끝, 최후, 종말, 죽음, 해고 (When something is over; dying)

 [Ex] If you fuck with me, it's gonna be curtains.

- **muck-up** 1. 실패, (일의) 망침 (Mistake; failure) 2. 망치다

 [Ex] However, the fact is that they have made a muck-up of it and, as a consequence, it needs to be withdrawn.

- non-starter 애당초 (성공할) 가능성이 없는 것

 [Ex] The United States is certain to reject the proposal as a non-starter.

Chapter 11

Thinking
생각, 사고

인간의 생각이나 사고와 관련된 informal expression, slang의 양은 그다지 많지 않은 편입니다만, 몇 가지 중요한 표현들은 반드시 기억해 놓으시기 바랍니다.

1 *Believe*

믿다

Formal

accredit; give credence to; give weight to

- go along with ~에 동의하다 (To believe; to agree)

  [Ex] I don't go along with her views on private medicine.

- sign up for ~에 서명하다, ~을 믿다 (To sign; to believe)

  [Ex] It's the work he signed up for when he became a priest.

Informal

- **buy** (의견·설명 따위를) 받아들이다[수용하다], 믿다 (To be convinced to believe something)

  [Ex] I told him we were just friends but he wasn't buying it.

- eat something up 의심 없이 믿다 (To believe unquestioningly)

  [Ex] Those newbies eat up rumors about his hobby.

- gulp down (남의 말이나 의견을) 믿어 버리다 (To believe; to agree)

  [Ex] Both an accuser and her witness lied repeatedly; the district attorney actively abetted the deception; the media gulped the lies down whole.

- lap something up ~을 덥석[선뜻] 받아들이다 (To believe or accept eagerly and uncritically)

  [Ex] Think critically and don't lap up everything they tell you.

- swallow (의심 없이) ~을 받아들이다, 곧이곧대로 듣다 (To believe a lie)

  [Ex] I think they swallowed it.

- swallow hook, line, and sinker 모든 경고 신호도 무시하고 덜컥 믿어 버리다 (미끼를 물다 / To accept in every respect, ignoring every warning sign)

  [Ex] He swallowed the stupid story hook, line and sinker.

② Understand
이해하다

Formal

comprehend; figure out; grasp; make sense of; deduce; discern; fathom;

- **get it** 이해하다 (To understand)

[Ex] He didn't laugh at your joke because he didn't get it.

- **get the drift** (어찌 되어 있는지 또는 남이 하는 말을) 알다, 이해하다 (To understand)

[Ex] My German isn't very good, but I got the drift of what she said.

- **get the message** (힌트, 암시 등의) 뜻을 알아채다 (To understand)

[Ex] Oh, I get the message so you don't need to say more.

- **get the picture** (특히 다른 사람의 설명을 듣고 상황을) 이해하다 (To understand)

[Ex] Luke never tells you the whole story, but you always get the picture.

Informal

- **Capish** 이해하다 (보통 의문문으로 사용, 이탈리아어 방언에서 유래)

[Ex] Joey expects his money by Monday. Capish?

- **catch (one's) drift** 말을 알아듣다 (To understand; usually used aggressively)

[Ex] Have the money by Tuesday, or bad things will happen. You catch my drift?

- **catch on to** 이해하다 (To understand)

[Ex] He is very quick to catch on to things.

- **click** (불현듯) 딱 분명해지다[이해가 되다] (To understand)

[Ex] Suddenly it clicked. We'd been talking about different people.

- cotton on to 이해하다 (To understand or realize something after some difficulty, especially without people telling you about it)

[Ex] I suddenly cottoned on to what he was doing.

- **dig** 이해하다 (To perceive and comprehend the nature and significance of; grasp; gather.)

[Ex] A: Ya dig? / B: Yeah, I can dig it

- **dig it** 알다, 이해하다 (To understand)

[Ex] Can you dig it?

- get a line on ~에 관한 지식[정보]을 얻다, ~을 얻어듣다 (To secure information about)

  [Ex] I've got a line on a good used car.

- get it in one 이해가 빠르다 (To succeed in grasping the issue at hand quickly)

  [Ex] A: I don't think this job really suits me. / B: So you're thinking of leaving? / A: Yes, Dick, you've got it in one.

- **get the hand of** ~의 방법을 배우다 (To learn how to do something)

- get wise to ~을 알다, 알아[탐지해]내다, 눈치채다, 박식한 체하다 (To understand)

  [Ex] Dealers have already got wise to the trend and increased their prices accordingly.

- get[have] a person's number 남의 정체[본심, 약점]를 알다[간파하다], 남을 꿰뚫어 보다

  [Ex] "We've got your number now." Sarah said. "We know just what you like and don't think we won't use it to our advantage."

- latch on to ~을 이해하다 (To understand)

  [Ex] I think we were a little bit slow to latch on to that.

- nail (the concept) (개념을) 이해하다 (To understand)

  [Ex] But we've finally nailed the key elements.

- pick up on ~을 이해하다[알아차리다] (To understand)

  [Ex] She failed to pick up on the humor in his remark.

- read somebody[something] 이해하다 (To understand)

  [Ex] I think you guys are reading me wrong, but that's OK.

- **see where somebody is coming from** ~의 처지를 이해하다, ~의 입장을 이해하다

  (To understand another's viewpoint)

  [Ex] I can see where you are coming from, Calleva, however I most disagree.

- wrap (one's) mind around 이해하다 (To understand)

  [Ex] We have things that need to get done that don't necessarily include following souls around town with you. Ok? Can you wrap your little head around that?

③ *Evaluate*

평가하다, 살펴보다

Formal

check; evaluate; look over; review; check out; size up; appraise; assess; take something's measure

Informal

- get a load of somebody[something] ~ 좀 봐[들어 봐] (To take a look at; examine)

[Ex] Get a load of that!

- **get an eyeful** (흥미롭거나 특이한 것을) 유심히 보다 (To obtain a full view of)

[Ex] Walk down the average city street and you'll get an eyeful of modernist ar-chitecture.

- give somebody[something] the up-and-down 아래위로 훑어보다

[Ex] A: "Did you see that guy checking you out?" / B: "Yeah, he totally gave me the up and down!"

- give somebody the once-over 한번 훑어보다 (To examine; to evaluate)

[Ex] I gave them a once-over, but they weren't much help.

- **keep a tab on** 주시하다 (To watch with vigilance)

[Ex] How do you evaluate and keep a tab on just exactly how the sub-contractors are delivering?

- **keep one's eyes peeled** 계속 경계하고 있다, 눈을 바짝 뜨고 있다 (To stay visually alert)

[Ex] We kept our eyes peeled for any signs of life.

- **kick the tires** 품질을 살펴보다, 검사하다 (To examine; to check out before making a purchase)

[Ex] People need to start kicking the tires; it's a buyer's market.

- **scope out** ~을 자세히 살피다 (To examine or investigate)

[Ex] I was scoping out that hot soccer player after practice.

4 *Know*

알다

Formal

be acquainted with; know; be on top of; be versed in

Informal

- **have down pat** ~을 완벽하게 숙지하고 있다

  [Ex] She has all our names and cellphone numbers down pat.

- know something backwards (and forwards) 속속들이 알다 (To know perfectly)

  [Ex] She knew the material for her presentation backwards and forwards.

- know something[someone] inside out 속속들이 알다 (To know perfectly)

  [Ex] I know Martin inside out but I have a few other people in mind.

- know something like the back of one's hand 속속들이 알다 (To know intimately)

  [Ex] Our forces are completely bogged down, in difficult terrain the enemy knows like the back of their hands.

- know the score 사정을 알다[이해하고 있다]

  [Ex] The people are watching; they know the score with this government.

5 *Find Out*
찾아내다

Formal

detect; determine; find out; reveal; uncover; ascertain; divine; perceive; reveal; unearth; unmask;

- ferret out ~을 캐내다[찾아내다] (To find out)

[Ex] We have not ferreted out all the facts, but we are comfortable with the charges filed today.

- sniff something out 냄새[후각]로 ~을 알아[찾아내다] (To uncover)

[Ex] Journalists are good at sniffing out a scandal.

Forget
잊다

Formal

- **let bygones be bygones** 지난 일은 잊어버리기로 하다

[Ex] Okay, Sally, let bygones be bygones. Let's forgive and forget.

Informal

- go blank (마음 따위가) 텅 비다 (To forget; have one's mind "go blank")

  [Ex] When my name was read out, my mind went blank.

- space out (특히 마약에 취해) 멍해 있다

  [Ex] I was supposed to pick him up at the airport but I spaced out.

Chapter 12

Money
돈, 금액

돈과 관련된 informal expressions, slang도 그 수가 많지는 않지만, 사람들의 실생활에서 가장 중심이 되는 것이므로, formal한 표현보다는 생동감을 줄 수 있는 informal한 표현들이 더 많이 사용되기도 합니다. 따라서 중요한 표현들은 반드시 기억해 두어야 합니다.

1 *Amount*
금액, 액수

1-1. Small Amount (적은 금액)

Formal

mite; small change; pin money; paltry sum; pittance

Informal

- **chicken feed** 하찮은 것[사람], 적은 양 (Small amount)

  [Ex] It's impossible to live on such a chicken feed salary.
- **peanuts** 아주 적은 액수 (A small number or amount; very little money)

  [Ex] He gets paid peanuts for doing that job.
- shoestring 소액의 돈 (Small amount of money)

  [Ex] They are surviving on a shoestring.

1-2. Large Amount (많은 금액의 돈)

Formal

fortune; riches; treasure; wealth; affluence; opulence

Informal

- arm and leg 거액의 돈, 막대한 경비 (A lot of money)

  [Ex] My surgery cost an arm and a leg.

- **big bucks** 많은 돈 (A large sum of money)

[Ex] He made big bucks playing the stock market.

- boodle 많은 돈 (A large but unspecified amount of money)

[Ex] The country was pulling out of debt, and the treasury had enough boodle.

- cool million 엄청나게 많은 돈 (A large but unspecified amount of money)

[Ex] He even managed to blow a cool million pounds of Labor party funds on a stillborn election campaign.

- **deep pockets** 충분한 자력, 강력한 자금 줄

[Ex] I heard Johnny's pockets run deep. You should ask him out!

- king's ransom 왕의 몸값, 막대한 금액, 한 재산 (A large amount of money)

[Ex] Although we in this place are not paid a king's ransom, we are paid significantly more than that.

- megabucks 엄청난 돈 (A large amount of money)

[Ex] He's making megabucks at his new job.

- mint 엄청난 돈 (A lot of money; Usually "a mint")

[Ex] He died with a mint of money.

- **tidy sum** 많은 양, 많은 금액 (A large amount)

[Ex] We have a tidy sum put away after 2 years of budgeting for our fuel bills in this way.

② *Cost*
가격, 원가

2-1. Free (공짜, 무료)

Formal

without charge

Informal

- comp (입장권, 음식 등의) 무료, 증정 (Received without charge; complimentary)

  [Ex] Harry's uncle got comped a steak dinner at Harrah's after winning at Craps.

- **free lunch** 공짜 (Lunch received without charge; usually used in "There's no (such thing as a) free lunch. 이 세상에 공짜는 없는 법이다.")

  [Ex] There's no such thing as a free lunch.

- **free ride** 무임승차, 불로소득 (Riding without paying; earnings without working)

  [Ex] I've had an opponent every time. I've never had a free ride. I've had to fight.

- **freebie** 공짜 (Something given away for free)

  [Ex] Jeanie got promotional freebies at a new spa and asked us if we wanted to go get massages.

- **giveaway** 공짜, 거저, 경품 (Free samples)

  [Ex] Her name was called as one of five finalists in the car giveaway.

2-2. Overcharge (바가지 씌우다)

Formal

cheat; pad

Informal

- gip[gyp] 1. 바가지 2. 바가지를 씌우다 (To cheat; to deceive)

  [Ex] That meal was a real gyp.

- gouge 바가지를 씌우다, 값을 부당하게 올리다 (To exact or extort a large amount money)

  [Ex] Big oil claims they are not gouging customers.

- **rip off** ~에게 바가지를 씌우다, 바가지(요금) (To give someone a bad bargain)

  [Ex] Premier League tickets are a rip off.

- sell somebody a lemon 고장 난 물건(특히 자동차)을 팔다

  [Ex] If you want to succeed in your business, never sell anybody a lemon.

- soak 많은 돈을 우려내다 (To cheat)

  [Ex] He was accused of soaking his clients.

③ *Wealth*
빈부

3-1. Poor (가난한, 돈이 없는, 쪼들리는)

Formal

badly off; in debt; penniless; broke; destitute; impecunious; indigent; penurious; poverty-stricken;

- **in the red** 빚지고, 적자로, 적자상태로

[Ex] James is horrible at selling things. If everyone were like him we'd be in the red in no time.

Informal

- **belly up** 도산하다 (Bankrupt; failed; dead)

[Ex] Last year the business went belly up after one of the partners resigned.

- **busted** 돈 한 푼 없는 (With no money left)

[Ex] I'm busted but no one helps me.

- cleaned out 돈을 다 털린 (With no money left)

[Ex] You guys have cleaned me out!

- down-and-out 빈털터리인, 노숙자 신세인 (With no money left)

[Ex] There are so many down and out bums on the streets here.

- **flat broke** 완전 거덜 난[쪽박을 차게 된] (Completely broke)

[Ex] There is no more money - we're broke, flat broke.

- **hard up** (특히 짧은 기간 동안) 돈에 쪼들리는 (Not having enough cash, money; broke)

[Ex] We're a bit hard up at the moment.

- in hock 저당 잡혀, 빚을 져서 (With no money left; be in debt)

[Ex] The government is in hock for trillions but doesn't worry too much about that.

- pinch 돈에[경제적으로] 쪼들림 (With no money left)

  [Ex] The Smiths used to go abroad every year, but they're feeling the pinch since he retired.

- **stone[stony]-broke** 빈털터리 (Completely without money)

  [Ex] I'm stony/stone broke at the moment.

- **strapped (for cash[money])** 빈털터리의 (Without money)

  [Ex] Village halls have been strapped for cash since 1997 as lottery money has been diverted to other causes.

- strapped out 돈이 떨어진 (Pressed for money)

  [Ex] I'm strapped out today.

- without a bean 땡전 한 푼 없는 (With no money left)

  [Ex] The old lady was evicted without a bean.

- without a red cent 땡전 한 푼 없는 (Extremely poor)

  [Ex] Then things go from bad to worse: the old lady dies, leaving them without a red cent to their name.

Slang

- piss-poor 찢어지게 가난한, 믿을 수 없을 정도로 품질이 낮은

  [Ex] The "piss poor" Americans you refer to constitute about 40% of the population of the USA.

- without a pot to piss in 찢어지게 가난한 (Extremely poor)

  [Ex] All my friends knew I didn't have a pot to piss in.

3-2. Rich (부유한, 부자인, 풍족한)

Formal

have money in the bank; well-heeled; well-to-do; on easy street; well-off; moneyed

- **in the black** (경영이) 흑자로 (Business term meaning a positive amount of money)

  [Ex] James is an amazing sales agent, so he helps keep the company in the black.

Informal

- **flush** (돈을) 많이 가진 (Rich; having money)

  [Ex] He/she is flush.

- heeled 돈이 많은 (well-heeled의 준말 / Shortening of well-heeled)

  [Ex] They all seem to be well heeled people.

- in clover 풍족한 (To be in a pleasant situation; to be in ease and luxury; to be in prosperity)

  [Ex] His bills were paid, his homework was done, and he was heading off on vacation: He was in clover!

- in the money 주가가 액면가보다 높은 상태에 있음

  [Ex] Sweet! My call options are back in the money. Now I'd better exercise them.

- **loaded** 아주 돈이 많은 (Really rich; "loaded" with money)

  [Ex] "Man, why you with that girl? She's a bitch and she's got you whipped!" / "She's loaded… you ever see that pimped-out Ferrari she drives around in?" (pimped-out; 멋진)

- rolling in dough 아주 돈이 많은 (Very rich)

  [Ex] French farmers are rolling in dough.

- rolling in money 아주 돈이 많은 (Very rich)

  [Ex] They may be short of water, but they are rolling in money.

- stinking of money 돈이 엄청 많은 (Very rich)

  [Ex] They are stinking of money.

- worth a bundle 가치가 높은 (Having a high value)

  [Ex] Dividend income, which can be worth a bundle, is not included.

4 Payment

지급

4-1. Pay (지급하다, 돈을 치르다)

Formal

chip in; dish out; foot the bill; pay out; bear the expense; remit

Informal

- ante up (돈을) 내다, 치르다 (To pay; to contribute one's share)

  [Ex] Some parents ante up big bucks to send their kids to prep school.
- come through with 갚다 (To pay)

  [Ex] The bank finally came through with the money.
- **cough up** (돈)을 마지못해 주다

  [Ex] Come on, cough up. It's your turn to pay.
- **fork out[over]** (특히 마지못해 ~에) 돈을 들이다 (To pay for)

  [Ex] Why fork out for a taxi when there's a perfectly good bus service?
- **kick in** (할당된) 돈을 내다, 헌금하다 (To contribute)

  [Ex] Can you kick in a few dollars for dinner?
- pony up 돈을 내다[지불하다] (To pay for; to contribute an amount of money)

  [Ex] Can you pony up some cash for the keg?
- **shell out** (~에 거금을) 들이다[쏟아붓다] (To pay)

  [Ex] I had to shell out quite a bit for that ring.

<u>4-2.</u> Avoid Paying (지불을 미루다, 지불을 거절하다)

Formal

defraud; shirk; swindle

Informal

- beat 돈을 떼먹다 (To cheat by not paying)

  [Ex] You got beat for 20 bucks.

- bilk (특히 돈을) 사취하다, (사람을) 속이다 (To cheat money)

  [Ex] They are charged with bilking investors out of millions of dollars.

- diddle 사기 치다 (To cheat or swindle)

  [Ex] He diddled me out of that job.

- do somebody out of 속이다, 사기 치다 (To cheat or swindle)

  [Ex] Nobody is going to do me out of anything.

5 *Ways to Get Money*
돈 얻는[버는] 방법

5-1. **Beg** (구걸하다)

Formal

beg; pass the hat; freeload; panhandle; solicit alms

Informal

- **bum** 남에게 기식하다, 빌어먹다

  [Ex] Poor Charlie had to go on the bum.

- cadge 구걸[걸식]하다 (To get items by sponging or begging)

  [Ex] Can I cadge a ciggy?

- grub 구걸하다 (To scrounge; to beg)

  [Ex] I am not surprised that the Tories are grubbing after the Asian vote.

- **mooch** 빌붙다, 빈대 붙다 (To obtain or try to obtain by begging)

  [Ex] He's been mooching cigarettes all night.

- scrounge (공짜로) 얻어 내다 (To get by asking or begging)

  [Ex] The government did not give them money, forcing them to scrounge for food.

- **sponge** (돈, 먹을 것 등을 얻기 위해) 빌붙다, 뜯어먹다 (To get money from other people)

  [Ex] He became fed up with having to sponge off his wife.

5-2. **Make a Profit** (이윤을 보다, 거금을 벌다)

Formal

bring home; bring in; earn; make a profit

- cash in 경제적으로 성공[번창]하다, (돈 따위를) 벌다 (To make a profit)

  [Ex] Warner is hoping to cash in on this billion people market but it won't be easy.

- clean up 거금을 벌다 (To make a large profit)

  [Ex] This film should clean up at the box offices.

- gravy 수월한 돈벌이, 노다지판 (Money or profit acquired easily, especially tips or bonuses)

  [Ex] We expect to at least make back our investment. Anything over that is gravy.

- **hit it big** 성공하다, 잘 되어가다, 큰 이윤을 남기다 (To make a large profit)

  [Ex] But friends of the actress say they knew she'd hit it big.

- line one's pockets 부정한 방법으로 자기 주머니를 채우다

  [Ex] The Bill's provisions will provide the best possible support for complainants; they are not about lining the pockets of the legal profession.

- make a bundle 떼돈 벌다 (To earn a great deal of money)

  [Ex] Technologies don't emerge unless there's someone who thinks he can make a bundle by helping them emerge.

- make a fast buck 돈을 손쉽게[금방금방] 벌다 (To enjoy a quick financial success)

  [Ex] We've all lost, except for those making a fast buck on the back of the current financial climate.

- **make a killing** 갑자기 큰돈을 벌다[크게 한몫 잡다] (To make a lot of money)

  [Ex] He made a killing in the stock market.

- make it big 크게 성공하다 (To make a large profit)

  [Ex] Since I got my foot in the door, I might as well make it big.

- make out like a bandit 큰 이윤을 남기다 (To make a large profit)

  [Ex] If the purchase price is low and the sale price is high enough, then the government makes out like a bandit.

- rake it in 한밑천 잡다[벌다], 돈을 긁어 들이다 (To make a large profit)

[Ex] Yes, after a blip last year, bankers are raking it in again.

- shake the money tree (큰) 이익을 낳다, 크게 벌다 (To make a large profit)

  [Ex] The businessman shook the money tree.

Slang

- ass-dough 쉽게 벌리는 돈, 앉아만 있어도 벌리는 돈

  [Ex] Bill: I have a great job! All I do is sit on my ass and make money! / Fred: Yep, good ol' ass dough. Your living the dream buddy. Doesn't get any better than ass dough.

6 *Money*
돈

Informal

- Benjamin 미국 100달러 지폐 (Short or slang expression for a 100 dollar bill because Benjamin Franklin's face is on the front side of it.)

  [Ex] What is in this bag? It's full of Benjamins!

- **bill** 100달러 (One hundred dollars)

  [Ex] That'll cost you six bills.

- **buck** 달러 (dollar, Money)

  [Ex] My Nintendo DS costs 150 bucks.

- c-note 미화 100달러 지폐 (A $100 bill; Origin: the Roman numeral for 100 is C.)

  [Ex] Do you have change for a c-note?

- cold cash 현금 (Ready money)

  [Ex] I got the cold cash to pay for that car.

- dime 10센트 백동화 (A US coin worth ten cents)

  [Ex] Deposit a dime and dial your number.

- dinero 돈, 현찰 (스페인어로 돈의 의미임 / Money; from the Spanish word for money)

  [Ex] I don't really need extra dinero when I have a life to live. Cash is trash.

- **dough** 돈, 현찰 (Money)

  [Ex] Dad works at a lumber mill. Mom answers phones at a radio station nearby. Neither of them was rolling in the dough.

- ducats 돈 (더커츠, 12~16세기에 유럽 대륙에서 사용하던 화폐의 단위 / Money)

  [Ex] Hey man, you got any ducats I can borrow?

- **green** 돈, 지폐 (greenback, Money; Paper currency in the United States is green in color.)

  [Ex] But if they buy Euros instead, the green could collapse.

- **greenback** 미국 달러화 지폐 (Paper currency of United States dollars)

  [Ex] That will set you back a few greenbacks.

- hard cash 현금 (A large sum of money consisting of coins)

[Ex] Companies are also reporting alarming shortages of hard cash as the credit crunch bites.

- kick-back 킥백, 리베이트, 뇌물

[Ex] The congressman received a ten-percent kick back for supporting the legislation that would give the mining company exclusive rights to the region.

- kopecks 러시아의 화폐 단위, 약간의 돈

[Ex] He admits that money can't buy happiness, saying he was happy back when he did not have a kopeck to his name.

- moola[moolah] 돈, 금전 (Money)

[Ex] Those shoes cost a lot of moola.

- shekels 세켈(이스라엘의 통화 단위), 돈

[Ex] Rounds for Kalashnikov sell for seven shekels each, out of range for the militias.

Chapter 13

Quantity and Size
양과 크기의 표현

American English speaker들은 숫자나 크기를 어떻게 잘 표현할까에 관심이 많습니다. 따라서 사물의 양과 크기를 informal expression이나 속어들을 사용하여 표현하는 것을 자주 접할 수 있습니다. 이번 장에서는 양과 크기에 관련된 다양한 표현들을 정리합니다.

1 How Many

1-1. Zero (영, 0)

Formal

naught; ought; void

Informal

- goose egg (경기에서) 무득점, 0점 (Zero point)

  [Ex] His parents grounded him due to a goose egg on math test.
- **nada** 아무것도 없음, 무無(nothingness, Nothing, Nothing new)

  [Ex] A: "Hey, what's up?" / B: "Nada."
- **nix** 아무것도 없음, 무 (Nothing)

  [Ex] There's nix to do!
- zilch 무無, 영零 (Nothing)

  [Ex] Government's reply to those problems is nothing, absolutely zilch.
- **zip** 무無, 영零 (Nothing)

  [Ex] The score was three-zip.

1-2. A Large Number (많은 수)

Informal

- bazillion 엄청난 수 (A very large number)

  [Ex] There are a bazillion ways to leak stuff from any office, for anyone with any tech savvy at all.

- gazillion 엄청난 수 (A very large number; gadzillion)

[Ex] When they submitted their idea to the Pepsi Refresh project, it got a gazillion votes.

- gadzillion (상상 속의) 무한대의 숫자

[Ex] Most dogs elsewhere in the remaining gadzillion square miles of the US are mutts.

- **jillion** 막대한 수(의) (zillion, An extremely large number or amount)

[Ex] The Southeast has about a jillion different sauce recipes and they vary from town to town.

- mucho 1. 많은, 풍족한 2. 대단히, 굉장히 ("Much" in Spanish)

[Ex] You are being mucho dramatic, my dear.

- squillion (수가) 엄청나게 많음

[Ex] But now squillions of people are desperate to look younger.

- **umpteen** 아주 많은, 무수한 (Many; countless)

[Ex] I've told you umpteen times, but you keep mistaking the same mistake.

- **zillion** 엄청난 수 (A very large number)

[Ex] Do I have to say "sorry" zillion times?

2 *How Much*
양

2-1. Small Amount (적은 양)

Formal

bit; chunk; few; fragment; mite; modicum

Informal

- beans 소량, 약간 (A small amount)

  [Ex] He doesn't know beans about it.

- dollop 소량, 약간 (A small amount)

  [Ex] The best science books are low on dogma and usually contain dollops of doubt.

- glob 한 방울의 작은 양 (A small round amount)

  [Ex] The container drops to the floor and thick globs of cheese roll out.

- **itty-bitty** 작은, 조그만 (Small; tiny)

  [Ex] A: I love you, sweetheart. You have the most adorable itty-bitty titties I've ever seen. / B: Gee, thanks. And you have the most adorable itty-bitty weenie I've ever seen.

- **lick** 조금, 소량 (A small amount)

  [Ex] I don't speak a lick of Russian.

- nibble (조금 베어 문) 한 입 (A small piece)

  [Ex] She ate just a nibble.

- skosh 적은, 적은 양의 (일본어에서 유래)

  [Ex] The "original" clip was a skosh too long, without enough insane laughing.

- **small beer** 보잘것없는 사람[것] (A trifling matter)

  [Ex] It is small beer in the totality of things.

- **small potatoes** 조금, 소량 (A small amount)

  [Ex] It is still small potatoes but it is growing almost exponentially.

- smidgen 아주 조금, 아주 작은 조각 (A small amount)

  [Ex] I speak French and Spanish fluently and have a smidgen of Russian and German.

- **tad** 적은 양 (A small amount)

  [Ex] Could you turn the sound down just a tad?

2-2. A Large Amount (많은 양)

Formal

good deal; great deal; mass; bounty; galore; plethora; crammed with; more than enough; overflowing with; jam-packed with; brimming with; replete with;

- and a half 많은 양(A large amount), 굉장한 것

[Ex] That was a game and a half!

- **bellyful** 배 가득함, 만복, (of) 충분함

[Ex] I've had a bellyful of his complaining. If he doesn't stop, I'm leaving.

- **bursting at the seams with** 솔기가 터져나갈 정도로 많다[크다] (Having a large amount)

[Ex] The MacMall catalog is bursting at the seams with the latest and the greatest Apple computers, iPods, accessories, software or consumer electronics you might need.

- bushels 많은 양 (A large amount)

[Ex] We don't fill up the rockets with bushels of money and send it off to Mars.

- chock-a-block with 꽉 들어찬, 꽉 찬 (Filled to capacity or beyond)

[Ex] The window display is chock-a-block with the latest literary fiction, as well as more idiosyncratic offerings.

- gobs 많은 양 (A large amount)

[Ex] There's gobs of bad language, not to mention bad dialogue, and sexual situations.

- **heaps** 많음 (A large amount)

[Ex] I have heaps of homework.

- oceans 엄청나게 많은 (양의) (A large amount of something)

[Ex] The oceans of money have washed through the hospitals and left them crusted in filth and menaced by debt.

- **piles** 많은 ~, ~ 무더기 (A large amount)

[Ex] I have piles of work to do today.

- slathers 대량, 다수, 듬뿍 (A large amount)

[Ex] He has slathers of money.

- **tons** 아주 많은 양 (Many or much)

[Ex] Tons of people die of starvation every day.

- up to the eyeballs with ~이 엄청 많은 (With a large amount of)

[Ex] The medics dosed me up to the eyeballs with medication.

- **wall-to-wall with** ~로 가득히 깔린

[Ex] The movie is wall-to-wall with violence, much of it augmented by special effects.

- whole lot 아주 많이 (A large amount of)

[Ex] There were a whole lot of people I didn't know.

- **filthy with** 더럽게 많은 (Having a very large amount of)

[Ex] The train itself was filthy with beer cans rolling up the aisle.

- **lousy with** ~가 지천으로 널린, 많이 있는 (So many with; so much with)

[Ex] This place is lousy with tourists in August.

- shedload 엄청난 양 (특히 돈 / A large amount)

[Ex] I've got shedloads of work to do.

- **stinking with** ~가 역겨울 정도로 많은 (With extremely large amount of)

[Ex] She is stinking with money.

- ass-load 많은 양 (A great quantity; More than a butt-load but less than a shit-load)

[Ex] I would have bought that comic book collection, but they wanted an ass-load of money for it.

- buttload 많은 양 (An extremely large quantity of anything that takes up space)

[Ex] I drank a buttload last night and had to get my stomach pumped from the resulting alcohol poisoning.

- **shitload** 대량, 다수, 잔뜩 (A large amount)

[Ex] I've made a shitload of money in the last week. Tate said he would cut me a check for the download fees at the end of the week.

- **up the ass** 완전히, 철저히, 엄청 많은

[Ex] I've got e-mails up the ass!

영어 표현에도 등급이 있다!

- up the gazoo 완전히, 철저히, 엄청 많은 (An excessive amount of something)

  [Ex] To start with, he's got academic troubles up the gazoo.
- up the wazoo 대량으로 (An excessive amount of something)

  [Ex] He's got money up the wazoo!
- **up to the ass with** ~이 엄청 많은 (With a large amount of)

  [Ex] She's got awards up the ass.

2-3. All (전체, 모두, 모조리)

Formal

grand total; sum total

Informal

- full monte[monty] (필요한) 모든 것, 발가벗은 알몸뚱이 (Everything you need; nakedness)

  [Ex] They'll do the full monty if you pay them enough.
- whole bag of tricks 전부, 모조리 다 (Everything)

  [Ex] Hotel managers are using a whole new bag of tricks to attract their guests.
- whole enchilada 전부, 모조리 다 (Everything)

  [Ex] We had a great time on vacation, and it only cost us $500 for the whole enchilada.
- whole hog 전부, 모조리 다 (Everything)

  [Ex] Well, I thought, I've already lost half my job, I might as well go the whole hog and lose it completely.
- whole kit and caboodle 전부, 모조리 다 (Everything)

  [Ex] Offloading the whole kit and caboodle into the private sector with a big government guarantee was never going to fly.
- **whole nine yards** 모든 것, (필요한 것이 다 들어간) 완전한 것 (Everything)

  [Ex] Full of outrageous fun and adventure, it goes the whole nine yards for family fun.
- whole shebang 전부, 모조리 다 (shebang은 '셔뱅'으로 발음함 / Everything)

  [Ex] The whole shebang from top to bottom are rotten to the core, regardless from what party they hail.

Chapter 14

Speed and Travel
속도, 이동

현대 사회의 속성이라 할 수 있는 speed의 추구와 과학 기술의 발달은 자동차 운전, 속도, 이동과 연관된 다양한 표현들의 등장을 가져왔습니다. 또한, 범죄의 발달로 도주, 탈출과 관련된 속어들도 자주 접하게 됩니다. 이번 장에서는 속도, 이동, 달림, 움직임, 탈출 등에 관련된 표현들을 정리합니다.

1 Moving Along

달림, 움직임

1-1. Speed in a Vehicle (차를 고속으로 몰다)

Informal

- barrel (along) (차)를 고속으로 몰다 (To speed)

  [Ex] A rusted, yellow Model-T barrels along the rickety dock.

- belt (along) 질주하다 (To move with great speed or to hurry)

  [Ex] He was really belting along.

- **burn rubber** 타이어에 불이 나게 달려가다

  [Ex] To run away from him, she burnt rubber.

- clip 질주하다, 빨리 날다, 빠른 속도 (To speed)

  [Ex] We were going at a good clip.

- **flat-out** 전속력의, 빠르게, 전력을 다한 (At full capacity; at maximum speed; totally; thoroughgoing)

  [Ex] Then I found out the girl he wanted me to work with does escort work so I flat-out turned him down.

- **floor it** 가속 페달을 힘껏 밟다 (To hit the acceleration pedal)

  [Ex] That fucker's getting away, FLOOR IT!

- Give her the gun! 차의 속도를 높여라! (To speed a car)

- Let her rip! (배, 차, 기계 따위를) 최고 속도로 몰아라! (To set something in top speed)

- **put the pedal to the metal** 차를 전속력으로 몰다 (To speed in a vehicle)

  [Ex] Look, we're running a little late so we kind of need to put the pedal to the metal.

- **Step on it!** (특히 빨리 차를 몰라는 뜻의 명령문으로) 세게[빨리] 밟아라! (To drive quickly)

- **Step on the gas!** (특히 빨리 차를 몰라는 뜻의 명령문으로) 세게[빨리] 밟아라!

영어 표현에도 등급이 있다!

1-2. Move or Dance Very Fast (아주 빨리 걷거나 춤을 추다)

Informal

- boogie 춤추다, 빨리 움직이다 (To dance or move quickly)

  [Ex] Jay is boogieing between Calista and Amy.

- hoof it (빨리) 걸어가다 (To walk fast)

  [Ex] I saw 'em comin' and hoofed it home. ('em = them; comin' = coming)

1-3. Go Very Fast (아주 빨리 가다)

Formal

be quick; cover ground; gallop; open the throttle;

- go flat-out 전속력을 다하다 (To go with full speed)

[Ex] I wasn't sure if I should start gradually and build myself up or jump in and go flat out.

- **go full blast** 전속력을 다하다 (To go (operate) at full capacity)

[Ex] I don't think he'll be urging his players to go full blast to win this game.

- go like a bat out of hell 엄청 빠르게 가다 (To go very fast)

[Ex] It's no wonder the witnesses got the impression that he was riding like a bat out of hell.

- go like a shot 엄청 빠르게 가다 (To go very fast)

[Ex] If I had rich friends who invited me on holiday I would go like a shot from a gun.

- go like blaze 엄청 빠르게 가다 (To go very fast)

[Ex] If I had the chance to go there, I'd go like blaze.

- go like greased lightning 아주 빨리 (신나게) 달리다 (To move very fast)

[Ex] After the phone call, he was out of the door like greased lightning.

- **make it snappy** (남에게 하는 말로) 빨리해 (Hurry up!)

[Ex] Could I get a refill on this Coke? And make it snappy.

- **scoot** 급히 가다, 급히 떠나다 (To go or leave quickly)

  [Ex] I'd better scoot or I'll be late.
- **zip** (차·총알 등이) '핑'하고 소리 내며 나아가다 (To move; go very fast)

  [Ex] A sports car zipped past us.
- zippy 아주 빠른 (Very fast)

  [Ex] Even with my zippy home wireless connection, the movie had an estimated two-hour download time.

Informal

- go like hell 엄청 빠르게 가다 (To go very fast)

  [Ex] You're driving just over the limit, but they're going like hell.
- go like the devil 엄청 빠르게 가다 (To go very fast)

  [Ex] I went like the devil, but I still missed the bus.
- **haul ass** 서두르다, 급히 떠나다 (To move at a rapid speed)

  [Ex] I saw him ten minutes ago, haulin' ass up Broadway to get here on time.
- shake a leg (남에게 하는 말로) 빨리빨리 시작해라[움직여라] (To hurry)

  [Ex] Alright, ladies, shake a leg. Keep truckin'.
- zap 재빠르게 가다 (To go[move] very fast)

  [Ex] The racing cars zapped past us.
- zing 빠르게 움직이다 (To move[go] very fast)

  [Ex] You could hear the thud as Essien's right boot connected and the ball zinged forwards.

1-4. Move Quickly and Effortlessly (빠르게 또는 힘 안 들이고 움직이다)

Formal

cruise; glide; sail

Informal

- **streak** 전속력으로[쏜살같이] 가다 (To run very quickly)

  [Ex] You can often see meteors streak across the sky from here.
- **waltz** 잽싸게 하다 (To move quickly and effortlessly)

  [Ex] He just waltzed off with my car!

1-5. Depart in a Hurry (서둘러 출발하다)

Formal

flee; bolt; cut loose; hotfoot; run like a bunny; scamper;

- **clear off** 달아나다, 가 버리다 (To leave)

  [Ex] He cleared off when he heard the police siren.

- **hightail (it)** 꽁지가 빠지게[몹시 서둘러] 떠나다 (To go or move in a great hurry)

  [Ex] Eventually she regained her composure, smiled awkwardly and hightailed it away from the scene.

- **scoot** 서둘러 가다 (To leave; to depart speedily)

  [Ex] Wow, is that the time? I've got to scoot!

- **skip town** 갑자기 떠나다, 몰래 도망치다(To leave without a trace), 마을을 도망치다

  [Ex] He was facing up to three years in prison when he skipped town before his sentencing in 1992.

Informal

- blow (지체 없이) 떠나가다, 줄행랑 치다 (To leave; to depart speedily)

  [Ex] Gotta blow, catch you later.

- breeze 갑자기 떠나다 (To leave quickly)

  [Ex] Yo this party is wack. I'm about to breeze.

- take a powder 갑자기 떠나다, 달아나다 (To run away; to leave)

  [Ex] He stole the jewelry and took a powder.

1-6. Escape (탈출하다)

Formal

flee; go scot-free; take flight;

- **break out** (~로부터) 도망치다, 탈옥하다 (To escape; leave)

  [Ex] A group of prisoners rushed an officer and managed to break out.

- make a break for it 탈주를 시도하다 (To try to escape)

  [Ex] Six prisoners shot a guard and made a break for it in a stolen car.

- blow(fly) the coop (~로부터) 도망치다, 탈옥하다 (To leave suddenly; to escape from prison)

  [Ex] I saw the news that some criminals blew the coop yesterday.

- bust out (~로부터) 도망치다, 탈옥하다

  [Ex] Oh shit! She's waking up. Let's bust out of here!

- leg it 달리다, 달아나다 (To run away)

  [Ex] Leg it – it's the police!

- **make oneself scarce** 빠르게 떠나다 (To leave quickly)

  [Ex] Her unmarried mother died shortly after she was born; her father has made himself scarce.

- skip one's bail 보석 중에 행방을 감추다 (To disappear while on bail)

  [Ex] Lilley skipped bail during the trial and was convicted in his absence.

- take it on the lam '걸음아 날 살려라.' 하고 도망치다 (To escape; to run away)

  [Ex] He took it on the lam.

1-7. To Go Away (가 버리다, 떠나다)

Formal

  head out; split; take leave; withdraw;

- sally forth (결연히 또는 신이 나서) 힘차게 떠나다

  [Ex] The French army passed out the mountain gorge and sallied forth into the open plain.

- take oneself off 떠나다, 달아나다 (To go away; to run away)

  [Ex] Why did your friend take himself off like that?

Informal

- **hit the road** 길을 나서다 (To leave)

  [Ex] We need to hit the road by 5.

- truck 움직이다, 출발하다 (To move or to go)

  [Ex] Alright, ladies, shake a leg. Keep truckin'.

- **truck it** 급하게 출발하다 (To leave in a hurry)

  [Ex] When I saw the teacher coming, I started truckin' it!

- vamoose 급히 떠나다 (To leave)

  [Ex] Hastert demanded a floor vote on the idea of vamoosing Iraq immediately.

1-8. Run away (도망가다)

Informal

run for the hills 도망가다 (To run away)

  [Ex] The rest of us would have taken the offer and ran for the hills.

2 *How Fast?*

매우 빨리, 아주 빠르게

Formal

at full tilt; in a jiffy; in nothing flat; pronto; apace; expeditiously; posthaste

Informal

- clip 한번에, 단숨에 (At one clip; at a clip)

  [Ex] Rockefeller gave away a hundred million dollars at a clip.

- **double-quick** 매우 급한[하게], 아주 빠르게 (Very fast)

  [Ex] Secretary of State needs to come back from the Maldives in double quick time.

- hell-bent for leather 맹렬한 기세로, 전속력으로, 무턱대고 (With full speed)

  [Ex] Kennedy, of course, is currently going hell for leather to get Hillary Clinton's seat in the Senate.

- lickety-split 급히 서둘러[서두르는], 재빨리[빠른], 전속력으로 (Very quickly)

  [Ex] I got out of that strip club lickety-split when I realized the dancer was actually a man.

- **on the double** 황급히, 신속히 (Very quickly)

  [Ex] I need to get those sneakers on the double.

Chapter 15

Defecation and Vomiting
배변, 구토

어쩔 수 없는 인간의 생리 현상이지만 배변과 관련되어서는 아무래도 직접 언급
하기를 꺼리는 경향이 있습니다. 따라서 많은 informal 표현들이나 속어를 사용
하여 배변 현상을 표현하고 있고, 더하여 단어나 문장의 의미를 강조하는 데도
많이 사용하고 있습니다. 따라서 배변에 관련된 주요 표현들은 잘 알아놓을 필
요가 있습니다. 이번 장에는 배변, 구토에 관련된 용어들을 정리했습니다.

1 *Feces*
대변

Formal

- **droppings** 똥 (주로 동물의 것 / Animal feces)

  [Ex] It is made of fallen leaves, animal droppings, and rotting plant matter.
- **stool** 대변大便, 똥 (Feces; poop)

  [Ex] How often is there stool in the diaper?

Informal

- dookie 똥 (Feces)

  [Ex] Don't step in that dookie!
- doo-doo 응가, 똥 (Excrement; feces; poop)

  [Ex] Jeeze, you just stepped in dog doodoo!
- **number two** (어린아이의 말로) 응가 (The act or an instance of defecation)

  [Ex] Mum, I need a number two.
- **poo** 응가, 똥

  [Ex] "Oh shit!" said the classy lady, "I just stepped in some doggie poo!"
- **poop** 똥 (Feces)

  [Ex] I got some poop on my shoe while walking through the park.

Slang

- cow pie 쇠똥 (A large pile of cow shit)

  [Ex] Watch out for that cow pie.
- **crap** 똥(shit), (a~) 용변, 배변, 설사 (A pile of shit)

  [Ex] I crap my pants all the time.
- crud 똥, 쓸모없는 것, 불쾌한 것 (A euphemism for crap)

  [Ex] Oh shi···cra···crud! I left my homework at the library!
- **shit** 똥, 대변 (Feces)

  [Ex] There is shit on the floor.
- turd 대변大便, 똥 (Feces)

  [Ex] She couldn't fill out any of these suits the way we do. It would be like putting wrapping paper on a turd.

2 *Flatulate, Fart, Pass Gas*
방귀 뀌다

Formal

- break wind 방귀 뀌다 (A replacement for "Fart"; Mostly used by people(s) over the age of 55)

  [Ex] What the heck is that smell? Did you just break wind?

- **fart** (특히 소리가 크게 나게) 방귀를 뀌다 (An instance of flatulence; "the passing of gas")

  [Ex] That was a pretty nasty fart, dude.

- **pass gas** 방귀 뀌다 (To flatulate)

  [Ex] It's considered normal to pass gas between 10 to 20 times a day.

- **pass wind** 방귀 뀌다 (To flatulate)

  [Ex] I have never been around so many people who pass wind so constantly.

Informal

- let the dogs out 방귀 뀌다 (To flatulate)

  [Ex] Who let the dogs out?

Slang

- bust ass 방귀 뀌다 (To flatulate; fart)

  [Ex] Dude, did you just bust ass?

- let one 방귀 뀌다 (To expel flatulence; to fart)

  [Ex] Hey, dude, didja let one just a moment ago? Man, I could smell your gas a mile away!

③ *Poop*

대변을 보다, 응가 하다

Formal

- **go number two** 응가를 하다 (To defecate; poop)

  [Ex] Mom, I need to go number two.

Informal

- make a teddy bear 대변을 보다 (To defecate; poop)

  [Ex] I gotta make a teddy bear.

- take a dookie 대변보다 (To defecate)

  [Ex] I'll be right back, I need to take a dookie.

- take a dump 대변보다 (To defecate)

  [Ex] I've got to go take a dump.

- take a poop 대변보다 (To defecate)

  [Ex] I've got to go take a poop.

Slang

- **take a crap** 대변보다 (To defecate)

  [Ex] I've got to go take a crap.

- **take a shit** 대변보다 (To defecate)

④ *Urinate, Pee, Piss*

소변을 보다, 쉬하다

Informal

- **go number one** 쉬하다 (To urinate)

  [Ex] Mom, I need to go number one.

- number one 쉬, 오줌 (Urination)

  [Ex] Kid: I have to go to the bathroom. / Parent: Number one or number two? / Kid: Number one.

- **pee** 오줌 누다, 쉬하다, 오줌(piss), 오줌 누기[싸기] (To urinate)

  [Ex] I need to pee.

- **piss** 오줌, 소변, 오줌 누기, 오줌 누다 (To urinate)

  [Ex] I had to go piss.

- **take a leak** 소변보다 (To urinate)

  [Ex] I need to take a leak.

- **take a piss** 소변보다 (To urinate)

  [Ex] He goes to the toilet and starts taking a piss.

- take a whiz 소변, 쉬하다 (To urinate)

  [Ex] I've got to go take a whiz.

- whiz 소변을 보다 (To urinate)

  [Ex] I've got to go whiz.

5 *Vomit*
토하다

Formal

- **barf** 토하다, 게우다, 토사물 (To vomit)

  [Ex] You got barf on your shoes.

- chuck 게우다 (To vomit)

  [Ex] I think I'm going to chuck.

- **dry heave** 헛구역질하다 (To attempt to vomit, but to expel no liquid)

  [Ex] If even one of you thinks about dry heaving in my car, you're all walking home.

- **puke** 게우다, 토하다, 토사물 (To vomit)

  [Ex] There's puke on the floor!

- retch 토하다, 게우다 (To vomit)

  [Ex] That guy is retching everywhere and it almost hit that dog!

- **throw up** 토하다, 게우다 (To vomit)

  [Ex] I threw up my breakfast.

- upchuck 토하다, 게우다 (To vomit)

  [Ex] He upchucked his lunch.

Informal

- hug the toilet 변기에 토하다 (To be on one's knees vomiting into a toilet)

  [Ex] He's huggin the toilet.

- **lose one's lunch** 토하다 (To vomit)

  [Ex] He lost his lunch when he saw the body.

- york 토하다, 게우다 (To vomit)

  [Ex] I drank so much last night, I yorked all over myself.

Chapter 16

Private Parts
음부, 성기 관련 표현들

남녀의 음부, 또는 성기에 대한 informal한 표현들과 속어적 표현들은 일상생활에서 아주 많이 접하게 됩니다. 특히, 남녀 성기 관련 속어들은 남성과 여성을 경멸적으로 표현하는 의미도 대부분 겸하고 있기 때문에 중요한 표현들입니다. 이런 속어들은 직접적으로 언급하면 안 되겠지만, 남들이 이야기하는 것이 무슨 의미인지는 반드시 이해할 수 있어야 합니다.

Buttocks, Butt, Ass

둔부, 엉덩이

Formal

- **behind** 엉덩이 (Buttocks)

  [Ex] He slapped her on the behind.

- **butt** 궁둥이, 엉덩이 (Ass; buttocks)

  [Ex] I missed the chair and fell flat on my butt.

Informal

- back end 엉덩이 (Buttocks)

  [Ex] That backend is a fantastic sight.

- **bottom** 엉덩이, 둔부 (Buttocks)

  [Ex] One of Adam's hands stroked Allie's sides and her bottom.

- caboose 엉덩이 (Buttocks)

  [Ex] She got one damn fine caboose.

- cheeks 궁둥이, 엉덩이 (Buttocks)

  [Ex] She knelt forward and used both of her hands to part the girl's cheeks.

- fanny 엉덩이 (Buttocks)

  [Ex] I'm going to swat you on the fanny, young man.

Slang

- arse 엉덩이, 둔부(ass, buttocks) (Australian, British and Irish word for a person's rear end)

  [Ex] I'm sitting on my arse.

- **ass** 궁둥이, 엉덩이 (Buttocks)

  [Ex] Adam marveled at her ass.

- **ass cheeks** 궁둥이, 엉덩이 (Buttocks)

  [Ex] That shit was so big that it hurt my ass cheeks on the way out.

영어 표현에도 등급이 있다!

- booty 엉덩이 (Buttocks)

[Ex] That girl over there has some large-ass booty!

- bum 엉덩이 (Buttocks; butt; ass)

[Ex] She has a real hang-up about his big bum.

- buns (특히 남자의) 엉덩이 (Buttocks)

[Ex] Nice buns.

- patootie 1. 엉덩이 2. 매력 있는 여자

[Ex] Unless they want to do it themselves, I don't give a rat's patootie if they mind or not.

- pooper 엉덩이 (Buttocks)

[Ex] She's got a nice pooper.

- trunk 엉덩이 (Buttocks)

[Ex] She had a nice trunk.

- tush 엉덩이 (Buttocks)

[Ex] She surprises him by grabbing his tush and pulling him into her.

- tushie 엉덩이 (Buttocks)

[Ex] Mommy is bad because she patted my tushie? What idiot came up with that, I wonder.

② Anus
항문

- asshole 항문 (Anus)

[Ex] My asshole itches.

- ass crack 항문 (The cleft between the buttocks)

[Ex] Your ass crack is showing.

- back door 항문 (Anus)

[Ex] I went in through the back door.

- brown eye 항문 (Anus)

[Ex] You've got to be gentle with the brown eye.

- brown star 항문 (Referred to as the anus, often characterized by 'striations' that are in a star pattern.)

[Ex] Wow, that girl has some nice striations on her brown star.

- bung hole 항문 (Anus)

[Ex] I need TP(toilet paper) for my bunghole.

- butthole 항문 (Anus)

[Ex] Her motions became frenzied and Derrick found his whole finger buried in Jenny's butthole.

- cornhole 항문 (Anus)

[Ex] I banged her cornhole last night.

- Hershey Highway 항문 (The anal cavity; usually used when speaking in a sexual manner about taking it in the ass.)

[Ex] Hey look at Adam, he is probably about ready to go down Misty's Hershey Highway again.

- O-ring 항문 (The anus)

[Ex] If you don't slow down, you'll blow my O-ring!

- poop chute 항문 (The anus; butthole)

[Ex] I'd stick it up her poop chute.

- pucker 항문 (Asshole)

[Ex] Jenny rested her hands on Derrick's knees and presented her pucker to him.

- rosebud 항문 (Anus)

[Ex] We're going to get on the bed, spread our ass cheeks and give you a good look at our little rosebud.

- turd cutter 항문 (Anus)

[Ex] That girl has a fine turd cutter.

③ *Breast*
(유방)

3-1. Breast (유방)

Formal

- **bust** 가슴 (Breasts)

[Ex] She's got a huge bust.

Slang

- bazonga 젖퉁이, 큰 젖퉁이 (Breast; Usually used in the plural)

[Ex] She's got some nice bazongas.

- **boob** 유방 (Breast)

[Ex] Serious question for you: are you a boob man, ass man, leg man? What's your preference?

[Ex] She got hit in the boob.

- **boob job** 유방 확대 수술 (Breast enhancement surgery)

[Ex] "I was going to be a dancer." Rebecca confided to Adam. "I have the legs for it, I think, but I didn't have enough up top and I wasn't willing to get a boob job."

- **booby** 유방 (Breast)

[Ex] She just wanted him to notice her butt and boobies.

- gazonga 젖, 유방 (Breast; Usually used in reference to a large breast)

[Ex] Man, she's got some huge gazongas!

- headlights 유방, 유두 (Breasts; boobs; tits, erect nipples)

[Ex] Man, it's cold out here. But check out those headlights.

- hooter (여자의) 가슴 (A breast; Usually used in the plural)

[Ex] Did you see the size of the hooters on her?

- jug 유방 (Breast)

 [Ex] Hey, dude, you see that girl's jugs?

- knockers 유방 (Breasts)

 [Ex] Check out the knockers on that chick!

- rack (여성의) 가슴 (Breasts)

 [Ex] Check out the rack on that woman!

- tit 유방 (Breast; Likely from the word "teat")

 [Ex] To see you today, in your loose T-shirt and shorts, a person might think you were soft, maybe even a little overweight. I mean, you have the tits and ass of a woman who weighs a lot more than you do.

- titty 유방 (Breast; Usually but not always used in the plural)

 [Ex] Excuse me: your titty is exposed.

3-2. Large Breasted (유방이 큰)

Informal

- loaded 가슴이 큰 (Large breasted)

 [Ex] Woah, that girl's loaded!

- stacked (여성이 특히) 가슴이 풍만한, 포동포동한 (Large breasted)

 [Ex] Pamela Anderson is stacked!

- top heavy 유방이 큰 (Large breasted)

 [Ex] But being top heavy doesn't mean sacrificing your right to sexy lingerie.

4 *Vagina, Clitoris*
여성의 성기

4-1. Vagina (질)

Informal

- **c' word** Cunt (여성 성기에 대한 완곡어법 / Cunt)

  [Ex] Interestingly enough, so far there haven't been any reports of angry Tea Party protesters shouting the "c" word at female lawmakers.

- **cherry** 처녀막, 동정 (A membrane in a woman's vagina, known more properly as a hymen)

  [Ex] I popped my girlfriend's cherry while I fingered her.

- front bottom 여성 성기 (Childish name for the female genitalia)

  [Ex] My furry front bottom is hurting, doctor.

- labia majora 대음순 (The two outer rounded folds of adipose tissue that lie on either side of the opening of the vagina.)

  [Ex] Karlien was still looking at the lips of Shelly's cunt, seemingly entranced by how prominent the labia majora was.

- tunnel of love 질, 여자의 성기 (Vagina)

  [Ex] I wanna be in your tunnel of love.

Slang

- axe wound 도끼 자국 (여성의 성기/ Vulva; vagina)

  [Ex] She's got a nice axe wound.

- bearded clam 여성의 성기 (Female genitalia)

  [Ex] He touched my bearded clam!

- **beaver** 여성의 성기 (여성을 비하하는 말 / Vagina; a derogatory term for a woman)

  [Ex] Let's go scope out some beaver.

- beef curtain 음순 (Big saggy pussy lips)

[Ex] Being stuck in a blizzard, I was very thankful my girlfriend had her warm beef curtains to keep my dick from getting frost-bitten and fall off.

- **box** 여성의 성기 (Vulva)

[Ex] Derrick dipped his head down to capture a nipple in his mouth as Jenny felt the first inch of the invader in her box.

- cameltoe 여성이 옷을 꼭 끼게 입어 앞부분이 선명하게 보이는 것 (The outline of a human female's labia majora, as seen through tightly fitting clothes; the visible cleft of the outer labia under tight clothing. (A "frontal wedgie" on a female))

[Ex] A: Do you know what a camel toe is? / B: Of course. Jesus, I'm not nine. I know all the dirty words and nicknames, too.

- coochie 여성의 성기 (Women's vagina)

[Ex] Man, I wanted some of that coochie but she wouldn't give it to me.

- cookie 여성의 성기 (Female genitalia; vagina)

[Ex] Her cookie was so nicely shaven, mmm mmm!

- cunny 여성의 음부[성기] (A diminutive of cunt derived from the latin word, cunnis)

[Ex] She felt her cunny jump, burning with its own great fire.

- **cunt** 여성의 음부[성기] (Female genitalia)

[Ex] Sarah took Adam's wrist and gently guided it to the folds of her own cunt.

- fanny (영국)여성의 음부[성기] (British slang for pussy)

[Ex] She takes it in the fanny but never the ass.

- fuck hole 여성 성기 (Female genitalia)

[Ex] My penis went into her fuckhole.

- gash 여성의 성기

[Ex] She had a lovely gash.

- hair pie 음문陰門 (Vulva)

[Ex] I'm having some hair pie for lunch.

- kooch (여성의) 음부 (Vagina)

[Ex] Your kooch is filthy.

- lunchmeat (여자의) 질 (Vagina)

[Ex] Damn, that stripper is fine as hell but she got way too much lunch meat!

- **muff** (여자의) 거웃이 난 자리 (Female genitalia; vagina)

[Ex] I bet she has a nice muff under that dress.

- pink canoe 여성의 음부 (Vagina)

[Ex] The gynecologist examined my pink canoe.

- poon (여성의) 음부 (Vagina; Also poon-tang)

[Ex] I gotta find me some poon.

- poontang (여성의) 음부 (Female genitalia)

[Ex] I want some of that fine poontang!

- **pussy** 여성의 음부, 성교, (성교 대상으로서의) 여성 (Vagina)

[Ex] And every day from 3:00 to 5:40 p.m. Karlie would suck a dick, give a hand-job or get her pussy licked.

- quiff (여성의) 성기 (Female genitalia)

[Ex] She's got a tight little quiff.

- quim (여성의) 성기 (Female genitalia)

[Ex] 1. Cassie's face was in Jenny's quim and Jenny was munching on Sahara's slick box. / 2. She's got a tight little quim.

- **slit** 여성 성기 (Female genitals)

[Ex] Every female has a slit.

- **snatch** 질膣, 여자의 성기 (Female genitalia)

[Ex] Her snatch smells.

- **twat** (여성의) 성기 (여자의 음부를 가리키는 비어 / Vulva)

[Ex] Last time, Rachelle popped her nipple out and flashed her barely covered twat at Adam half a dozen times.

4-2. Clitoris (클리토리스)

Slang

- bald man in a boat 클리토리스 (Clitoris)

[Ex] Licking the bald man in the boat will make your woman CUM!

- bean 클리토리스 (Clitoris)

[Ex] She was flicking her bean all night.

- bud 클리토리스 (Clitoris)

[Ex] Sarah exploded when Karlie started to gently flick her tongue over the bud.

- clit 음핵陰核, 클리토리스 (Clitoris)

[Ex] The tip of his finger split her lips and he caressed her clit gently.

- lady boner 여성의 성적 흥분 상태 (Sexual arousal in women; A figurative erection)

[Ex] Jake has such a beautiful smile that I get a lady boner just by thinking about it!

- man in the boat 클리토리스 (Clitoris)

[Ex] While you are tearing it up from behind, reach around and rub that "Little Man in the Boat".

⑤ Penis
남성의 성기

Informal

- **hard-on** (남자 성기의) 발기 (An erect penis)

  [Ex] She used some of the soap from her body and started to stroke Adam's hard-on again.

- wee wee 남성의 성기, (아동어로) 고추 (Penis)

  [Ex] Hey, stop staring at my wee-wee.

- weenie 남성의 성기, (아동어로) 고추 (Penis)

  [Ex] Hey! You have a very small weenie!

- willy (특히 아동어로) 고추 (Penis)

  [Ex] Stop clutching your willy. It's disgusting.

Slang

- bone (발기한) 남성의 성기, 발기 (The penis, especially when erect)

  [Ex] He gave her his bone.

- **boner** 발기한 남성의 성기, 발기 (An erection)

  [Ex] My boner is showing through my pants.

- **cock** 음경陰莖 (Penis)

  [Ex] He's practically got a Saturn V rocket for a cock.

- **dick** 남성의 성기 (Penis)

  [Ex] Adam's dick jumped of its own volition.

- ding-a-ling 남자의 성기 (Penis)

  [Ex] The little boy was withering on the ground because, his ding-a-ling got hurt by the baseball.

- dinky 남자의 성기 (Penis)

  [Ex] Wow, your dinky is really small!

- dipstick 남자의 성기 (Penis)

  [Ex] I saw his dipstick in the moonlight and my word did I get a fright. And that on a Saturday night!

- doinker 남성의 성기 (A large object such as a PENIS)

  [Ex] I have a huge DOINKER.

- dong 음경 (Penis)

  [Ex] She has tried to put that monster dong in her pussy and it wouldn't fit.

- joystick 남성의 성기 (Penis)

  [Ex] Why don't you come play with my joy stick?

- love muscle 남성의 성기 (Penis)

  [Ex] My old lady and I do it so infrequently, my love muscle is beginning to atrophy.

- **member** 음경 (Penis)

  [Ex] Adam felt a hand on his rampant member.

- one-eyed monster 남성의 성기 (Penis)

- packer 남성의 성기 (Penis)

  [Ex] You made me look at that kid's packer.

- **pecker** 음경 (Penis)

  [Ex] "Slight groping is permitted." Allie said. "Nothing beyond that, don't try to finger bang Shelly or give Sean a handjob. But if you brush against Shelly sweet little mound or Sean or Walt's pecker, that's cool."

- peter 남성의 성기 (Penis)

- pole 남성의 성기 (Penis)

  [Ex] Man, that guy is such a pole.

- **prick** 남근男根, 음경 (Penis)

  [Ex] The end of Adam's prick was wet with pre-cum.

- rod 남성의 성기 (Penis)

  [Ex] I woke up this morning with a wicked rod!

- salami 남성의 성기 (Penis)

  [Ex] I can't mess with a guy who has a small salami!

- **schlong** 남근男根, 음경 (A penis which is a fairly good length)

  [Ex] John ruined his sister's wedding when he drunkenly whipped out his schlong in front of everyone at the reception.

- schlort 단소 음경 (A short penis; A play on the word schlong)

  [Ex] A schlong is better than a schlort.

- schmeckel 남성의 성기 (Pejorative, derivative of schmuck; Jewish derivative for penis)

  [Ex] Johnny pulled his pants down to reveal his schmeckel.

- schwartz 남성의 성기 (Penis; From Jewish)

  [Ex] I see your schwartz is as big as mine.

- shaft 남성의 성기 (Penis)

  [Ex] Wow, he's got a big shaft.

- shlong[schlong] 남성의 성기 (Penis)

  [Ex] You got a big shlong!

- tent pole 발기 (An erection)

  [Ex] I woke up hearing someone knock on the door. Forgetting about the morning wood phenomenon, I went to answer it and after about ten seconds realized that she was totally staring at the tent pole bulging in my boxers.

- wanger 음경 (Penis)

  [Ex] Yo, that kid has a XL wanger.

- wanker 음경 (Penis)

  [Ex] Crikey, he's got a huge wanker!

- wankie 음경 (Penis)

  [Ex] He got a small wankie.

- whang 음경 (Penis)

  [Ex] Suck my whang.

- **wood** 발기한 남성의 성기, 발기 (An erection)

  [Ex] Girl, you're so hot. You're giving me wood.

- woody 남성의 발기 (A male's erection)

  [Ex] Ashley gives me a woody.

Testicle, Scrotum
고환, 음낭

Informal

- **ball** 고환睾丸 (Testicle)

  [Ex] Adam felt warm fingers caressing his balls. Allie keeping him erect, he thought.

- **sack** 고환 (Testicles; Sentence implies to be masculine and not feminine.)

  [Ex] Man, I just got hit really hard in the sack. I think I'm going to throw up.

Pubic Hair
음모

Slang

- **pube** 음모陰毛, 거웃 (A pubic hair)

  [Ex] Carly found a pube in the lasagna.

Chapter 17

Sexual Activities
성행위 관련 표현들

Sex와 관련된 속어들은 공식적인 석상이나 예의를 갖춰야 할 장소에서의 대화 중에는 절대 사용하면 안 됩니다. 하지만 최근 많은 발전을 한 인터넷과 대중 매체에서 예전에 비해 Sex와 관련된 속어들을 많이 사용하고 있어 우리도 더 많이 이런 속어들을 접하게 됩니다. 이번 장에서 살펴볼 informal, slang 표현들은 타인에게 언급하지 않더라도 남들이 사용할 때는 무슨 의미인지 이해해야 합니다.

1 Sexual Practices

성행위 방법

1-1. Oral sex (구강성교)

Slang

- **69** 남녀 동시 구강성교 행위 (To receive and perform oral sex at the same time)

  [Ex] The two girls were in a 69, licking each other's pussies.

- anilingus (성적 흥분을 위한) 항문을 입으로 자극하기

  [Ex] Anilingus (from anus + lingus (Latin Lingere: to lick), also spelled analingus, also referred to or described as anal to oral contact or anal to oral sex, is a form of oral sex involving contact.

- **B.J.** 구강성교 (Blow job의 두문자 / Acronym for "blowjob", i.e. fellatio)

  [Ex] Tom: Dude, I just got the sweetest B.J., she did it like a pro. / Jack: Oh really? Who was she? I want some of that B.J. action.

- **blow** 펠라치오[구강성교]를 하다 (To perform fellatio)

  [Ex] Will you stop acting like I'm blowing bums for rock, for Christ's sake?

- **blow job** 구강口腔성교[성애], 펠라치오 (Fellatio)

  [Ex] Yet she was certain that a blowjob, which she didn't really want to do, could give her things she never imagined.

- bob head 펠라치오[구강성교]를 하다 (To practice fellatio, oral sex)

  [Ex] Marcia doesn't like to bob head.

- box lunch 컨니링거스 (입술이나 혀로 여성의 성기를 애무하는 행위 / Cunnilingus)

  [Ex] Damn, my girl was just begging for a box lunch…. I didn't mind giving her one.

- butt-fuck (~와) 항문성교(를 하다) (Assfuck)

  [Ex] She got butt fucked.

- cabeza 펠라치오 (Literally means head in Spanish, pronounced as cuh-bay-sa)

  [Ex] Yo dude, that hot Latin chick in my Spanish 2 class gave me some cabeza! dude… me gusta mucho….

영어 표현에도 등급이 있다!

- chicken head 펠라티오를 자주 하는 여자 (A female who performs fellatio frequently)

[Ex] That girl is a chicken head – she's blown everyone on this street.

- **cunnilingus** 컨니링거스 (여성에 대한 구강성교)

[Ex] I performed cunnilingus on her until my tongue couldn't move anymore. She appreciated it very much.

- **deep throat** 펠라치오 (Fellatio; Deep fellatio)

[Ex] When she performed deep throat on me, it made me forget all other blowjobs.

- **eat** (여성)에게 구강성교를 하다, ~의 성기를 핥다 (Lick someone's vagina)

[Ex] Yo girl, I'm 'bout to get waxed cuz Styles gonna eat me tonight!

- eat hair pie (여성)에게 구강성교를 하다 (To perform cunnilingus)

[Ex] Tyrone decided on dessert after having sex with Takeshia. He ate Takeshia's hair pie.

- eat up (여성)에게 구강성교를 하다 (To performing oral sex on a female)

[Ex] I ate up Sarah like a bowlful of Jell-O.

- **fellatio** 펠라치오 (남성 성기에 하는 오럴 섹스)

[Ex] My girlfriend doesn't swallow after fellatio.

- fellatrix 펠라티오(남성 성기에 하는 오럴 섹스)를 하는 여성

[Ex] She was a good fellatrix.

- get head 구강성교를 받다 (To receive oral sex)

[Ex] I got some head last night.

- give face 구강성교를 해주다 (To perform cunnilingus; GO DOWN ON)

[Ex] This girl I talked to wanted me to give her face and I said hell no!

- **give head** 구강성교를 해주다 (To perform fellatio)

[Ex] She pulled some dorky guy aside after school and gave him head at the library.

- **go down on** 구강성교를 하다 (To perform oral sex)

[Ex] I think I would offer to go down on you once a month for that amount.

- gobble one's knob 펠라치오하다 (To perform fellatio)

[Ex] Have you gobbled his knob yet?

- have a box lunch (여성에게) 오럴 섹스를 하다 (To perform cunnilingus; GO DOWN ON)

[Ex] The wife came home for a nooner, but I decided to have a box lunch instead.

- head-bang 격하게 구강성교하다 (To perform aggressive fellatio)

[Ex] I'm down for some head-bangin' tonight.

- Lewinsky 구강성교 (To suck one's manhood; Originated from a 1998 sex scandal between US President Bill Clinton and White House intern Monica Lewinsky.)

  [Ex] Bro. I got the best Lewinsky last night!

- muff dive 여성에게 구강성교를 하다 (To give oral sex to a girl; to go down on her; to perform cunnilingus)

  [Ex] I'm going muff divin'.

- munch on 컨니링거스를 하다 (To perform cunnilingus; eat out)

  [Ex] Yesterday, I was munchin' on that chick for an hour.

- **oral** 구강성교 (Oral sex)

  [Ex] Is she into oral?

- play the skin flute 펠라치오하다 (To perform fellatio)

  [Ex] Tom: Dude, that chick totally plays the skin flute. Dave: And doesn't miss a single beat!

- salad tossing 항문 구강성교 (Analingus)

  [Ex] She's into salad tossing.

- **sixty nine** 남녀 동시 구강성교 (Simultaneous oral sexual stimulation: from the physical position of head to tail)

  [Ex] Sixty-nine is a popular sexual position.

- smoke pole 펠라치오를 하다 (To perform fellatio)

  [Ex] Hey, ya wanna smoke my pole?

- **suck** 구강성교를 하다 (To perform fellatio or cunnilingus)

  [Ex] You can suck it right into your hot little mouth. You can lick it right up and keep him so he can do this to you, Love.

- suck off 구강성교를 하다 (To perform fellatio; for a male to receive oral sex)

  [Ex] Yo, I got a suck off, from that bitch last night.

- swallow 정액을 삼키다 (To swallow a man's ejaculate during oral sex)

  [Ex] When Sally swallowed Harry's load, he knew she was the one.

- toss salad 항문 구강성교를 하다 (To perform analingus; Rim)

  [Ex] She just tossed his salad.

1-2. Anal sex (항문 성교)

- **anal** 항문 성교 (Anal sex)

  [Ex] Are you into anal?

- ATM 항문 대 구강성교 (Ass to Mouth Sex)

  [Ex] He ATM'ed her.

- bite the pillow 항문 성교의 상대가 되다 (To be on the receiving end of anal sex)

  [Ex] Mike bites the pillow!

- BUFU 항문 성교 (Butt fuck)

  [Ex] No, Jenny didn't break her legs. She's in the wheelchair cuz mandingo bufued her last night.

- buggery (남성간의) 항문 성교 (Anal intercourse)

  [Ex] The perp got 5 years for committing buggery and posting on the internet.

- **butt fuck** 항문 성교 (Anal sex)

  [Ex] Sheryl almost died when Tom asked her if she wanted to butt fuck.

- butt love 항문 성교 (Anal sex)

  [Ex] Did we just make butt love?

- chocolate cha-cha 항문 성교 (Anal Sex)

  [Ex] Hey man, wanna do the chocolate cha-cha?

- corn hole 항문 성교 (Anal sex)

  [Ex] After I cornhole you, you won't shit right for a week.

- dookie love 항문 성교 (To have anal sex)

  [Ex] I'm not into dookie love.

- fifth base 항문 성교 (In the "sex as baseball" metaphor, anal sex)

  [Ex] Man, that girl has an onion ass. I hope I get to fifth base on that shit!

- Greek sex 항문 성교 (Anal sex)

- ride the hershey highway 항문 성교하다 (To have anal sex)

  [Ex] A: Yo man, are you going to get a little tonight? / B: No dude, she is ragging. / A: Oh, so you're going to ride the Hershey Highway?

- slip through the backdoor 항문 성교를 하다 (To perform anal sex)

  [Ex] Last night, I slipped through her backdoor.

- take it up the ass 항문 성교의 상대가 되어주다 (To be on the receiving end of anal sex)

1-3. Orgy (난교)

- circle jerk (3명 이상 사이의) 상호 수음 (A masturbation party; can be with guys or girls. Everyone usually sits in a circle and jacks off in the company of other people.)

  [Ex] I am planning a circle jerk next week if any of y'all are interested.

- **daisy chain** 난교亂交, 그룹 섹스 (A group sex formation involving multiple partners, with the participants lying in a circle, putting their mouth to the genitals of the next person.)

  [Ex] The shoot ended with a six-girl daisy chain. Derrick thought it might be the hottest thing he'd ever seen.

- pull a[the] train (여자가) 차례차례 여러 남자와 성행위를 하다

  [Ex] "That little slut." Allie remarked with a laugh. "Blowing high school guys? She's going to be pulling a train on the Padres if they're not careful.

1-4. Adventurous Sex (모험적인 성행위)

- a.c./d.c. 양성애兩性愛의 (Bisexual)

  [Ex] Hey, did you hear about Brittney, I think she's AC DC!

- B. and D. 학대·피학대 변태 성욕 행위 (Bondage & Discipline)

  [Ex] Though it's still a fairly taboo subject, B and D is rather common.

- **BDSM** 속박과 훈육, 새디즘과 마조히즘 (Acronym for "bondage, dominance, sadism(submission), masochism")

  [Ex] In a BDSM relationship the partner who has the active (i.e. controlling) role in a session or in the entire relationship is described as the "top", a role that often involves inflicting pain, degradation or subjugation.

- **foot job** 여성이 남성의 성기를 발로 애무하는 행위

  [Ex] In return for the foot rub, she gave me a foot job.

- **gangbang** (한 여성을 상대로) 난교亂交하다, 윤간하다, 윤간에 끼다

  [Ex] I would love to be in a gangbang with that chick.

- nooner 점심 시간 동안의 섹스 (Sex during the lunch break)

  [Ex] A: What did you do for lunch? / B: I wen't home for a nooner.

- phone fuck 폰 섹스 (To engage in phone sex)

  [Ex] Dude, last night I phone fucked this crazy bitch.
- swinger 부부 교환행위를 하는 사람

  [Ex] On our first date Tom and I went to a swinger club.
- **threesome** 스리섬 (세 명이 함께 하는 성행위 / A session of sex involving 3 people)

  [Ex] My best friend asked me to join she and her husband for a threesome.
- titty fuck 젖가슴 사이 마찰 성교 (A session of "sex" with breasts that are pushed together)

  [Ex] That was a nice titty fuck.
- voyeur (성적으로) 엿보기 좋아하는 사람, 관음자觀淫者

  [Ex] Her fingers were underneath her dress, her panties at her feet. She felt like a voyeur but she wasn't embarrassed. She would have loved to go join them.
- water sport 배뇨排尿를 수반하는 성행위 (Sexual play with urine)

  [Ex] Though Matt and Coop had been known to engage in water sports on occasion Jake thought the whole concept was disgusting.

1-5. Homosexual (동성애)

Slang

- drag king 남장 여성 (A (usually homosexual) female dressed in man's clothing)

  [Ex] Sarah performed as a drag king in the local bar, under the name Alexander.
- drag queen 여장女裝을 (좋아)하는 호모 (남성 동성애자)

  [Ex] He told me he just likes to go out and score the occasional blowjob from a street hooker and he had no idea that drag queens did their business over by Macarthur Park.
- **dyke** 여성 동성애자, (남자역의) 레즈비언 (A lesbian)

  [Ex] OMG, is she really a dyke?
- fag (남성) 동성애자(의)

  [Ex] You're a fag! She's a fag! I'm the only straight one here!
- faggot 남성 동성애자 (A male homosexual; Extremely offensive)

  [Ex] That Elton John is such a faggot!
- **gay** 동성애자, 게이 (A homosexual person)

  [Ex] Child: Mom, Dad, I have something to tell you. I'm gay. / Parents: We will love you no matter what your sexual preference is.
- **GLBT** 동성, 양성, 성전환자의 두음문자 (Acronym for "Gay, lesbian, bisexual, transgendered")

  [Ex] Statistics of discrimination against GLBT youth are even worse.

- **homo** 동성애자 (A homosexual person)

  [Ex] He knows what he'd like to do to "queers" and "homos".
- **lez** 동성애를 하는 여자(lesbian) (Short for lesbian)

  [Ex] Kate loves Laura. She's a lez.
- **queer** 퀴어, (특히 남자) 동성애자 (Homosexual; homosexual person)

  [Ex] I've also been called poof, faggot, queer, little girl.

1-6. Position (체위)

Formal

- **missionary position[style]** 정상체위 성교 자세

  [Ex] My girlfriend says I should be more adventurous in bed, but I love the missionary position.

Slang

- bucking bronco 성교시 후배위 체위의 일종 (The Bucking Bronco is an sex position in which the man mounts the girl from the back. The girl will then proceed to buck up and down like a wild bronco.)

  [Ex] I decided to try the Bucking Bronco last night on my girlfriend, and she threw me off like a monkey throwing shit!
- cow girl 여성 상위체위

  [Ex] Briana Banks, loves riding the cock, she's a true cow girl.
- **doggy style** 후배위 성교 자세

  [Ex] I did her doggy style.
- ride one's dick 여성상위의 체위로 성교하다

  [Ex] That girl was riding my dick last night.

2 Party, Event, Gathering, Meeting 파티

- ABC party 옷만 빼고는 다 입을 수 있는 파티 ("Anything But Clothes" party, where you wear anything but clothes. ex: trashbags, saran wrap, lampshades, trashcans, tape, cardboard boxes, etc.)

  [Ex] Dude, that ABC party last night was raging, there's nothing better than seeing girls with just a piece of tape on dancing around!

- **booty call** 성관계를 가지려고 갖는 만남 또는 그것을 위한 전화 (A last-minute or previously unplanned request to meet up with someone with the intention of having sex)

  [Ex] He called me at 3 a.m. last night for a booty call.

③ Kiss, Make out

키스, 애무

Informal

- **1st base** (데이트에서) 키스(에 성공)하다 (To kiss, make out at a date)

  [Ex] He got to the 1st base with her.

- **2nd base** (데이트에서) 가슴을 만짐[만지는 데 성공하다] (To put one's hands up a person's shirt, with hand-on-skin contact, e.g. the fondling of breasts)

  [Ex] He got to 2nd base on the 1st date.

- **3rd base** (데이트에서) 성기를 만짐[만지는 데 성공하다] (To stimulate the genitals with one's hand)

  [Ex] He got to 3rd base.

- **feel up** (특히 원치 않는 사람의) 몸을 만지다[더듬다]

  [Ex] Haley: It looks like you were felt up by that creepy guy around the corner. / Alex: Ew! Why him? / Haley: 'Cause he's got, like, freakishly tiny hands.

- **French kiss** 짙은 입맞춤 (Kiss with an open mouth, usually placing one's tongue in the other person's mouth)

  [Ex] They were outside French kissing.

- get on 열정적으로 입 맞추다 (To kiss passionately; MAKE OUT.)

  [Ex] She got on that guy last night.

- **make out** (~를[와]) 애무하다 (To "French kiss" (i.e. kiss with tongue contact) for a period of time)

  [Ex] I can't believe my dad. First he's saying that I need to respect the sanctity of marriage, and then he's making out with her on the balcony.

- pucker up 입을 오므리다 (입을 오므려 키스할 준비를 하다 / To prepare for a kiss.)

  [Ex] Pucker up baby!

- smooch 키스(하다), 애무(하다), 페팅(하다 / Pet) (To kiss)

  [Ex] You're the cutest boy in school. We're gonna have an awesome summer. Smooches, Brenda.

- **XOXO** 포옹과 키스 (채팅 약어/ An abbreviation for hugs and kisses, usually placed at the end of a letter)

  [Ex] And who am I? That's one secret I'll never tell···. You know you love me. XOXO, Gossip Girl.

4 *Partner*
섹스 파트너

- **one night stand** 하룻밤의 섹스, 하룻밤의 섹스 상대

[Ex] He kept calling me, but I was like, "Dude, it was just a one night stand."

Slang

- go hogging 약간 마음에 들지 않는 여자라도 찾다 (To go out seeking less desirable girls.)

[Ex] Let's give the fat girls a chance and go hogging.

- cock tease 몸만 달아오르게 하는 여자 (성관계를 원하는 듯 유혹하면서 끝내 허락하지 않는 여자를 가리키는 욕설)

[Ex] She is such a cock tease.

- **lay** (정사情事 상대로서의) 여자, 성행위 (A sexual partner; Almost always used with an adjective.)

[Ex] She's a great lay.

- mack 여자를 잘 유혹하는 남자, 뚜쟁이, 유객꾼, 매춘알선자, 여자에게 말을 걸며 다가가다[구애하다] (One who is good with the opposite sex, usually a male)

[Ex] Jeff is such a mack. He gets all the girls.

- prick tease 몸만 달아오르게 하는 여자 (성관계를 원하는 듯 유혹하면서 끝내 허락하지 않는 여자를 가리키는 욕설)

[Ex] She's such a prick tease.

5 *Have a Sex*

섹스하다

Informal

- action 성교 (Sex)

  [Ex] Hey, you get any action last night?

- all the way (이성과) 갈 데까지 가다, 성교하다 (Copulation, especially in "go all the way")

  [Ex] I did not go all the way with him, however.

- do it 성관계를 갖다 (To have sex)

  [Ex] A: So did you do it? / B: You mean have sex? Yes.

- **fool around** (이성과) 놀아나다

  [Ex] Chris and I fool around in his car before he drops me off.

- get some 성교하다 (To engage in sexual activity)

  [Ex] I got some from that girl last night.

- go all the way (~와) 갈 데까지 다 가다, 성관계까지 하다 (To have sexual intercourse)

  [Ex] Have you guys gone all the way yet?

- hit it 섹스하다 (To have sex)

  [Ex] They met at the club and went back to her place to hit it.

- home run 섹스하다

  [Ex] A: Did you get to 3rd base? / B: Actually, I hit a home run!

- **hook up** 성관계를 갖다

  [Ex] They hooked up last night after the party.

- **mess around** (특히 그래선 안 될 상대와) 성관계를 갖다

  [Ex] We were messing around in his car when a security guard knocked on the window.

- **roll in the hay** 성교 (A session of sex)

  [Ex] I'm kind of in the mood for a roll in the hay.

- score (여자)를 손에 넣다 (To have sex)

  [Ex] Guess who scored last night?

- **shack up** 동서同棲하다, 불의의 관계를 가지다

[Ex] I don't think his father was too thrilled when he shacked up with his girl-friend.

Slang

- ball 성교하다 (To have intercourse)

[Ex] If I put a sock on the doorknob, don't come in: it means I'm going to ball my girlfriend.

- **bang** (여성)과 성교하다 (To have sexual intercourse)

[Ex] I banged that girl I took home from the bar last night!

- boff 성교하다 (To have sex)

[Ex] Did you finally boff her?

- boink 성교하다 (To have sex with someone)

[Ex] He boinked her last week.

- dig out 성관계를 갖다 (To have sex with someone)

[Ex] I'd like to dig her out.

- doink 섹스하다 (To have sex)

[Ex] I doinked her.

- frig 성교하다 (Alternate version of "fuck")

[Ex] I was frigging all day and all night.

- **fuck** 성교하다

[Ex] Fuck me, shove it up as far as it will go at every stroke you give.

- get any (섹스) 좀 하다 (주로 의문문으로 사용됨 / To have sex. Used as a question)

[Ex] You gotten any lately?

- **get in (one's) pants** 성관계를 갖다 (To have sex with; Also "get into (one's) pants")

[Ex] Guys you meet in bars, they'll say anything to get in your pants.

- get it on (~와) 섹스하다 (To engage in coitus)

[Ex] She's gettin' it on with that guy.

- **get laid** 섹스하다 (To have sex)

[Ex] I'm not looking to get married, man, I just want to get laid.

- get one's hump on 섹스하다 (To have sex)

[Ex] We went back to my place and got our hump on.

- get physical 성관계를 갖다 (To have intimate[sexual] contact)

[Ex] Are you aware that your daughter and my son have been getting physical? I mean, can you imagine anything that inappropriate?

- get some booty 성교하다 (To have sexual intercourse)

[Ex] He got some booty last night.

- hoochie coochie 섹스(하다) (Sex or sexual play)

[Ex] Frank: Where's Dave? I thought he was partying with us tonight! / Jim: He'll be back in a minute, he's doing the hoochie-coochie.

- hump 성교하다 (To have sex with)

[Ex] It looked like he was humping her.

- pull a train (여자가) 차례차례 여러 남자와 성행위를 하다

[Ex] "That little slut." Allie remarked with a laugh. "Blowing high school guys? She's going to be pulling a train on the Padres if they're not careful."

- **quickie** 짧은 시간에 갖는 성관계

[Ex] Pat and I had a quickie during his lunch break.

- **screw** 섹스하다 (To have sex)

[Ex] She's pretty. Look, if she was there in '92, and if she looked anything like that, I promise you I totally screwed her.

- shag 섹스, 성교 (A session of sex)

[Ex] Fancy a shag?

- **wham bam, thank you ma'am** 짧고 형식적이며 일회적인 섹스 (A brief sexual encounter)

[Ex] The guys just want 'wham, bam, thank-you ma'am.' They don't care about building a relationship.

6 *Masturbation*
자위

6-1. Masturbate (자위하다)

Slang

- **beat it** 자위하다 (To masturbate)

  [Ex] I like to beat it while watching lesbian porn.

- **beat off** 자위하다 (To masturbate)

  [Ex] I've heard he beats off twice a day.

- **beat one's meat** 자위하다 (To masturbate)

  [Ex] Give me some lotion, I need to beat my meat.

- diddle 자위하다 (To masturbate; jerk off)

  [Ex] It was rare for her to diddle her pussy without also fingering her asshole.

- finger (~의) 성기를 손으로 애무하다 (To finger fuck)

  [Ex] Karlie had never kissed another girl. Then again, she had never had two other girls finger her pussy either.

- finger bang (~의) 성기를 손으로 애무하다 (To finger fuck)

  [Ex] Before we had intercourse, he proceeded to arouse me first by finger banging my vagina.

- finger-fuck (~의) 성기를 손으로 애무하다 (To stimulate the female genitals with one's fingers.)

  [Ex] That was a good finger-fuck.

- fist (성기에) 손을 집어넣다 (To insert the fist into the rectum or vagina for sexual purposes)

  [Ex] Man: I'm a big fan of fisting.

- fist fuck (성기에) 손을 넣는 행위를 하다

  [Ex] Jim fist fucked his girlfriend in her twat.

- **frig** 수음하다 (To masturbate)

  [Ex] I was at this girl's house last night and after we were kissing I gently got my fingers into her pants and frigged her.

- **hand job** 수음手淫

  [Ex] That little slut Kimmy was giving a hand job to every guy on the swim team last night!

- **jack it** 자위하다 (To masturbate)

   [Ex] Were you jacking it in the bathroom?

- **jack off** 자위하다 (To masturbate; jerk off)

   [Ex] He likes to jack off every night.

- **jerk it** 자위 행위를 하다 (To masturbate; Usually applied only to males)

   [Ex] He's jerking it in our dorm room.

- **jerk off** 자위 행위를 하다 (To masturbate; Usually used in reference to male masturbation)

   [Ex] Five minutes before my shift ended I was jerking off playing solitaire on my computer.

- jill off (주로 여성이) 자위하다 (To masturbate; Applied only to female masturbation; Variant of "jack off")

   [Ex] I am so horny, I need to jill off.

- rub one off 자위하다 (To masturbate)

   [Ex] Go take a shower and rub one off, you'll feel better.

- rub one out 자위하다 (To masturbate)

   [Ex] I was so horny I had to rub one out.

- **spank it** 자위하다 (To masturbate; Most commonly applied to males.)

   [Ex] You weren't out on a date last night – you were home spankin' it.

- **wack off** 자위하다 (To masturbate; Typically only used for male masturbation.)

   [Ex] I was really horny so I wacked off.

- **whack off** 자위하다, 수음하다

   [Ex] Leave me alone! Go whack off or something.

6-2. Artificial Penis (모조 성기)

Slang

- **dildo** 모조 남근, 남근 대용품 (A sex toy for women)

   [Ex] You are going to wake up with my Derrick Driller dildo in your asshole.

- strap on 부착용 모조 성기

   [Ex] I could get a big strap on and you could have a big cock in your pussy and a bigger cock right in your tiny little asshole.

7 *Climax*

절정

7-1. Climax, Ejaculate (사정하다)

Slang

- big O 오르가즘 (An orgasm)

  [Ex] Did you give her the big O?

- blast 사정하다 (To ejaculate)

  [Ex] I just blasted her in the ass.

- blow one's load 사정하다 (To ejaculate)

  [Ex] I accidentally blew my load on her pillow.

- bust one's nuts 사정하다 (To ejaculate)

  [Ex] I won't stop 'til I bust my nuts.

- bust a load 사정하다 (To ejaculate)

  [Ex] I busted a load in my pants.

- bust a nut 사정하다 (To ejaculate)

  [Ex] I won't stop 'til I bust a nut.

- bukkake 안면 사정 행위

  [Ex] I know you love bukkake.

- **come** 정액精液, 사정하다(ejaculate) (To ejaculate)

  [Ex] She came all over me.

- creampie 질내 사정 (A genre of pornography that features ejaculating inside the man's sexual
  partner; as a result, a man's ejaculating inside their sexual partner.)

  [Ex] I gave her a creampie.

- **cum** 사정하다 (To ejaculate)

  [Ex] He hated to cut her short but he knew he was going to cum and cum hard
  any moment.

- facial 얼굴에 사정하는 성행위 (The sex act of ejaculating on a person's face.)

[Ex] There's a good facial scene in this movie.

- **get it** (남자가) 오르가슴에 이르다, 사정射精하다 (To climax)

[Ex] It is very easy to get it off the internet; my secretary did so this morning with no difficulty at all.

- get off 오르가슴에 도달하다[하게 하다], 흥분시키다 (To climax)

[Ex] She would do her best to get Adam off with her mouth, and swallow every fucking drop, or to make sure Shelly had an incomplete ride before Adam filled her little pussy with his juice.

- get one's cookies 짜릿한 쾌감을 느끼다 (To climax)

[Ex] Sarah had plenty of time to go get her cookies.

- get one's nut off 사정하다 (To ejaculate)

- **get (one's) rocks off** 사정하다, 성교하다 (To enjoy in a sexual sense)

[Ex] You are into some weird porn. But⋯ whatever gets your rocks off, man.

- **jizm** 사정하다 (To ejaculate)

[Ex] He jizmed all over the place.

- **jizz** 사정하다 (To ejaculate)

[Ex] He jizzed all over.

- nut 사정하다 (To ejaculate)

[Ex] The first time we did it, we had extra lubricant because the guy nutted a second or two after the first inch was in.

- shoot one's load 사정하다 (To ejaculate)

[Ex] She looked so good I thought I was going to shoot my load in my pants!

- shoot (one's) wad 사정하다 (To ejaculate)

- **spend** 정액, 사정하다 (To ejaculate; sperm)

[Ex] She hadn't said anything but Karlie could tell from the look on Sarah's face that the driver had known exactly what she was doing, fingering her twat and eating the remnants of Adam's spend.

- splurge 사정하다 (To ejaculate)

[Ex] He splurged on his bed sheets.

- squirt (여성이) 사정하다 (To ejaculate; used for woman)

[Ex] "Oh yes." she said as he dropped to his knees on the floor and pushed her knees apart. "Fuck yes! Eat my snatch! Make me squirt in your fuckin' face!"

- wad 사정하다 (To ejaculate)

[Ex] Have you not wadded in months?

7-2. Semen (정액)

- **come** 정액精液 사정하다 (Semen; to ejaculate)

  [Ex] She came all over me.

- **cum** 정액(come) (Semen)

  [Ex] He then squirted his warm load of cum right down my throat.

- **jism[jizm]** (남자의) 정액 (Semen)

  [Ex] She watched as he spewed his jism.

- **load** 사정한 정액 (A unit of semen: the output of one male's ejaculation)

  [Ex] Hey, guys, the management needs everybody to get out, because they caught a guy jerking off in here and they're going to send in a crew to wipe down the loads.

- nut butter 정액 (호두 버터와 비슷해서)

  [Ex] That guy smells like nut butter.

- **pre-cum** 정액 사출 전에 분비되는 무색투명 액체

  [Ex] He saw his cock had left trails of pre-cum across her stomach.

- scum 정액 (Semen)

  [Ex] That guy's scum is nasty.

- **seed** 정액 (Semen)

  [Ex] Derek Wolf planted his seed in his wife. She accepted all of his seed. His seed is growing.

- snowball 여성이 구강 사정 후의 남성의 정액을 키스로 교환하는 행위

  [Ex] She gave him a snowball.

- **spend** 정액 (Semen)

  [Ex] She was so hot I thought I would shoot off my spend just looking at her.

- spooge 정액 (Semen)

  [Ex] There were spooge stains on the back seat.

- spunk 정액 (Semen)

  [Ex] He jacked off and shot spunk all over his hand.

- **swallow** 구강성교 중 남성의 정액을 삼키다 (To swallow a man's ejaculate during oral sex.)

  [Ex] Does she swallow?

- wad 정액 (Semen)

  [Ex] I just shot a wad in the shower.

8 *Condom*

콘돔 관련

- no glove, no love 콘돔 없이는 섹스 없다 (If there isn't a condom present, don't have sex.)

  [Ex] I hope your date goes well tonight. And remember: no glove, no love.

- raincoat 콘돔 (A condom)

  [Ex] Did you wear a raincoat?

- **rubber** 콘돔 (A condom)

  [Ex] Always wear a rubber during sex.

- **skin** 콘돔 (A condom)

  [Ex] I need to buy some skins right now.

Slang

- bareback 콘돔을 쓰지 않는 성교 (Unprotected sex)

  [Ex] 1. I saw a test that was 6 days old. That is too old for me to go bareback. / 2. She likes it bareback.

- hit it raw 콘돔 없이 섹스하다 (To have sex without a condom)

  [Ex] Can I hit it raw?

영어 표현에도 등급이 있다!

Sexually Endowed
성기가 큰

Sexually Aroused
성적으로 흥분한

Informal
- sex up 성욕을 불러일으키다, 성적 매력을 더하게 하다

  [Ex] I want to sex you up, girl.

Slang
- **horny** 성적性的으로 흥분한, 발정한 (Sexually aroused)

  [Ex] I am so horny I just need fucked. Can we do that?
- randy (성적으로) 흥분한 (Horny; to be sexually aroused or in a horny state of mind)

  [Ex] I'm feeling so randy right now!

Sexual Movements

성적인 동작들

Informal

- **bumps and grinds** (쇼의 댄서 등이) 허리 부분을 쑥 내밀고 비트는[돌리는] 동작

  [Ex] One boy was up close to a girl's back, bumping and grinding to the pounding beat of the music.

- come-on 유혹의 몸짓, 유혹하는 것

  [Ex] She was definitely giving him the come-on.

- **flash** (사람들 앞에서) 성기[유방, 팬티 따위]를 슬쩍 보이다

  [Ex] "If I had to guess, he probably likes Shelly's boobies best." Rachelle said. "Every time I've seen him tonight he's been sneaking a peek. I wish she would just flash him and get it over with."

- **flasher** (길거리에서 여성들을 향해 성기를 드러내 보이는) 노출증 환자

  [Ex] There's a flasher who ties sausage to his willy.

Slang

- dry hump 옷을 입은 상태로 성행위 흉내 냄

  [Ex] I dry humped her last night, so maybe I'll get the real thing tonight!

- dry sex 옷을 입은 상태로 성행위 흉내 냄 (To stimulated sex, without the removal of clothes)

  [Ex] They had dry sex.

- **go commando** (겉옷 속에) 속옷을 입지 않다, 노팬티다

  [Ex] I reached behind me and yanked her exercise shorts down her legs, only to find she'd also gone commando - no underwear, maybe in anticipation of this moment.

- tribbing 여자 동성애자 간의 성기 마찰 행위

Picture & Movie
Sex 관련 사진, 영화

Informal

- **porn** 포르노 (영화 또는 잡지 / Pornography)

  [Ex] I was watching porn on my computer.

- **POV** Point of view 시점, 1인칭 관점 제작 포르노 영화

  [Ex] I've never done a real boy-girl scene. I've restricted myself to POV blowjobs but I've decided to move full into the industry.

Slang

- beaver shot 두 다리를 벌려 성기를 드러낸 여자 사진

  [Ex] I'm sure she'll want to say hi but I'll make sure she dresses appropriately. I might give you a beaver shot but you've seen hers for the last time until she's legal.

13 *Misc.*

sex 관련 기타

- bean count (여성들의) 가슴을 쳐다보다 (To stare at breasts)

  [Ex] We just sat on the porch bean counting.

- **knock** (여성)을 범하다, 임신시키다 (To impregnate)

  [Ex] You got knocked? Who ya baby daddy?

Slang

- moose knuckle (주로) 남성 국부의 외관이 옷 위로 드러나는 것 (A slang term that refers to the outline of a human male's genitals showing through clothes at the crotch. It is the male equivalent of cameltoe.)

  [Ex] Damn those tight pants show his moose knuckle.

- take it out in trade (빚을) 섹스로 갚다

  [Ex] A: "Carl! This is beautiful! How much does this cost?" asked a wide-eyed Marilyn. / B: "For you, nothing!" / A: "Carl, I'm serious!" / B: "Well, I'll take it out in trade." I replied, waggling my eyebrows lewdly.